William Cobbett, known as "the poor man's friend," was born near
Farnham in Surrey in 1763. He was the third son of a small farmer and
owner of the Jolly Farmer public house which still exists today. Cobbett
was largely self-educated. After spending a few months as a London law
clerk he enlisted in the West Norfolk regiment in 1784. He served for
seven years in Nova Scotia, rising to the rank of sergeant-major. He
received an honourable discharge in 1791, but soon afterwards made an
accusation of corruption against some of his former officers. Faced with
the risk that the charge might lead to his own prosecution, he left
England, first for France where he spent "the happiest six months" of his
life, and then for America, where he began his lifelong journalistic
career. His *Porcupine's Gazette* had the largest circulation of any contemporary newspaper in America.

He returned to England in 1800, and in 1802 launched *Cobbett's
Weekly Political Register*, in which he promoted an increasingly radical
view of political, economic and social affairs. For attacking flogging in
the army he spent two years in prison. When his subsequent campaigns
against corruption, waste and censorship seemed likely to lead to further
imprisonment he left again for America in 1817. Returning in 1819, he
twice stood unsuccessfully for Parliament under the unreformed electoral
system, for Coventry in 1820, and Preston in 1826. But his views became
increasingly accepted in the years leading up to the Reform Bill of 1832;
a libel charge to silence him was unsuccessful in a court action in 1830,
when he conducted his own defence masterfully. In the Reform
Parliament he was elected member for Oldham. He toured Ireland in
1834 and died in 1835. He married Nancy Reid in 1792; they had four
sons and two daughters.

Cobbett is one of the most prolific writers in English. His published
works include: *The Life and Adventures of Peter Porcupine* (1796), *A Year's
Residence in America* (1818), *Cottage Economy* (1822), *Rural Rides* (1830),
Advice to Young Men (1830), and an *English and French Grammar* (1818
and 1824). *A History of the Protestant "Reformation" in England and Ireland*
first appeared as published monthly letters between 1824 and 1827.

WILLIAM COBBETT

A HISTORY OF THE
PROTESTANT REFORMATION

Abridged by Hugh Arnold
With a new introduction by Molly Townsend

Illustrated by Mary Tyler

Fisher Press

Published by Fisher Press, Post Office Box 41,
Sevenoaks, Kent TN15 6YN, England

A *History of the Protestant "Reformation" in England and Ireland* was first published as a series of monthly letters between 1824 and 1827
First published as a Fisher Paperback 1994

British Library Cataloguing in Publication Data
A catalogue record for this book is available from the British Library

ISBN 1 874037 10 8

Typesetting consultant: Grand Designs, London
Printed by Antony Rowe Ltd., Chippenham, Wiltshire

ACKNOWLEDGEMENTS

We are grateful to the Norfolk Museums Services (Norwich Castle Museum) for permission to reproduce the watercolour, Byland Abbey, by John Sell Cotman on the cover; and to the Trustees of the National Portrait Gallery for permission to reproduce the portrait of William Cobbett by an unknown artist in the vignette.

NOTE ON THE ABRIDGEMENT

This abridgement of one of Cobbett's finest works is designed for the ordinary reader. I decided to undertake the task when my daughter was studying the Reformation at school; she had been encouraged to read Cobbett's work, which I have always admired. But the full text, which appeared as a series of letters between 1824 and 1827, with paragraph numbers up to 479, many digressions on contemporary politics, and some repetitions arising from the nature of its original form of publication and from Cobbett's love of polemic, made the work appear less accessible than I would have wished. My abridgement is based on Cardinal Gasquet's edition of 1896. The aim has been to preserve the essential elements of Cobbett's narrative flow and argument. Some of the more important digressions, analyses of particular points, or supporting evidence, have been kept, but reproduced in 8 Appendices. Since the books and authors to whom Cobbett refers may not all be familiar to contemporary readers I have also included a bibliography with basic details of the writers and works concerned. I dedicate the abridgement to May Frith.

HUGH ARNOLD

INTRODUCTION

"When I went to France," Cobbett wrote," I was full of all the prejudices that Englishmen suck in with their mother's milk against the French and against their religion: a few weeks convinced me that I had been deceived in respect to both. I found the people among whom I lived honest, pious, and kind to excess."

The six months in France which William Cobbett referred to in that passage was from March to September 1792. Thirty-two years later, in 1824, he published his *A History of the Protestant Reformation*, perhaps the most damning indictment of England's secession from the Roman Catholic Church ever penned. The doubts sown in his mind in France when he was twenty-nine years old were to become certainties by the time he reached the age of sixty-one.

Cobbett was not, and made no pretence, to be a theologian. By upbringing and inclination he wished to be a farmer, and throughout his life he devoted all the time he could spare to agricultural pursuits. But he was conscious and proud of being an Englishman, and as an Englishman he believed passionately that it was his duty to do all in his power to promote the well-being of his fellow countrymen. In a letter to one of his sons he wrote that he hoped to see him when he grew up employing his time and talents "in aiding the cause of truth and justice, in affording protection to defenceless innocence, and in drawing down vengeance on lawless oppression." It was with these precepts in his own mind that Cobbett became one of the foremost political commentators of his time, exposing injustice, maladministration, corruption and hypocrisy in high places, and crying out against the parlous state of the common people. It was with these precepts in his mind that Cobbett embarked on a study of the history of the Protestant Reformation.

It was inevitable that Cobbett, always alert to expose injustice and oppression, should involve himself in the cause of Catholic Emancipation. His book was the culmination of his efforts to redress the wrongs inflicted on his Catholic fellow countrymen. The penal laws against Catholics, begun in the sixteenth century under Elizabeth and modified during subsequent reigns, had been on the statute books for over two hundred years when Cobbett was born. By the middle of the the eighteenth century so successful had they been that the Catholic population in England had become an insignificant minority and many of the severe punishments, fines and restrictions imposed on those practising the Catholic religion had been mitigated. Even so, when Cobbett was writing his *History*, Catholics were still excluded from both House of Parliament and debarred from holding any office under the Crown. Furthermore, in all the squibs and cartoons touching on the Catholic religion, the Pope was always depicted as an evil-looking man, often with a devil or two sitting on his shoulders, and was invariably set against a background of flames and instruments of torture, to remind the people of the hideous fate which would fall on England if it were to revert to the Old Faith and fall under the jurisdiction of the Pope of Rome.

In the 1770's, the fortunes of Britain were at a low ebb. The British army was bogged down in the United States, constantly outmanoeuvred by Washington's troops; its navy depleted by American and French deprivations; its West Indian colonies overrun by the French. Unable, because of the penal laws, to serve in the army and navy, the English Catholics, aided by their Protestant friends, began to petition for a relaxation of the laws under which they suffered. "We do not," they said, "presume to point out the particular means by which we may be allowed to testify our zeal to Your Majesty," but ask only that they might be allowed to demonstrate "the purity of our intentions." Such a profession of loyalty at a time when the power of Britain was being so successfully challenged overseas, fell gratefully on the the ears of the harassed King and Parliament. In 1778 a Catholic Relief Act was passed removing most of the restrictions on owning and inheriting land, and abolishing most of the laws which punished Catholics for practising their religion. The Act applied only to England. It was when it was suggested that it might be extended to Scotland that all hell broke loose. Early in 1779, Protestant mobs attacked shops, houses and factories owned by Catholics in Edinburgh and Glasgow. So extensive were the persecutions, the Scottish Catholics, fearful for their safety, appealed to the the government to withdraw the proposal to extend the Bill to Scotland, and it was dropped.

Such a success inspired those English who were antipathetic to Popery, to press for the repeal of the Relief Act in England, and when a petition to that effect was turned down by Parliament, Lord George Gordon, the leader of the newly created Protestant Association, called for a mass meeting to march with him to the Houses of Parliament to deliver a monster petition. On June 2nd 1780, sixty thousand Protestants assembled south of the Thames, and with flags flying, bagpipes playing, and chanting psalms and hymns, crossed Blackfriars and Westminster Bridges and converged on Parliament. Shouting the slogan of "No Popery," the crowd attacked and manhandled Members of Parliament whom they thought to be sympathetic to the Catholics. When news came that Parliament had decided to postpone considering their petition, they gave vent to their disappointment. Some marched to Lincoln's Inn Fields and despoiled and set fire to the Roman Catholic Chapel of the Sardinian Embassy there; others perpetrated a similar outrage at the chapel of the Bavarian Embassy.

So began the terrible nights and days of the Gordon Riots of June 1780. Not to wear the blue cockade of the Protestant Association, not to shout "No Popery" back when addressed by the rioters, not to illuminate one's windows to celebrate some fresh outrage, any of these was to subject oneself and one's family to broken windows or worse. Houses were forced open, shops and warehouses believed to be owned by Catholics set on fire. The most fearful climax came when a large distillery in Holborn was set alight and the flames, according to one eye-witness, "surpassed those of Mount Vesuvius." As the casks spilled their contents the very streets caught alight, and men, women and children, some of them alight themselves, slaked their thirst and died in the burning liquor.

The Gordon Riots occurred when Cobbett was seventeen years old, and before he had left his home in Surrey. At that time he was working on his father's small farm and was probably unaware of the events in London. Three years later, in 1783, he enlisted as a soldier. He served in Canada for eight years, visited France to perfect himself in the French language, and then settled in the United States where he quickly established himself as a powerful political journalist. He returned to England in 1800 and continued his career as a writer, founded his famous weekly paper *The Political Register*, and plunged wholeheartedly into the maelstrom of political controversy.

In the early 1800's many attempts were made to relieve Catholics from the remaining Penal Laws. During the General Election of 1807 some of the candidates favoured granting Catholic emancipation — a restoration to Catholics of their political rights — and, though the reaction was nothing like that of the Gordon Riots, "No Popery" was chalked on the doors of houses known to be in favour of relief. "No Popery" notices appeared on walls in all big cities. Public houses hung out banners exhorting people to come inside and sign "No Popery" petitions in return for free drinks. The cry of "Church and King in danger" was heard throughout the land. Cobbett looked on in dismay:

"One side cries out that the Church is in danger, and the other that they are persecuted for righteousness sake. One side seems to dread the faggots in Smithfield, and the other to be in bodily fear of Satan himself. That there should be men of talent so lost to all sense of shame as to come forward publicly and carry on debates on it is truly shocking."

That election resulted in the defeat of pro-Catholic candidates and a strongly Protestant ministry was formed.

It was against this background that Cobbett began his enquiries into the origins of the break with Rome and the establishment of the Church of England. His *A History of the Protestant Reformation* is unlike any history written before or since. Published in parts from 1824 onwards, it traces the history of the Established Church from its inception in the reign of Henry VIII. to the time when the book was written. Passionately partisan, yet meticulous in its quotations from statute books and contemporary sources, didactic in tone, yet respecting the intelligence of its readers, uncompromising in its detail of atrocities, yet humorous in the midst of its denunciations, it is unique. Cobbett tells how when he first began to delve into the history of the English Church, his reaction was one of astonishment and disbelief. Is it possible, he asks himself, that what we have been led to believe about the dark ages of Catholicism, and the enlightened ages which followed the break with Rome is a monstrous lie? Yet the more he read, the more he became convinced that indeed it was so, and the stronger his desire to share his discoveries with his fellow countrymen.

When reading *A History of the Protestant Reformation* it is important to keep in mind the circumstances in which and the purpose for which it was written. The circumstances were the fear and abhorrence of the Catholic religion prevailing at the time among a large proportion of the people; the purpose, to allay those fears and so pave the way for the abolition of the Penal Laws under which the Catholics were still suffering. "In books of all sizes," Cobbett tells us, "and from the pulpit of every church, we have been taught from our infancy that the beast, the man of sin, and the scarlet whore mentioned in Revelations, were names which God himself had given to the Pope."

It would be true to say that nearly all Cobbett's writings sprang from his most earnest desire to expose wrongs and to persuade his readers both that the wrongs existed, and even more importantly that they were capable of being redressed. It is not uncommon for histories to be written from a partisan point of view, nor is it uncommon for certain unpalatable facts to be suppressed. What is rare in Cobbett's history is that from the first page to the last the reader is never allowed to forget that wicked deeds have been done and reparation for those deeds is urgently necessary. So, right from the beginning, Cobbett takes us by the hand, and begs us to retrace with him the steps he took on his voyage of exploration into the history of the Reformation and its aftermath. And what a remarkable journey it turns out to be. Can one ever forget the description of the seventy year old Countess of Salisbury running round the block "with her grey locks hanging round her shoulders and breast" while her executioner pursued her with his axe? Or the relish with which Cobbett describes the tergiversations of those divines who first forswore their old religion and swore allegiance to Henry VIII. as Supreme Head of the Church, then, under Mary, took on sackcloth and ashes to beg the Pope's pardon for their apostasy, only to turn their coats yet again under Elizabeth.

If, today, we are astonished at Cobbett's thesis that the Protestant Reformation was an "alteration greatly for the worse"; that the "Reformation", as it is called, was "engendered in beastly lust, brought forth in hypocrisy and perfidy, and cherished and fed by plunder, devastation, and by rivers of innocent English and Irish blood," what must have been the feelings of his contemporary readers, steeped in anti-Catholic bigotry, when they opened the book! For them it must have seemed that history, as they knew it, was being stood on its head. But, and herein lies his genius as a popular writer, Cobbett is the gentlest and most patient of teachers. He does not expect us to believe him all at once, he anticipates our initial incredulity, craves our indulgence for the present, and promises to make good his claims later if we will continue to keep him company on the way ahead. He treats us as his friends and equals, as people like himself who, when we know the facts, will support him in his attempt to redress the wrongs inflicted on our innocent fellow countrymen.

Initially the book was published serially in separate numbers, and quickly sold about forty thousand copies for each number. It was reprinted in Ireland and America and later translated into French, German, Italian and Spanish. Four years after its publication, the Bill for Catholic Emancipation was passed, the Penal Laws were abolished, Catholics were allowed to stand for Parliament, to serve on juries, to hold positions under the Crown, and to practice their religion openly. It would be foolish to pretend that when Wellington and Peel, those hitherto staunch anti-Catholics, submitted the Bill to Parliament, they were greatly influenced by Cobbett's argument in *A History of the Protestant Reformation*. It was the Irish dimension —the determination of the Irish Catholics led by Daniel O'Connell, and the fear of civil war there that turned the scales. But Cobbett had prepared the ground. To him goes much of the credit that when the Bill was passed there was no rioting, no attempt either then or afterwards to repeal the Act. So let us read it in the spirit in which it was written and judge it as Cobbett himself wished it to be judged.

"It is not for the rich and the powerful of my countrymen that I have spoken; but for the poor, the persecuted, the proscribed...when I considered the long, long triumph of calumny over the religion of those to whom we owe all that we possess that is great and renowned...it would be baseness to hold my tongue, and baseness superlative would it have been if I had been restrained by fear of the shafts of falsehood and of folly."

MOLLY TOWNSEND

CHAPTER ONE

Before we proceed further let us clearly understand the meaning of these words: Catholic, Protestant and Reformation. Catholic means universal, and the religion which takes this epithet was called universal because all Christian people of every nation acknowledged it to be the only true religion, and because they all acknowledged one and the same head of the Church, and this was the Pope, who, though he generally resided at Rome, was head of the Church in England, in France, in Spain, and, in short, in every part of the world where the Christian religion was professed. But there came a time, when some nations, or rather parts of some nations, cast off the authority of the Pope, and of course no longer acknowledged him as head of the Christian Church. These nations, or parts of nations, declared, or protested, against the authority of their former head, and also against the doctrines of that Church, which until now had been the only Christian Church. They therefore called themselves Protestors or Protestants; and this is now the appellation given to all who are not Catholics. As to the word Reformation, it means an alteration for the better; and it would have been hard indeed if the makers of this great alteration could not have contrived to give it a good name.

Now, my friends, a fair and honest enquiry will teach us that this was an alteration greatly for the worse. Were there, for the entering of this enquiry, no motive other than that of the bare love of justice, that motive alone would, I hope, be sufficient with the far greater part of Englishmen. When we consider these things, that fair and honest enquiry, on which a bare love of justice might well induce us to enter, presses itself upon us as a duty which we owe to ourselves, our children and our country.

But before I enter on this series of deeds and of consequences, it is necessary to offer you some observations of a more general nature, and calculated to make us doubt, at least, of the truth of what we have heard against the Catholic religion. Our minds have been so completely filled with abuse of this religion, that at first we can hardly bring ourselves to listen to anything said in defence of it, or in apology for it. Those whom, you will, by and by, find in possession of the spoils of the Catholic Church and, indeed, of those of the Catholic nobles and gentlemen, not forgetting those of the poor; these persons have always had the strongest possible motive for causing the people to be brought up in the belief that the Catholic religion was, and is, something to inspire us with horror. From our very infancy, on the knees of our mothers, we have been taught to believe that to be a Catholic was to be a false, cruel, and bloody wretch; and "popery and slavery" have been rung in our ears, till, whether we looked on the Catholics in their private or their public capacity, we have inevitably come to the conclusion that they were everything that was vicious and vile.

But, you may say, why should anybody, and particularly our countrymen, take such pains to deceive us? Why should they, for so many years, take the trouble to write and publish books of all sizes, from big folios down to half-penny tracts, in order to make us think ill of this Catholic religion? Now, my friends, take an instance in answer to this why. The immense property of the Catholic Church in Ireland, in which, mind, the poor had a share, was taken from the Catholics and given to the Protestant bishops and parsons. These have never been able to change the religion of the main body of the people of that country; and there these bishops and parsons are enjoying the immense revenues without having scarcely any flocks. This produces great discontents, makes the country continually in a state of ferment, causes enormous expenses to England, and exposes the whole kingdom to great danger in case of war. Now, if those who enjoy these revenues, and their close connections in this country, had not made us believe that there was something very bad, wicked and horrible in the Catholic religion, should we not, long ago, have asked why they put us to all this expense for keeping that religion down? They never told us, and they never tell us, that this Catholic religion was the only religion known to our own forefathers for nine hundred years. If they had told us this, we should have said that it could not possibly have been so very bad a religion, and that it would be better to leave the Irish people still to enjoy it; and that, since there were scarcely any Protestant flocks, it would be better for us all if the Church revenues were to go again to the original owners.

Ah! my friends! here we have the real motive for all the abuse, all the hideous calumnies that have been heaped upon the Catholic religion, and upon all that numerous body of our fellow-subjects who adhere to that ancient faith. When you think of the power of this motive, you will not be surprised at the great and incessant pains that have been taken to deceive us. Even the Scripture itself has been perverted in order to blacken the Catholics. In books of all sizes and from the pulpit of every church we have been taught from our infancy that the "beast, the man of sin, and the scarlet whore," mentioned in Revelations, were names which God himself had given to the Pope; and we have all been taught to believe of the Catholic Church that her worship was "idolatrous," and that her doctrines were "damnable."

Now, let us put a plain question or two to ourselves, and to these our teachers. Will these modest assailants of the faith of their and our ancestors assert to our faces, that, for twelve hundred years at least, there were no true Christians in the world? Will they tell us that Christ, who promised to be with the teachers of His word to the end of the world, wholly left them, and gave up hundreds upon hundreds of millions of people to be led in darkness to their eternal perdition, by one whom His inspired followers had denominated the "man of sin" and the "scarlet whore"? Will they, indeed, dare to tell us that Christ gave up the world wholly to "Antichrist" for twelve hundred years? Yet this they must do, they must thus stand forward with bold and unblushing blasphemy; or they must confess themselves guilty of the most atrocious calumny against the Catholic religion.

Then, coming nearer to home, and closer to our own bosoms, our ancestors became Christians about six hundred years after the death of Christ. And how did they become Christians? Who first pronounced the name of Christ to this land? Who converted the English from paganism to Christianity? Some Protestant saint, doubtless, warm from a victory like that of Skibbereen? No, no! The work was begun, continued, and ended by the Popes, one of whom sent over some monks (of whom we shall see more by-and-by) who settled at Canterbury, and from whose beginnings the Christian religion spread, like the grain of mustard-seed, rapidly over the land. Whatever therefore any other part of the world might have known of Christianity before the Pope became the settled and acknowledged head of the Church, England at any rate never had known of any Christian religion other than that at the head of which was the Pope; and in this religion, with the Pope at its head,

England continued to be firmly fixed for nine hundred years.

Away, then, my friends, with this foul abuse of the Catholic religion, which, after all, is the religion of about nine-tenths of all the Christians in the world! Away with this shameful calumny, the sole object of which is, and always has been, to secure a quiet possession of the spoils of the Catholic Church and of the poor; for we shall, by-and-by, clearly see how the poor were despoiled at the same time that the Church was.

Now we know very well, that we who belong to this Protestant Church believe, or profess to believe, that the New Testament, as printed and distributed amongst us, contains the true and genuine "word of God;" that it contains the "words of eternal life;" that it points out to us the means, and the only means, by which we can possibly be saved from everlasting fire. This is what we believe. Now, how did we come by this New Testament? Who gave us this real and genuine "word of God?" From whom did we receive these "words of eternal life?" They are questions of great importance; because, if this be the book, and the only book, which contains instructions relative to the means of saving our souls, it is manifest that it is a matter of deep interest to us who it was that this book came from to us, through what channel we received it, and what proof we have of its authenticity.

After the death of Christ there was a long space of time before the gospel was put into anything like its present shape. It was preached in several countries, and churches were established in those countries, long before the written gospel was known much of, or at least long before it was made use of as a guide to the Christian Churches. At the end of about four hundred years, the written gospels were laid before a Council of the Catholic Church, of which the Pope was the head. But there were several gospels besides those of Matthew, Mark, Luke, and John! All these, long after the death of the authors, were, as I have just said, laid before a Council of the Catholic Church, and that Council determined which of the gospels were genuine and which not. It retained the four gospels of Matthew, Mark, Luke and John: it determined that these four should be received and believed in, and that all the rest should be rejected.

So a Protestant Society "for promoting Christian Knowledge" is without any other gospel; without any other word of God; without any guide to eternal life; without any other than that which the Society, as well as all the rest of us, have received from a Church which such a Society calls "idolatrous," and the head of which it calls "the beast, the man of sin, the scarlet whore, and Antichrist!"

To our law-Church Prayer Book there is a calendar pre-fixed, and in this calendar there are, under different days of the year, certain names of holy men and women. Their names are put here in order that their anniversaries may be attended to, and religiously attended to, by the people. Now, who are these holy persons? Some Protestant saints to be sure? Not one! What, not saint Luther, nor saint Cranmer, nor saint Edward the Sixth, nor the "virgin" saint Elizabeth? Not a soul of them; but a whole list of Popes, Catholic bishops, and Catholic holy persons, female as well as male. Several virgins, but not the "virgin Queen," nor any one of the Protestant race. At first sight this seems odd, for this calendar was made by act of Parliament. But the truth is, it was necessary to preserve some of their names, so long revered by the people, in order to keep them in better humour, and to lead them by degrees into the new religion.

Enough! Aye, and much more than enough to make us sorely repent of having so long been the dupes of the crafty and selfish revilers of the religion of our fathers. Were there ever presumption, impudence, inconsistency and insinceri-ty equal to those of which we have just taken a view? When we thus open our eyes and look into the matter, we are astonished, and ashamed of our credulity; and this, more especially, when we reflect that the far greater part of us have suffered ourselves to be misled by men not possessing a tenth part of our own capacity, by a set of low-minded, greedy creatures, but indefatigable; never losing sight of the spoil, and day after day, year after year, close at the ears of the people from their very childhood, din, din, din, incessantly, until from mere habit the monstrous lie got sucked in for gospel truth.

Having now shown that the censure heaped on the religion of our forefathers is not only unjust, but absurd and monstrous; having shown that there could be no good reason for altering the religion of England from Catholic to Protestant; having exposed the vile and selfish calumniators, and duly prepared the mind of every just person for that fair and honest enquiry, I should now enter on my enquiry, and show in the first place how this "Reformation," as it is called, was engendered. But there is yet one topic to be touched on in this preliminary chapter of my little work.

Truth has, with regard to this subject, made great progress in the public mind in England within the last dozen years. Men are not now to be carried away by the cry of "No-Popery," and the "Church in danger;" and it is now, by no means rare to hear Protestants allow that, as to faith, as to morals, as to salvation, the Catholic religion is quite good enough; and a very large part of the people of England are forward to declare that the Catholics have been most barbarously treated, and that it is time that they had justice done them.

But, with all these just notions, there exists, amongst Protestants in general, an opinion that the Catholic religion is unfavourable to civil liberty, and also unfavourable to the producing and the exerting of genius and talent. As to the former, I shall, in the course of this work, find a suitable place for proving, by the melancholy experience of this country, that a total want of civil liberty was unknown in England as long as its religion was Catholic; and that the moment it lost the protection of the Pope its kings and nobles became horrid tyrants, and its people the most abject and most ill-treated of slaves. This I shall prove in due time and place; and I beg you, my friends, to bear in mind that I pledge myself to this proof.

And now to the other charge against the Catholic religion; namely that it is unfavourable to the producing of genius and talent, and to the causing of them to be exerted. I am going, in a minute, to prove that this charge is not only false, but ridiculously and most stupidly false; but before I do this, let me observe that this charge comes from the same source with all the other charges against the Catholics. "Monkish ignorance and superstition" is a phrase that you find in every Protestant historian, from the reign of Elizabeth to the present hour. It has, with time, become a sort of magpie-saying, like "glorious revolution," "happy constitution," " good old king," "envy of surrounding nations," and the like. But there has always, false as the notion will presently be proved to be, there has always been a very sufficient motive for inculcating it. Blackstone, for instance, in his *Commentaries on the Laws of England*, never lets slip an opportunity to rail against "monkish ignorance and superstition." Blackstone was no fool. At the very time when he was writing these *Commentaries*, and reading them to the students at Oxford, he was, and he knew it, living upon the spoils of the Catholic Church and the spoils of the Catholic gentry, and also of the poor! He knew that well. He knew that if every one had had his due he would not have been fattening where he was. He knew besides, that all who heard his lectures were aware of the spoils that he was wallowing in. These considerations were quite sufficient to induce him to abuse the Catholic Church, and to affect to look back with contempt to Catholic times.

For cool, placid, unruffled impudence, there have been no people in the world to equal the "Reformation" gentry; and Blackstone seems to have inherited this quality in direct line from some altar-robber of the reign of that sweet young Protestant saint, Edward the Sixth. If Blackstone had not actually felt the spoils of the Catholics sticking to his ribs, he would have recollected that all those things which he was eulogizing, Magna Charta, trial by jury, the offices of sheriff, justice of the peace, constable, and all the rest of it, arose in the days of "monkish ignorance and superstition." If his head had not been rendered muddy by his gourmandizing on the spoils of the Catholic Church, he would have remembered that Fortescue, and that that greatest of all our lawyers, Lyttleton, were born, bred, lived and died in the days of "monkish ignorance and superstition." But, did not this Blackstone know, that the very roof under which he was abusing our Catholic forefathers, was made by these forefathers? Did he not, when he looked up to that roof, or when he beheld any of those noble buildings which, in defiance of time, still tell us what those forefathers were, did he not, when he beheld any of these, feel that he was a pigmy in mind, compared with those whom he had the impudence to abuse?

When we hear some Jew or Orangeman talk about "monkish ignorance and superstition," we turn from him with silent contempt: but Blackstone is to be treated in another manner. It was at Oxford where he wrote, and where he was reading, his *Commentaries*. He well knew, that the foundations for learning at Oxford were laid and brought to perfection, not only in monkish times, but, in great part, by monks. He knew, "that the abbeys were public schools for education, each of them having one or more persons set apart to instruct the youth of the neighbourhood, without any expense to the parents." He knew, that "each of the greater monasteries had a peculiar residence in the universities; and, whereas there were, in those times, nearly three hundred halls and private schools at Oxford, besides the colleges, there were not above eight remaining towards the middle of the seventeenth century," that is to say, in about a hundred years after the enlightening "Reformation" began. At this time (1824) there are, I am informed, only five halls remaining, and not a single school.

I shall, in another place, have to show more fully the folly and, indeed, the baseness of railing against monastic institutions generally; but I must here confine myself to this charge against the Catholic religion, of being unfavourable to genius, talent, and, in short, to the powers of the mind. It is a strange notion; and one can hardly hear it mentioned without suspecting that, somehow or other, there is plunder at the bottom of the apparently nothing but stupid idea. Those who put forward this piece of rare impudence do not favour us with reasons for believing that the Catholic religion has any such tendency. They content themselves with the bare assertion, not supposing that it admits of anything like disproof. They look upon it as assertion against assertion; and, in a question which depends on mere hardness of mouth, they know that their triumph is secure. But this is a question that does admit of proof, and very good proof too. The "Reformation" in England was pretty nearly completed by the year 1600. By that time all the "monkish ignorance and superstition" were swept away. The monasteries were all pretty nearly knocked down, young King Edward's people had robbed all the altars, and Elizabeth had put the finishing hand to the pillage. So that all was, in 1600, become as Protestant as heart could wish. Very well; the kingdom of France remained buried in "monkish ignorance and superstition" until the year 1787; that is to say, 187 years after happy England stood in a blaze of Protestant light! Now, then; if we carefully examine into the number of men remarkable for great powers of mind, men famed for their knowledge or genius; if we carefully examine into the number of such men produced by France in these 187 years, and the number of such men produced by England, Scotland, and Ireland, during the same period; if we do this, we shall get a pretty good foundation for judging the effects of the two religions, with regard to their influence on knowledge, and genius—what is generally called learning.

"Oh, no!" exclaim the fire-shovels. "France is a great deal bigger, and contains more people, than these islands; and this is not fair play!" Do not be frightened, good fire-

shovels. According to your own account, these islands contain twenty-one millions; and the French say they have
thirty millions. Therefore, when we have got the numbers,
we will make an allowance of one third in our favour
accordingly. If, for instance, the French have not three
famous men to every two of ours, then I shall confess that
the law-established Church, and its family of
Muggletonians, Cameronians, Jumpers, Unitarians,
Shakers, Quakers, and the rest of the Protestant litter, are
more favourable to knowledge and genius, than is the
Catholic Church.

But how are we to ascertain these numbers? Very well. I
shall refer to a work which has a place in every good library
in the kingdom; I mean the *Universal, Historical, Critical
and Bibliographical Dictionary*. This work, which is everywhere received as authority as to facts, contains lists of persons of all nations, celebrated for their published works. But
then, to have a place in these lists the person must have
been really distinguished; his or her works must have been
considered as worthy of universal notice. From these lists I
shall take my numbers, as before proposed. It will not be
necessary to go into all the arts and sciences; eight or nine
will be sufficient. It may be as well, perhaps, to take the
Italians as well as the French; for we all know that they
were living in most shocking "monkish ignorance and
superstition;" and that they, poor unfortunate and unplundered souls, are so living unto this very day.

Here, then, is the statement: and you have only to
observe, that the figures represent the number of persons
who were famous for the art or science opposite the name
of which the figures are placed. The period is from the year
1600 to 1787, during which period France was under what
has been called the "dark despotism of the Catholic
Church," and what Blackstone calls "monkish ignorance
and superstition:" and, during the same period, these islands
were in a blaze of light, sent forth by Luther, Cranmer,
Knox, and their followers.

Here then is the statement:

	England, Scotland & Ireland	France	Italy
Writers on Law	6	51	9
Mathematicians	17	52	15
Physicians & Surgeons	13	72	21
Writers on natural history	6	33	11
Historians	21	139	22
Dramatic writers	19	66	6
Grammarians	7	42	2
Poets	38	157	34
Painters	5	64	44
Total	132	676	164

Here is that very "scale" which a modest Scotch writer spoke of the other day, when he told the public that, "throughout Europe, Protestants rank higher in the scale of intellect than Catholics, and that Catholics in the neighbourhood of Protestants are more intellectual than those at a distance from them." This is a fine specimen of upstart Protestant impudence. The above "scale" is, however, a complete answer to it. Allow one-third more to the French on account of their superior populousness, and then there will remain to them 451 to our 132! So that they had, man for man, three and a-half times as much intellect as we, though they were buried all the while in "monkish ignorance and superstition," and though they had no Protestant neighbours to catch the intellect from! Even the Italians surpass us in this rivalship of intellect; for their population is not equal to that of which we boast, and their number of men of mind considerably exceeds that of ours. But, do I not, all this while misunderstand the matter? And, by intellect, does not the Scotchman mean the capacity to make, not books and pictures, but checks, bills, bonds, exchequer bills, inimitable notes, and the like? Does he not mean loan-jobbing, and stock-jobbing, insurance-broking, annuities at ten per cent., kite-flying, and all the "intellectual"

proceedings of 'Change Alley? Ah! in that case, I confess
he is right. On this scale Protestants do rank high indeed!

Here then, my friends, sensible and just Englishmen, I
close this introduction. I have shown you how grossly we
have been deceived, even from our very infancy. I have
shown you, not only the injustice, but the absurdity of the
abuse heaped by our interested deluders on the religion of
their and our fathers. I have shown you enough to convince
you that there was no obviously just cause for an alteration
in the religion of our country. I have, I dare say, awakened
in your minds a strong desire to know how it came to pass,
then, that this alteration was made; and in the following
pages it shall be my anxious endeavour to fully gratify this
desire. But, observe, my chief object is to show that this
alteration made the main body of the people poor and miserable compared with what they were before; that it impoverished and degraded them; that it banished at once that
"old English hospitality," of which we have since known
nothing but the name; and that in lieu of that hospitality it
gave us pauperism, a thing the very name of which was
never before known in England.

CHAPTER TWO

We never understand the nature and constituent parts
of a thing so well as when we ourselves have made
the thing: next to making it is the seeing of it made; but if
we have neither of these advantages, we ought at least, if
possible, to get a true description of the origin of the thing
and of the manner in which it was put together. I have to
speak to you of the Catholic Church generally, then of the
Church in England, under which head I shall have to speak
of the parish churches, the monasteries, the tithes and
other revenues of the Church. It is, therefore, necessary
that I explain to you how the Catholic Church arose, and

how churches, monasteries, tithes and other church revenues came to be in England. When you have this information you will well understand what it was which was devastated by Henry VIII. and the "Reformation" people. And I am satisfied that when you have read this one number of my little work, you will know more about your country than you have learned, or ever will learn, from the reading of hundreds of those bulky volumes, called Histories of England.

The Catholic Church originated with Jesus Christ Himself. He selected Peter to be head of his Church. This Apostle's name was Simon, but his Master called him Peter, which means a stone or rock; and He said, "on this rock will I build my Church." Look at the Gospel of Saint Matthew xvi., 18, 19, and at that of Saint John xxi., 15, and onward; and you will see that we must deny the truth of the Scriptures, or acknowledge that there was a head of the Church promised for all generations.

Saint Peter died a Martyr at Rome in about 60 years after the birth of Christ. But another supplied his place; and there is the most satisfactory evidence that the chain of succession has remained unbroken from that day to this. When I said in Chapter 1 that it might be said that there was no Pope seated at Rome for the first three hundred years, I by no means meant to admit the fact, but to get rid of a pretence which at any rate could not apply to England, which was converted to Christianity by missionaries sent by a Pope, the successor of other Popes who had been seated at Rome for hundreds of years. The truth is, that, from the persecutions which for the first three hundred years the Church underwent, the Chief Bishops, successors of St. Peter, had not always the means of openly maintaining their supremacy; but they always existed, there was always a Chief Bishop, and his supremacy was always acknowledged by the Church; that is to say, by all the Christians then in the world.

Of later date, the Chief Bishop has been called in our

language, the Pope, and in the French, Pape. In the Latin he is called Papa, which is a union and abbreviation of the two Latin words, Pater Patrum, which means Father of Fathers. Hence comes the appellation of Papa, which children of all Christian nations give to their fathers; an appellation of the highest respect and most ardent and sincere affection. Thus, then, the Pope, each as he succeeded to his office, became the chief or head of the Church; and his supreme power and authority were acknowledged by all the bishops and by all the teachers of Christianity in all the nations where that religion existed. The Pope was, and is, assisted by a body of persons called Cardinals or Great Councillors; and at various and numerous times Councils of the Church have been held in order to discuss and settle matters of deep interest to the unity and well-being of the Church. These Councils have been held in all the countries of Christendom. Many were held in England. The Popes themselves have been taken promiscuously from men of all the Christian nations. Pope Adrian IV. was an Englishman, the son of a very poor labouring man: but having become a servant in a monastery, he was there taught and became himself a monk. In time he grew famous for his learning, his talents and piety, and at last became the head of the Church.

The Popedom, or office of Pope, continued in existence through all the great and repeated revolutions of kingdoms and empires. The Roman empire, which was at the height of its glory at the beginning of the Christian era, and which extended, indeed, nearly over the whole of Europe and part of Africa and Asia, crumbled all to pieces, yet the Popedom remained; and at the time when the devastation, commonly called the "Reformation" of England began, there had been, during the fifteen hundred years, about two hundred and sixty Popes, following each other in due and unbroken succession.

The history of the Church in England, down to the time of the "Reformation," is a matter of deep interest to us. A mere look at it, a bare sketch of the principal facts, will show how false, how unjust, how ungrateful those have been who have vilified the Catholic Church, its Popes, its monks and its priests. It is supposed by some, and indeed with good authorities on their side, that the Christian religion was partly introduced into England so early as the second century after Christ. But we know for a certainty that it was introduced effectually in the year 596; that is to say, 923 years before Henry VIII. began to destroy it.

England, at the time when this religion was introduced, was governed by seven kings, and that state was called the Heptarchy. The people of the whole country were pagans. Yes, my friends, our ancestors were pagans; they worshipped gods made with hands; and they sacrificed children on the altars of their idols. In this state England was when the Pope of that day, Gregory I., sent forty monks, with a monk of the name of Austin (or Augustin) at their head, to preach the Gospel to the English.

Now, please to bear in mind that this great event took place in the year 596. The Protestant writers have been strangely embarrassed in their endeavours to make it out, that up to this time, or thereabouts, the Catholic Church was pure and trod in the steps of the Apostles; but that after this time that Church became corrupt. They applaud the character and acts of Pope Gregory; they do the same with regard to Austin: shame would not suffer them to leave their names out of the calendar; but still they want to make it out, that there was no pure Christian religion after the Pope came to be the visible and acknowledged head and to have supreme authority. There are scarcely any two of them that agree upon this point. Some say that it was 300, some 400, some 500, and some 600 years before the Catholic Church ceased to be the true Church of Christ. But none of them can deny, nor dare they attempt it, that it was the Christian religion as practised at Rome; that it was the Roman Catholic religion that was introduced into England in the year 596, with all its dogmas, rites, ceremonies and observances, just as they all continued to exist at the time of the "Reformation," and as they continue to exist in that Church even unto this day. Whence it clearly follows, that if the Catholic Church were corrupt at the time of the "Reformation," or be corrupt now, be radically bad now, it was so in 596; and then comes the impious and horrid inference that "All our fathers who first built our churches, and whose bones and flesh form the earth for many feet deep in all the churchyards, are now howling in the region of the damned."

"The tree is known by its fruit." Bear in mind, that it was the Catholic faith, as now held, that was introduced into England by Pope Gregory the Great; and bearing this in mind, let us see what were the effects of that introduction, let us see how that faith worked its way, in spite of wars, invasions, tyrannies, and political revolutions.

Saint Austin, upon his arrival, applied to the Saxon king within whose dominions the county of Kent lay. He obtained leave to preach to the people, and his success was great and immediate. He converted the king himself, who was very gracious to him and his brethren, and who provided dwellings and other necessaries for them at Canterbury. Saint Austin and his brethren, being monks, lived together in common, and from this common home went forth over the country, preaching the gospel. As the community was diminished by death, new members were ordained to keep up the supply; and besides this, the number was in time greatly augmented. A church was built at Canterbury. Saint Austin was of course, the Bishop, or Head Priest. He was succeeded by other bishops. As Christianity spread over the island, other communities, like that at Canterbury, were founded in other cities; as at London, Winchester, Exeter, Worcester, Norwich, York, and so of all the other places where there are now Cathedrals, or Bishops' churches.

As to the mode of supporting the clergy in those times, it was by oblations or free gifts, and sometimes by tithes, which land-owners paid themselves, or ordered their tenants to pay, though there was no general obligation to yield tithes for many years after the arrival of St. Austin. In this collective or collegiate state the clergy remained for many years. But, in time, as the land-owners became converted to Christianity, they were desirous of having priests settled near to them, and always upon the spot ready to perform the offices of religion. The land was then owned by comparatively few persons. The rest of the people were vassals, or tenants, of the land-owners. The land-owners, therefore, built churches on their estates, and generally near their own houses, for the benefit of themselves, their vassals, and tenants. And to this day we see, in numerous instances, the country church close by the gentleman's house. When they built the churches, they also built a house for the priest, which we now call the parsonage-house; and, in most cases, they attached some plough-land, or meadow-land, or both, to the priest's house, for his use; and this was called his glebe, which word, literally taken, means the top earth, which is turned over by the plough. Besides these, the land-owners, in conformity with the custom then prevalent in other Christian countries, endowed the churches with the tithe of the produce of their estates.

Hence parishes arose. Parish means a priestship, as the land on which a town stands is a township. So that the great man's estate now became a parish. He retained the right of appointing the priest, whenever a vacancy happened; but he could not displace a priest, when once appointed; and the whole of the endowment became the property of the Church, independent of his control. It was a long while, even two centuries, or more, before this became the settled law of the whole kingdom; but at last it did become such. But to this possession of so much property by the Church certain important conditions were attached; and to these conditions it behoves us of the present day to pay particular attention; for we are, at this time, more than ever feeling the want of the performance of those conditions.

There never can have existed a state of society; that is to say, a state of things in which proprietorship in land was acknowledged, and in which it was maintained by law; there never can have existed such a state without an obligation on the land-owners to take care of the necessitous and to prevent them from perishing for want. The land-owners in England took care of their vassals and dependents. But when Christianity, the very basis of which is charity, became established, the taking care of the necessitous was deposited in the hands of the clergy. Upon the very face of it, it appears monstrous that a house, a small farm, and the tenth part of the produce of a large estate, should have been given to a priest who could have no wife and, of course, no family. But, the fact is that the grants were for other purposes as well as for the support of the priests. The produce of the benefice was to be employed thus: "Let the priests receive the tithes of the people and keep a written account of all that have paid them; and divide them in the presence of such as fear God, according to canonical authority. Let them set apart the first share for the repairs and ornaments of the church; let them distribute the second to the poor and the stranger, with their own hands, in mercy and humility; and reserve the third part for themselves." These were the orders contained in a canon issued by a Bishop of York. At different times, and under different bishops, regulations somewhat different were adopted; but there were always two-fourths, at the least, of the annual produce of the benefice to be given to the necessitous, and to be employed in the repairing or in the ornamenting of the church.

Thus the providing for the poor became one of the great duties and uses of the Church. This duty rested before on the land-owners. It must have rested on them; for, as Blackstone observes, a right in the indigent "to demand a supply sufficient to all the necessities of life from the more opulent part of the community is dictated by the principles of society." This duty could be lodged in no hands so fitly as in those of the clergy; for thus the work of charity, the feed-ing of the hungry, the clothing of the naked, the adminis-tering to the sick, the comforting of the widow, the foster-ing of the fatherless, came always in company with the per-formances of services to God. For the uncertain disposition of the rich, for their occasional and sometimes capricious charity, was substituted the certain, the steady, the impar-tial hand of a constantly resident and unmarried adminis-trator of bodily as well as of spiritual comfort to the poor, the unfortunate, and the stranger.

We shall see, by-and-by, the condition that the poor were placed in, we shall see how all the labouring classes were impoverished and degraded, the moment the tithes and other revenues of the Church were transferred to a Protestant and married clergy; and we shall have to take a full view of the unparalleled barbarity with which the Irish people were treated at that time; but I have not yet noticed another great branch or constituent part of the Catholic Church: namely, the monasteries, which form a subject full of interest and worthy of our best attention.

The persons belonging to a monastery lived in common; they lived in one and the same building; they could possess no property individually; when they entered the walls of the monastery, they left the world wholly behind them; they made a solemn vow of celibacy; they could devise nothing by will; each had a life-interest, but nothing more, in the revenues belonging to the community; some of the monks and friars were also priests, but this was not always the case; and the business of the whole was to say masses and prayers, and to do deeds of hospitality and charity.

This mode of life began by single persons separating themselves from the world and living in complete solitude, passing all their days in prayer, and dedicating themselves wholly to the serving of God. These were called hermits, and their conduct drew towards them great respect. In time, such men, or men having a similar propensity, formed themselves into societies, and agreed to live together in one house and to possess things in common. Women did the same. And hence came those places called monasteries. The piety, the austerities, and particularly the works of kindness and of charity performed by those persons, made them objects of great veneration; and the rich made them, in time, the channels of their benevolence to the poor. Kings, queens, princes, princesses, nobles, and gentlemen founded monasteries; that is to say, erected the buildings and endowed them with estates for their maintenance. Others, some in the way of atonement for their sins and some from a pious disposition, gave while alive, or bequeathed at their death, lands, houses, or money, to monasteries already erected. So that in time the monasteries became the owners of great landed estates; they had the lordship over innumerable manors, and had a tenantry of prodigious extent, especially in England, where the monastic orders were always held in great esteem, in consequence of Christianity having been introduced into the kingdom by a community of monks.

England, more, perhaps, than any other country in Europe, abounded in such institutions, and these more richly endowed than anywhere else. In England there was,

on average, more than twenty (we shall see the exact number by-and-by) of those establishments to a county! Here
was a prize for an unjust and cruel tyrant to lay his lawless
hands upon, and for "Reformation" gentry to share
amongst them! Here was enough, indeed, to make robbers
on a grand scale cry out against "monkish ignorance and
superstition"! No wonder that the bowels of Cranmer,
Knox, and all the rest, yearned so piteously as they did,
when they cast their pious eyes on all the farms and
manors, and on all the silver and gold ornaments, belonging to these communities! We shall see by-and-by with
what alacrity they ousted, plundered, and pulled down: we
shall see them robbing, under the basest pretences, even
the altars of the country parish churches, down to the very
smallest of those churches, and down to the value of five
shillings. But we must first take a view of the motives
which led the tyrant, Henry VIII, to set their devastating
and plundering faculties in motion.

This king succeeded his father, Henry VII, in the year
1509. He succeeded to a great and prosperous kingdom, a
full treasury, and a happy and contented people, who
expected in him the wisdom of his father without his
avarice, which seems to have been that father's only fault.
Henry VIII. was eighteen years old when his father died. He
had had an elder brother, named Arthur, who, at the early
age of twelve years, had been betrothed to Catherine,
fourth daughter of Ferdinand, King of Castile and Arragon.
When Arthur was fourteen years old, the Princess came to
England, and the marriage ceremony was performed; but
Arthur, who was a weak and sickly boy, died before the year
was out, and the marriage never was consummated; and,
indeed, who will believe that it could be? Henry wished to
marry Catherine, and the marriage was agreed to by the
parents on both sides; but it did not take place until after
the death of Henry VII. The moment the young King came
to the throne, he took measures for his marriage. Catherine
being, though only nominally, the widow of his deceased

brother, it was necessary to have from the Pope, as supreme head of the Church, a dispensation in order to render the marriage lawful in the eye of the canon law. The dispensation, to which there could be no valid objection, was obtained, and the marriage was, amidst the rejoicings of the whole nation, celebrated in June, 1509, in less than two months after the King's accession.

With this lady, who was beautiful in her youth, and whose virtues of all sorts seem scarcely ever to have been exceeded, he lived in the married state seventeen years, before the end of which he had had three sons and two daughters by her, one of whom only, a daughter, was still alive, who afterwards was Mary, Queen of England. But now, at the end of seventeen years, he being thirty-five years of age, and eight years younger than the queen, and having cast his eyes on a young lady, an attendant on the queen, named Anne Boleyn, he, all of a sudden, affected to believe that he was living in sin because he was married to the widow of his brother, though, as we have seen, the marriage between Catherine and the brother had never been consummated, and though the parents of both the parties, together with his own Council, unanimously and unhesitatingly approved of his marriage, which had, moreover, been sanctioned by the Pope, the head of the Church, of the faith and observances of which Henry himself had, as we shall hereafter see, been, long since his marriage, a zealous defender.

But the tyrant's passions were now in motion, and he resolved to gratify them, cost what it might in reputation, in treasure, and in blood. He first applied to the Pope to divorce him from his queen. He was a great favourite of the Pope, he was very powerful, there were many strong motives for yielding to his request; but that request was so full of injustice, it would have been so cruel towards the virtuous queen to accede to it, that the Pope could not and did not grant it. He, however, in hopes that time might induce the tyrant to relent, ordered a court to be held by his Legate and Wolsey, in England, to hear and determine the case. Before this court the Queen disdained to plead, and the Legate, dissolving the court referred the matter back to the Pope, who still refused to take any step towards the granting of the divorce. The tyrant now became furious, resolved upon overthrowing the power of the Pope in England, upon making himself the head of the Church in this country, and upon doing whatever else might be necessary to insure the gratification of his desires and the glutting of his vengeance.

By making himself the supreme head of the Church, he made himself, he having the sword and the gibbet at his command, master of all the property of that Church, including that of the monasteries! His counsellors and courtiers knew this; and as it was soon discovered that a sweeping confiscation would take place, the parliament was by no means backward in aiding his designs, everyone hoping to share in the plunder. The first step was to pass acts taking from the Pope all authority and power over the Church in England, and giving to the King all authority whatever as to ecclesiastical matters. His chief adviser and abettor was Thomas Cranmer, a name which deserves to be held in everlasting execration; a name which we could not pronounce without almost doubting of the justice of God, were it not for our knowledge of the fact that the cold-blooded, most perfidious man expired at last amidst those flames which he himself had been the chief cause of kindling.

The tyrant, being now both Pope and King, made Cranmer archbishop of Canterbury, a dignity just then become vacant. Of course, this adviser and ready tool now became chief judge in all ecclesiatical matters. But here was a difficulty; for the tyrant still professed to be a Catholic; so that his new Archbishop was to be consecrated according to the usual pontifical form, which required of him to swear obedience to the Pope. And here a transaction took place that will at once show us of what sort of stuff the "Reformation" gentry were made. Cranmer, before he went to the altar to be consecrated, went into a chapel, and there made a declaration on oath, that by the oath he was about to take, and which, for the sake of form, he was obliged to take, he did not intend to bind himself to anything that tended to prevent him from assisting the King in making any such "reforms" as he might think useful in the Church of England! I once knew a corrupt Cornish knave, who, having sworn to a direct falsehood (and that he, in private, acknowledged to be such) before an Election Committee of the House of Commons, being asked how he could possibly give such evidence, actually declared, in so many words, "that he had, before he left his lodging in the morning, taken an oath that he would swear falsely that day." He, perhaps, imbibed his principles from this very Archbishop, who occupies the highest place in lying Fox's lying book on Protestant Martyrs.

Having provided himself with so famous a judge in ecclesiastical matters, the King lost, of course, no time in bringing his hard case before him and demanding justice at his hands! Hard case, indeed; to be compelled to live with a wife of forty-three, when he could have, for next to nothing, and only for asking for, a young one of eighteen or twenty! A really hard case; and he sought relief, now that he had got such an upright and impartial judge, with all imaginable despatch. What I am now going to relate of the conduct of this Archbishop and of the other parties concerned in the transaction is calculated to make us shudder with horror, to make our very bowels heave with loathing, to make us turn our eyes from the paper and resolve to read no further. But we must not give way to these feelings if we have a mind to know the true history of the Protestant "Reformation." We must keep ourselves cool; we must reason ourselves out of our ordinary impulses; we must beseech nature to be quiet within us for a while: for, from first to last, we have to contemplate nothing that is not of a kind to fill us with horror and disgust.

It was now four or five years since the King and Cranmer had begun to hatch the project of the divorce; but, in the meanwhile, the King had kept Anne Boleyn, or, in more modern phrase she had been "under his protection," for about three years. And here let me state that in Dr. Bayley's *Life of Bishop Fisher* it is positively asserted, that Anne Boleyn was the King's daughter, and that Lady Boleyn, her mother, said to the King, when he was about to marry Anne, "Sir, for the reverence of God, take heed what you do in marrying my daughter, for, if you record your own conscience well, she is your own daughter as well as mine." To which the king replied, "Whose daughter soever she is, she shall be my wife." Now, though I believe this fact, I do not give it as a thing the truth of which is undeniable. I find it in the writings of a man who was the eulogist (and justly) of the excellent Bishop Fisher, who suffered death because he stood firmly on the side of Queen Catherine. I believe it; but I do not give it, as I do the other facts that I state, as what is undeniably true. God knows, it is unnecessary to make the parties blacker than they are made by the Protestant historians themselves, in even a favourable record of their horrid deeds.

The King had had Anne about three years "under his protection," when she became, for the first time, with child. There was, now, therefore, no time to be lost in order to "make an honest woman of her." A private marriage took place in January, 1533. As Anne's pregnancy could not be long disguised, it became necessary to avow her marriage, and therefore it was also necessary to press onward the trial for the divorce, for it might have seemed rather awkward, even amongst "Reformation" people, for the King to have two wives at a time! Now, then, the famous ecclesiastical judge, Cranmer, had to play his part; and if his hypocrisy did not make the devil blush, he could have no blushing faculties in him. Cranmer, in April, 1533, wrote a letter to the King, begging him, for the good of the nation and for the safety of his own soul, to grant his permission to try the question of the divorce, and beseeching him no longer to live in the peril attending an "incestuous intercourse!" Matchless, astonishing hypocrite! He knew, and the King knew that he knew,

and he knew that the King knew that he knew it, that the
King had been actually married to Anne three months
before, she being with child at the time when he married her.

The King graciously condescended to listen to this
ghostly advice of his pious primate, who was so anxious
about the safety of his royal soul, and, without delay, he,
as head of the Church, granted the ghostly father,
Cranmer, who in violation of his clerical vows, had, in
private, a woman of his own; to this ghostly father the
King granted a licence to hold a spiritual court for the
trial of the divorce. Queen Catherine, who had been
ordered to retire from the court, resided at this time at
Ampthill, in Bedfordshire, at a little distance from
Dunstable. At this latter place Cranmer opened his court,
and sent a citation to the Queen to appear before him,
which citation she treated with the scorn that it deserved.
When he had kept his "court" open the number of days
required by the law, he pronounced sentence against the
Queen, declaring her marriage with the King null from
the beginning; and having done this, he closed his farcical
court. We shall see him doing more jobs in the divorcing
line; but thus he finished the first.

The result of this trial was, by this incomparable judge,
made known to the King, whom this wonderful hypocrite
gravely besought to submit himself with resignation to the
will of God, as declared to him in this decision of the spiritual court, acting according to the laws of holy Church!
The pious and resigned King yielded to the admonition;
and then Cranmer held another court at Lambeth, at which
he declared that the King had been lawfully married to
Anne Boleyn, and that he now confirmed the marriage by
his pastoral and judicial authority, which he derived from
the successors of the Apostles! We shall see him by-and-by,
exercising the same authority to declare this new marriage
null and void from the beginning, and see him assist in bas-
tardizing the fruit of it; but we must now follow Anne
Boleyn (whom the Protestant writers strain hard to white-

wash) till we have seen the end of her.

She was delivered of a daughter (who was afterwards Queen Elizabeth) at the end of eight months from the date of her marriage. This did not please the king, who wanted a son, and who was quite monster enough to be displeased with her on this account. The couple jogged on apparently without quarrelling for about three years; a pretty long time, if we duly consider the many obstacles which vice opposes to peace and happiness. The husband, however, had plenty of occupation, for being now, "head of the church," he had a deal to manage; he had, poor man, to labour hard at making a new religion, new articles of faith, new rules of discipline, and he had new things of all sorts to prepare. Besides which, he had, as we shall see later, some of the best men in his kingdom, and that ever lived in any kingdom or country, to behead, hang, rip up, and cut into quarters. He had, moreover, as we shall see, begun the grand work of confiscation, plunder and devastation. So that he could not have a great deal of time for family squabbles.

If, however, he had not time to jar with Anne, he had no time to look after her, which is a thing to be thought of when a man marries a woman half his own age; and that this "great female reformer," as some of the Protestant writers call her, wanted a little of husband-like vigilance, we are now going to see. The freedom, or rather the looseness, of her manners, so very different from those of that virtuous queen whom the English court and nation had had before them as an example for so many years, gave offence to the more sober, and excited the mirth and set a-going the chat of persons of another description. In January, 1536, Queen Catherine died. She had been banished from the court. She had seen her marriage annulled by Cranmer, and her daughter and only surviving child bastardized by act of parliament; and the husband, who had had five children by her, that "Reformation" husband, had had the barbarity to keep her separated from, and never to suffer her, after her banishment, to set her eyes on that only child! She died, as she had lived, beloved and revered by every good man and woman in the kingdom, and was buried, amidst the sobbings and tears of a vast assemblage of the people, in the Abbey-church of Peterborough.

The King, whose iron heart seems to have been softened, for a moment, by a most affecting letter, which she dictated to him from her death-bed, ordered the persons about him to wear mourning on the day of her burial. But our famous "great female reformer" not only did not wear mourning, but dressed herself out in the gayest and gaudiest attire; expressed her unbounded joy; and said that she was now in reality a queen! Alas, for our "great female reformer!" in just three months and sixteen days from this day of her exultation, she died herself; not, however, as the real queen had died, in her bed, deeply lamented by all the good, and without a soul on earth to impute to her a single fault, but on a scaffold, under a death-warrant signed by her husband, and charged with treason, adultery, and incest!

In the month of May, 1536, she was along with the King, amongst the spectators at a tilting-match at Greenwich, when, being incautious, she gave to one of the combatants, who was also one of her paramours, a sign of her attachment, which seems only to have confirmed the King in suspicions which he before entertained. He instantly quitted the place, returned to Westminster, ordered her to be confined at Greenwich that night, and to be brought by water to Westminster the next day. But she was met, by his order, on the river, and conveyed to the Tower; and, as if it were to remind her of the injustice which she had so mainly assisted in committing against the late virtuous queen; as it were to say to her, "see, after all, God is just," she was imprisoned in the very room in which she had slept the night before her coronation!

From the moment of her imprisonment her behaviour indicated anything but conscious innocence. She was charged with adultery committed with four gentlemen of the King's household, and with incest with her brother, Lord Rochford, and she was, of course, charged with treason, those being acts of treason by law. They were all found guilty, and all put to death. But, before Anne was executed, our friend, Thomas Cranmer, had another tough job to perform. The King, who never did things by halves, ordered, as "head of the Church," the Archbishop to hold his "spiritual court," and to divorce him from Anne!

He cited the King and Queen to appear in his "court"! (Oh! that court!) His citation stated that their marriage had been unlawful, that they were living in adultery, and that, for the "salvation of their souls," they should come and show cause why they should not be separated. They were just going to be separated most effectually; for this was on May 17, and Anne, who had been condemned to death on the 15th, was to be, and was, executed on the 19th! They both obeyed this citation, and appeared before him by their proctors; and, after having heard these, Cranmer, who, observe, afterwards drew up the Book of Common Prayer, wound up the blasphemous farce by pronouncing, "in the name of Christ and for the honour of God," that the marriage "was, and always had been, null and void!" Good God! But we must not give way to exclamations, or they will interrupt us at every step. Thus was the daughter, Elizabeth, bastardized by the decision of the very man who had not only pronounced her mother's marriage lawful, but who had been the contriver of that marriage! And yet Burnet has the impudence to say that Cranmer "appears to have done every thing with a good conscience!"

On the 19th Anne was beheaded in the Tower, put into an elm coffin, and buried there. At the place of execution she did not pretend that she was innocent; and there appears to me to be very little doubt of her having done some at least of the things imputed to her: but, if her marriage with the King had "always been null and void"; that is to say, if she had never been married to him, how could she, by her commerce with other men, have been found guilty of treason? On the 15th she is condemned as the wife of the King, and on the 17th she is pronounced never to have been his wife, and on the 19th she is executed for having been his unfaithful wife! However, as to the effect which this event has upon the character of the "Reformation," it signifies not a straw whether she were guilty or innocent of the crimes now laid to her charge; for, if she were innocent, how are we to describe the monsters who brought her to the block? How are we to describe that "head of the Church" and that Archbishop, who had now the management of the religious affairs of England? It is said that the evening before her execution, she begged the lady of the lieutenant of the Tower to go to the Princess Mary, and beg her to pardon her for the many wrongs she had done her. There were others to whom she had done wrongs. She had been the cause, and the guilty cause, of breaking the heart of the rightful queen; she had caused the blood of More and of Fisher to be shed; and she had been the promoter of Cranmer, and his aider and abettor in all those crafty and pernicious councils, by acting upon which an obstinate and hard-hearted King had plunged the kingdom into confusion and blood. The King, in order to show his total disregard for her, and, as it were, to repay her for her conduct on the day of the funeral of Catherine, dressed himself in white on the day of her execution; and, the very next day, was married to Jane Seymour, at Marevell Hall, in Hampshire.

CHAPTER THREE

Sunk as the country was by the members of the Parliament, hoping to share, as they finally did, in the plunder of the Church and the poor; selfish and servile as was the conduct of the courtiers, the king's councillors, and the people's representatives; still there were some men to raise their voices against the illegality and cruelty of the divorce of Catherine, as well as against that great preparatory measure of plunder, the taking of the spiritual supremacy from the Pope and giving it to the king. The bishops, all but one, which one we shall presently see dying on the scaffold rather than abandon his integrity, were terrified into acquiescence, or, at least, into silence. But there were many of the parochial clergy, and a large part of the monks and friars, who were not thus acquiescent or silent. These, by their sermons and by their conversations, made the truth pretty generally known to the people at large; and though they did not succeed in preventing the calamities which they saw approaching, they rescued the character of their country from the infamy of silent submission.

Of all the duties of the historian, the most sacred is that of recording the conduct of those who have stood forward to defend helpless innocence against the attacks of powerful guilt. This duty calls on me to make particular mention of the conduct of the two friars, Peyto and Elstow. The former, preaching before the King at Greenwich, just previous to his marriage with Anne, and taking for his text the passage in the first book of Kings, where Micaiah prophecies against Ahab, who was surrounded with flatterers and lying prophets, said, "I am that Micaiah, whom you will hate because I must tell you truly that this marriage is unlawful; and I know that I shall eat the bread of affliction and drink the water of sorrow; yet, because the Lord hath put it in my mouth I must speak it. Your flatterers are the four hundred prophets, who, in the spirit of lying, seek to deceive you. But take good heed lest you, being seduced, find Ahab's punishment, which was to have his blood licked up by dogs. It is one of the greatest miseries in princes to be daily abused by flatterers." The King took this reproof in silence; but the next Sunday a Dr. Curwin preached in the same place before the King, and having called Peyto dog, slanderer, base beggarly friar, rebel and traitor, and having said that he had fled for fear and shame, Elstow, who was present and who was a fellow-friar of Peyto, called out aloud to Curwin and said, "Good sir, you know that Father Peyto is now gone to a provincial council at Canterbury, and not fled for fear of you; for tomorrow he will return. In the meanwhile I am here as another Micaiah, and will lay down my life to prove all those things true which he hath taught out of Holy Scripture; and to this combat I challenge thee before God and all equal judges; even unto thee, Curwin, I say, which art one of the four hundred false prophets into whom the spirit of lying is entered, and seekest by adultery to establish a succession, betraying the King into endless perdition."

Stowe, who relates this in his Chronicle, says that Elstow "waxed hot, so that they could not make him cease his speech until the King himself bade him hold his peace." The two friars were brought the next day before the King's council who rebuked them and told them that they deserved to be put into a sack and thrown into the Thames. Whereupon Elstow said smiling, "Threaten these things to rich and dainty persons, who are clothed in purple, fare deliciously, and have their chiefest hope in this world; for we esteem them not, but are joyful that, for the discharge of our duty, we are driven hence: and, with thanks to God, we know the way to heaven to be as ready by water as by land."

It is impossible to speak with sufficient admiration of the conduct of these men. Ten thousand victories by land or sea would not bespeak so much heroism in the winners of those victories as was shown by these friars. If the bishops, or only a fourth part of them, had shown equal courage, the tyrant would have stopped in that career which was now on the eve of producing so many horrors. The stand made against him by these two poor friars was the only instance of bold and open resistance until he had actually got into his murders and robberies; and, seeing that there never was yet found even a Protestant pen, except the vile pen of Burnet, to offer so much as an apology for the deeds of this tyrant, one would think that the heroic virtue of Peyto and Elstow ought to be sufficient to make us hesitate before we talk of "monkish ignorance and superstition." Recollect, that there was no wild fanaticism in the conduct of those men, that they could not be actuated by any selfish motive, that they stood forward in the cause of morality, and in defence of a person whom they had never personally known, and that, too with certainty of incurring the most severe punishments, if not death itself. Before their conduct how the heroism of the Hampdens and the Russells sinks from our sight!

We now come to the consideration of that copious source of blood, the suppression of the Pope's supremacy. To deny the King's supremacy was made high treason, and to refuse to take an oath acknowledging that supremacy was deemed a denial of it.

The Scripture tells us that Christ's Church was to be one. We, in repeating the Apostles' Creed, say, "I believe in the Holy Catholic Church." Catholic, as we have seen in Chapter 1 means universal. And how can we believe in a universal Church without believing that that Church is one, and under the direction of one head?

How is the faith of all nations to continue to be one, if there be in every nation a head of the Church, who is to be appealed to, in the last resort, as to all questions, as to all points of dispute, which may arise? How, if this be the case, is there to be "one fold and one shepherd"? How is there to be "one faith and one baptism"? How are the "unity of the spirit and the bond of peace" to be preserved? We shall presently see what unity and what peace there were in England, the moment the King became the head of the Church.

If, however, we still insist that the Pope's supremacy and its accompanying circumstances produced ignorance, superstition and slavery, let us act the part of sincere, consistent and honest men. Let us knock down, or blow up, the cathedrals and colleges and old churches: let us sweep away the three courts, the twelve judges, the circuits and the jury boxes; let us demolish all that we inherit from those whose religion we denounce, and whose memory we affect so heartily to despise; let us demolish all this, and we shall have left —all our own— the capacious jails and penitentiaries, the stock-exchange, the hot, ankle and knee-swelling and lung-destroying cotton-factories; the whiskered standing army and its splendid barracks; the parson-captains, parson-lieutenants, parson-ensigns and parson-justices, the poor-rates and the pauper-houses; and, by no means forgetting that blessing which is peculiarly and doubly and "gloriously" Protestant, —the National Debt. Ah! people of England, how have you been deceived!

We have been told of "the thunders of the Vatican" till we have almost believed that the Pope's residence was in the skies; and, if we had believed it quite, the belief would not have surpassed in folly our belief in numerous other stories hatched by the gentry of the "Reformation." The truth is, that the Pope had no power but that which he derived from the free will of the people. The people were frequently on his side in his contests with kings; and by this means, they, in numerous instances, preserved their rights against the attempts of tyrants. If the Pope had had no power there must have sprung up an oligarchy, or something else, to check the power of the king; or every king might have been a Nero, if he would. We shall soon see a worse than Nero in Henry VIII; we shall soon see him laying all law prostrate at his feet; and plundering his people, down even to the patrimony of the poor.

Thus, then, this so much abused papal supremacy was a most salutary thing: it was the only check, then existing, on despotic power, besides being absolutely necessary to that unity of faith without which there could be nothing worthy of the name of a Catholic Church. To abjure this supremacy was an act of apostacy, and also an act of base abandonment of the rights of the people. To require it of any man was to violate Magna Charta and all the laws of the land; and to put men to death for refusing to comply with the request was to commit unqualified murder. Yet without such murder, without shedding innocent blood, it was impossible to effect the object. Blood must flow. Amongst the victims to this act of outrageous tyranny were Sir Thomas More and Bishop Fisher. The former had been the Lord High Chancellor for many years. The character given of him by his contemporaries, and by every one to the present day, is that of as great perfection for learning, integrity, and piety, as it is possible for a human being to possess. He was the greatest lawyer of his age, a long-tried and most faithful servant of the King and his father, and was, besides, so highly distinguished beyond men in general for his gentleness and humility of manners, as well as for his talents and abilities, that his murder gave a shock to all Europe. Fisher was equally eminent in point of learning, piety, and integrity. He was the only surviving privy-councillor of the late King, whose mother (the grandmother of Henry VIII.), having outlived her son and daughter, besought, with her dying breath, the young king to listen particularly to the advice of this learned, pious, and venerable prelate; and, until that advice thwarted his brutal passions, he was in the habit of saying that no other prince could boast of a subject to be compared with Fisher. He used, at the council-board, to take him by the hand and call him his father; marks of favour and affection which the bishop repaid by zeal and devotion which knew no bounds other than those prescribed by his duty to God, his king, and his country. But that sacred duty bade him object to the divorce and to the King's supremacy; and then the tyrant, forgetting, at once, all his services, all his devotion, all his unparalleled attachment, sent him to the block, after fifteen months of imprisonment, during which he lay, worse than a common felon, buried in filth and almost destitute of food; sent him, who had been his boast, and whom he had called his father, to perish under the axe; dragged him forth, with limbs tottering under him, his venerable face and hoary locks begrimed, and his nakedness scarcely covered with the rags left on his body; dragged him thus forth to the scaffold, and, even when the life was gone, left him to lie on that scaffold like a dead dog! Savage monster! Rage stems the torrent of our tears, hurries us back to the horrid scene, and bids us look about for a dagger to plunge into the heart of the tyrant.

And yet, the calculating, cold-blooded, and brazen Burnet has the audacity to say that "such a man as Henry VIII. was necessary to bring about the Reformation!" He means, of course, that such measures as those of Henry were necessary; and, if they were necessary, what must be the nature and tendency of that "Reformation"?

The work of blood was now begun, and it proceeded with steady pace. All who refused to take the oath of supremacy, — that is to say, all who refused to become apostates, — were considered and treated as traitors, and made to suffer death accompanied with every possible cruelty and indignity. As a specimen of the works of Burnet's necessary reformer, and to spare the reader repetition on the subject, let us take the treatment of John Houghton, prior of the Charterhouse in London, which was then a convent of Carthusian monks. This prior, for having refused to take the oath, which, observe, he could not take without committing perjury, was dragged to Tyburn. He was scarcely suspended when the rope was cut, and he fell alive on the ground. His clothes were then stripped off; his bowels were ripped up; his heart and entrails were torn from his body and flung into a fire; his head was cut from his body; the body was divided into quarters and parboiled; the quarters were then subdivided, and hung up in different parts of the city; and one arm was nailed to the wall over the entrance into the monastery!

Such were the means which Burnet said were necessary to introduce the Protestant religion into England! How different, alas! from the means by which the Catholic religion had been introduced by Pope Gregory and Saint Austin! These horrid butcheries were perpetrated, mind, under the primacy of Fox's great martyr, Cranmer, and with the active agency of another ruffian, named Thomas Cromwell, whom we shall soon see sharing with Cranmer the work of plunder, and finally sharing, too, in his disgraceful end.

We must now, before we state more particulars relating to Luther and the sects that he gave rise to, see how the King of England dealt with those of his subjects who had adopted the heresy.

The Protestants immediately began to disagree amongst themselves; but they all maintained that faith alone was sufficient to secure salvation, while the Catholics maintained that good works were also necessary. If Luther had begun twelve years later the King would have been a Protestant at once, especially after seeing that this new religion allowed Luther and seven other of his brother leaders in the "Reformation" to grant, under their hands, a licence to the Landgrave of Hesse to have two wives at one and the same time! So complaisant a religion would have been, and doubtless was, at the time of the divorce, precisely to the King's taste; but, as I have just observed, it came twelve years too soon for him; for, not only had he not adopted this religion, but had opposed it as a sovereign; and, which was a still more serious affair, had opposed it as an author! He had, in 1521, written a book against it. His vanity and his pride were engaged in the contest; to which may be added, that Luther, in answering his book, had called him "a pig, an ass, a dunghill, the spawn of an adder, a basilisk, a lying buffoon dressed in a king's robes, a mad fool with a frothy mouth and a whorish face;" and had afterwards said to him, "you lie, you stupid and sacriligious king."

His book against Luther had acquired him the title of "Defender of the Faith," of which we shall see more by-and-by. He could not, therefore, without recantation, be a Protestant; and, indeed, his pride would not suffer him to become the proselyte of a man who had, in print too, proclaimed him to be a pig, an ass, a fool, and a liar. Yet he could not pretend to be a Catholic. He was therefore compelled to make a religion of his own. This was doing nothing, unless he enforced its adoption by what he called law. Laws were made by him and by his servile and plundering parliament, condemning to the flames as heretics all who did not expressly conform, by acts as well as by declarations, to the faith and worship which, as head of the Church, he invented and ordained. Amongst his tenets there were such as neither Catholics nor Protestants could, consistently with their creeds, adopt. He therefore sent both to the stake, and sometimes, in order to add mental pangs to those of the body, he dragged them to the fire on the same hurdle, tied together in pairs, back to back, each pair containing a Catholic and a Protestant. Was this the way that Saint Austin and Saint Patrick propogated their religion? Yet, such is the malignity of Burnet, and of many, many others, called Protestant "divines," that they apologize for, if they do not absolutely applaud, this execrable tyrant, at the very moment that they are compelled to confess that he soaked the earth with Protestant blood and filled the air with the fumes of their roasting flesh.

Throughout the whole of this bloody work, Cranmer, who was the primate of the King's religion, was consenting to, sanctioning, and aiding and abetting in, the murdering of Protestants as well as Catholics; though, and I pray you mark it well, Hume, Tillotson, Burnet, and all his long lists of eulogists, say, and make it matter of merit in him, that all this while he was himself a sincere Protestant in his heart! And, indeed, we shall, by-and-by see him openly avowing those very tenets, for the holding of which he had been instrumental in sending, without regard to age or sex, others to perish in the flames. The progress of this man in the paths of infamy needed incontestable proof to reconcile the human mind to a belief in it. Before he became a priest he had married; after he became a priest, and had taken the oath of celibacy, he, being then in Germany and having become a Protestant, married another wife. Being the primate of Henry's Church, which still forbade the clergy to have wives, and which held them to their oath of celibacy, he had his wife brought to England in a chest, with holes bored in it to give her air! As the cargo was destined for Canterbury, it was landed at Gravesend, where the sailors, not apprised of the contents of the chest, set it up on end, and the wrong end downwards, and had nearly broken the neck of the poor frow! Here was a pretty scene! A German wife and children, kept in hugger-mugger on that spot which had been the cradle of English Christianity; that spot where St. Austin had inhabited, and where Thomas à Becket had sealed with his blood his opposition to a tyrant who aimed at the destruction of the Church and at the pillage of the people! Here is quite enough to fill us with disgust: but when we reflect that this same primate, while he had under his roof his wife and her children was engaged in assisting to send Protestants to the flames because they dissented from a system that forbade the clergy to have wives,

we swell with indignation; —not against Cranmer, for, though there are so many of his atrocious deeds yet to come, he has exhausted our store; not against Hume, for he professed no regard for any religion at all; but against those who are called "divines," and who are the eulogists of Cranmer; against Burnet, who says that Cranmer "did all with a good conscience;" and against Dr. Sturges, or, rather, the Dean and Chapter of Winchester, who clubbed their "talents" in getting up the Reflections on Popery, who talk of the "respectable Cranmer," and who have the audacity to put him, in point of integrity, upon a level with Sir Thomas More!

The King received the title from the Pope, as a reward for his written defence of the Catholic faith against Luther. The Pope conferred on him this title, which was to descend to his posterity. The title was given by Pope Leo X., in a bull or edict, beginning with these words: "Leo, servant of the servants of the Lord, to his most dear son, Henry, King of England, Defender of the Faith, all health and happiness." The bull then goes on to say, that the King having in defence of the faith of the Catholic Church written a book against Martin Luther, the Pope and his Council had determined to confer on him and his successors the title of Defender of the Faith. "We," says the bull, "sitting in this Holy See, having with mature deliberation considered the business with our brethren, do with their unanimous counsel and consent grant unto your Majesty, your heirs and successors, the title of Defender of the Faith; which we do by these presents, confirm unto you; commanding all the faithful to give your Majesty this title."

But there is a little more to be said about this title of Defender of the Faith, which, for some reason or other that one can hardly discover, seems to have been, down to our time, a singularly great favourite. Edward VI, —though his two "Protectors," who succeeded each other in that office, and whose guilty heads we shall gladly see succeeding each other on the block, abolished the Catholic faith by law; though the Protestant faith was, with the help of foreign troops, established in its stead; and though the greedy ruffians of his time robbed the very altars, under the pretext of extirpating that very faith of which his title called him the Defender; —continued to wear this title throughout his reign. Elizabeth continued to wear this title during her long reign of "mischief and misery," as Whitaker justly calls it, though during the whole of that reign she was busily engaged in persecuting, in ruining, in ripping up the bowels of those who entertained that faith of which she styled herself the Defender, in which she herself had been born, in which she had lived for many years, and to which she adhered openly and privately till her self-interest called upon her to abandon it. She continued to wear this title while she was tearing the bowels out of her subjects for hearing mass, while she was refusing the last comforts of the Catholic religion to her cousin, Mary, Queen of Scotland, whom she put to death by a mockery of law and justice, after, as Whitaker has fully proved, having long endeavoured in vain, to find amongst her subjects a man base and bloody enough to take her victim off by assassination. This title was worn by that mean creature, James I, who took as his chief councillor the right worthy son of that father who had been the chief contriver of the murder of his innocent mother, and whose reign was one unbroken series of base plots and cruel persecutions of all who professed the Catholic faith. But, not to anticipate further matter which will, hereafter, find a more suitable place, we may observe that amongst all our sovereigns the only real Defenders of the Faith, since the reign of Mary, have been King George III. and his son; the former, by assenting to a repeal of a part of the penal code, and by his appointing a special commission to try, condemn,and execute the leaders of the ferocious mob who set fire to, and who wished to sack London, in 1780, with the cry of "no popery" in their mouths and from pretended zeal for the Protestant religion, and the latter, by his sending, in 1814, a body of English troops to assist as a guard of honour at the re-instalment of the Pope. Let us hope that his defence of the faith is not to stop here; but that unto him is reserved the real glory of being the Defender of the Faith of all his subjects, and of healing for ever those deep and festering wounds which, for more than two centuries, have been inflicted on so large and so loyal a part of his people.

The King's predecessors had another title. They were called Kings of France; a title of much longer standing than that of Defender of the Faith. That title, a title of great glory, and one of which we were very proud, was not won by "Gospellers" or Presbyterians. It was, along with the Three

Feathers, which the King so long wore, won by our brave Catholic ancestors. It was won while the Pope's supremacy, while confessions to priests, while absolutions, indulgences, masses, and monasteries existed in England. It was won by Catholics in "the dark ages of monkish ignorance and superstition." It was surrendered in an age enlightened by "a heaven-born" Protestant and pledge-breaking minister. It was won by valour and surrendered by fear.

CHAPTER FOUR

When we left the King and Cranmer at their bloody work, we had come to the year 1536, and to the 27th. year of the King's reign. In the year 1528 an act had been passed to exempt the King from paying any sum of money that he might have borrowed; another act followed this for a similar purpose, and thus thousands of persons were ruined. His new Queen, Jane Seymour, brought him, in 1537, a son, who was afterwards king, under the title of Edward VI; but the mother died in childbirth and, according to Sir Richard Baker, "had her body ripped up to preserve the child"! In this great "Reformation" man all was of a piece, all was consistent; he seemed never to have any compassion for the sufferings of any human being; and this is a characteristic which Whitaker gives to his daughter Elizabeth.

Having a son for a successor, he with his Parliament enacted in 1537 that Mary and Elizabeth, his two daughters, were illegitimate, and that in case of a want of lawful issue the king should be enabled, by letters patent or by his last will, to give the crown to whomsoever he pleased! To cap the whole, to complete a series of acts of tyranny such as were never before heard of, it was enacted in 1537, and in the 28th. year of his reign, that except in cases of mere private right "the King's proclamation should be of the same force as Acts of Parliament"! Thus, then, all law and justice were laid prostrate at the feet of a single man, and that man a man with whom law was a mockery, on whom the name of justice was a libel, and to whom mercy was wholly unknown.

It is easy to imagine that no man's property or life could have security with power like this in the hands of such a man. Magna Charta had been trampled under foot from the moment that the Pope's supremacy was assailed. The famous act of Edward the Third, for the security of the people against unfounded charges of high treason, was wholly set aside. Numerous things were made high treason which were never before thought criminal at all. The trials were for a long while a mere mockery, and at last they were altogether, in many cases, laid aside and the accused were condemned to death, not only without being arraigned and heard in their defence, but in numerous cases without being apprised of the crimes or pretended crimes for which they were executed. He spared neither sex nor age if the parties possessed, or were suspected of possessing, that integrity which made them disapprove of his deeds. To look awry excited his suspicion, and his suspicion was death. England, before his reign so happy, so free, knowing so little of crime as to present to the judges of assize scarcely three criminals in a county in a year, now saw upwards of sixty thousand persons shut up in her jails at one and the same time. The

purlieus of the court of this "first-born son of the
Reformation" were a great human slaughter-house; his people, deserted by their natural leaders, who had been bribed
by plunder or the hope of plunder, were the terrified and
trembling flock; while he, the master-butcher, fat and
jocose, sat in his palace issuing orders for the slaughter,
while his high priest, Cranmer, stood ready to sanction and
to sanctify all his deeds.

A detail of these butcheries could only disgust and weary
the reader. One instance, however, must not be omitted;
namely, the slaughtering of the relations and particularly
the mother of Cardinal Pole. The Cardinal, who had, when
very young and before the King's first divorce had been agi-
tated, been a great favourite with the King, and had pursued his studies and travels on the Continent at the King's
expense, disapproved of the divorce and of all the acts that
followed it; and though called home by the King he refused
to obey. He was a man of great learning, talent and virtue,
and his opinions had great weight in England. His mother,
the Countess of Salisbury, was descended from the
Plantagenets, and was the last living descendant of that
long race of English kings. Margaret, Countess of Salisbury,
was the daughter of George, Duke of Clarence, brother of
King Edwards IV. So that the Cardinal, who had been by
the Pope raised to that dignity on account of his great
learning and eminent virtues, was thus a relation of the
King, as his mother was of course, and she was, too, the
nearest of all his relations. But the Cardinal was opposed to
the King's proceedings; and that was enough to excite and
put in motion the deadly vengeance of the latter. Many
were the arts that he made use of, and great in amount was
the treasure of the people that he expended, in order to
bring the Cardinal's person within his grasp; and these having failed, he resolved to wreak his ruthless vengeance on
his kindred and aged mother. She was charged by the base
Thomas Cromwell (of whom we shall soon see enough)
with having persuaded her tenants not to read the new

translations of the Bible, and also with having received bulls from Rome, which the accuser said were found at Cowdray House, her seat in Sussex. Cromwell also showed a banner which had, he said, been used by certain rebels in the north, and which he said he found in her house. All this was, however, so very barefaced that it was impossible to think of a trial. The judges were then asked whether the Parliament could not attaint her; that is to say, condemn her without giving her a hearing. The judges said that it was a dangerous matter; that they could not in their courts act in this manner, and that they thought the Parliament never would. But being asked whether, if the Parliament were to do it, it would remain good in law, they answered in the affirmative. That was enough. A bill was brought in, and thus was the Countess, together with the Marchioness of Exeter and two gentlemen, relations of the Cardinal, condemned to death. The two latter were executed, the Marchioness was pardoned, and the Countess shut up in prison as a sort of hostage for the conduct of her son. In a few months, however, an insurrection having broken out on account of his tyrannical acts, the King chose to suspect that the rebels had been instigated by Cardinal Pole, and forth he dragged his mother to the scaffold. She, who was upwards of seventy years of age, though worn down in body by her imprisonment, maintained to the last a true sense of her character and noble descent. When bidden to lay her head upon the block: "No," answered she, "my head shall never bow to tyranny: it never committed treason; and if you will have it, you must get it as you can." The executioner struck at her neck with his axe, and as she ran about the scaffold with her gray locks hanging down her shoulders and breast, he pursued, giving her repeated chops, till at last he brought her down!

Is it a scene in Turkey or in Tripoli that we are contemplating? No; but in England, where Magna Charta had been so lately in force, where nothing could have been done contrary to law; but where all power ecclesiastical as well as lay being placed in the hands of one man, bloody butcheries like this, which would have roused even a Turkish populace to resistance, could be perpetrated without the smallest danger to the perpetrator. Hume, in his remarks upon the state of the people in this reign, pretends that the people never hated the King, and, "that he seems even in some degree to have possessed to the last their love and affection." He adds that it may be said with truth that the "English in that age were so thoroughly subdued that, like Eastern slaves, they were inclined to admire even those acts of violence and tyranny which were exercised over themselves and at their own expense." This unreliable historian everywhere endeavours to gloss over the deeds of those who destroyed the Catholic Church both in England and Scotland. Too cunning, however, to applaud Henry himself, he would have us believe that, after all, there was something amiable in him, and this belief he would have us found on the fact of his having been to the last seemingly beloved by his people.

Nothing can be more false than this assertion, if repeated insurrections against him, accompanied with the most bitter complaints and reproaches, be not to be taken as marks of popular affection. And as to the remark that the English "in that age were so thoroughly subdued," while it seems to refute the assertion as to their affection for the tyrant, it is a slander which the envious Scotch writers all delight to put forth and repeat. One object always uppermost with Hume is to malign the Catholic religion: it therefore did not occur to him that this sanguinary tyrant was not effectually resisted, as King John and other bad kings had been, because this tyrant had the means of bribing the natural leaders of the people to take part against them, or, at the least, to neutralise those leaders. It did not occur to him to tell us that Henry VIII. found the English as gallant and just a people as his ancestors had found them, but that having divided them by holding out to the great an enormous mass of plunder as a reward for abandoning the rights of the people, the people became, as every people without leaders must become, a mere flock or herd to be dealt with at pleasure. The malignity and envy of this Scotchman blinded him to this view of the matter, and induced him to ascribe to the people's admiration of tyranny that submission which, after repeated struggles, they yielded merely from the want of those leaders of whom they were now for the first time wholly deprived. What? have we never known any country consisting of several millions of people, oppressed and insulted, even for ages, by a mere handful of men? And are we to conclude that such a country submits from admiration of the tyranny under which they groan? Did the English submit to Cromwell from admiration; and was it from admiration that the French submitted to Robespierre? The latter was punished, but Cromwell was not, —he, like Henry, died in his bed; but to what mind, except to that of the most malignant and perverse, would it occur that Cromwell's impunity arose from the willing submission and the admiration of the people?

We have already seen how monasteries arose and what sort of institutions they were. There were in England at the time we are speaking of, 645 of these institutions, besides 90 colleges, 110 hospitals, and 2,374 chantries and free chapels. The whole were seized on, first and last, taken into the hands of the King, and by him granted to those who aided and abetted him in the work of plunder.

I pray you my friends, sensible and just Englishmen, to observe here that this was a great mass of landed property, that this property was not by any means used for the sole benefit of monks, friars and nuns, that for the far greater part its rents flowed immediately back amongst the people at large, and that if it had never been an object of plunder England never would, and never could, have heard the hideous sound of the words pauper and poor-rate.

You have, without doubt, fresh in your recollection all the censures, sarcasms, and ridicule which we have from our very infancy heard against the monastic life. What drones the monks and friars and nuns were, how uselessly they lived, how much they consumed to no good purpose whatever, and particularly how ridiculous and even how wicked it was to compel men and women to live unmarried, to lead a life of celibacy, and thus either to deprive them of a great natural pleasure, or to expose them to the double sin of breach of chastity and breach of oath.

Now this is a very important matter. It is a great moral question, and therefore we ought to endeavour to settle this question; to make up our minds completely upon it before we proceed any further. The monastic state necessarily was accompanied with vows of celibacy; and therefore it is, before we give an account of the putting down of these institutions in England, necessary to speak of the tendency and, indeed, of the natural and inevitable consequences of those vows.

It has been represented as "unnatural" to compel men and women to live in the unmarried state, and as tending to produce propensities to which it is hardly proper even to allude. In the first place, the Catholic Church compels nobody to make such vow. It only says that it will admit no one to be a priest, monk, friar, or nun, who rejects such vow. Saint Paul strongly recommends to all Christian teachers an unmarried life. The Church has founded a rule on this recommendation, and that, too, for the same reason that the recommendation was given; namely, that those who have flocks to watch over, or, in the language of our own Protestant Church, who have the care of souls, should have as few as possible of other cares, and should by all means be free from those incessant and sometimes racking cares which are inseparable from a wife and family. What priest who has a wife and family will not think more about them than about his flock? Will he, when any part of that family is in distress from illness or other cause, be wholly devoted, body and mind, to his flock? Will he be as ready to give alms or aid of any sort to the poor as he would be if he had no family to provide for? Will he never be tempted to swerve from his duty in order to provide patronage for sons and for the husbands of daughters? Will he always as boldly stand up and reprove the lord or the squire for their oppressions and vices as he would do if he had no son for whom to get a benefice, a commission, or a sinecure? Will his wife never have her partialities, her tattlings, her bickerings, amongst his flock, and never on any account induce him to act towards any part of that flock contrary to the strict dictates of his sacred duty? And to omit hundreds —yes, hundreds —of reasons that might in addition be suggested, will the married priest be as ready as the unmarried one to appear at the bedside of sickness and contagion? Here it is that the calls on him are most imperative, and here it is that the married priest will —and with nature on his side —be deaf to those calls. From amongst many instances that I could cite, let me take one. During the war of 1776, the king's house at Winchester was used as a prison for French prisoners of war. A dreadfully contagious fever broke out amongst them. Many of them died. They were chiefly Catholics, and were attended in their last moments by two or three Catholic priests residing in that city; but amongst the sick prisoners there were many Protestants, and these requested the attendance of Protestant parsons. There were the parsons of all the parishes at Winchester. There were the dean and all the prebendaries; but not a man of them went to console the dying Protestants, in consequence of which several of them desired the assistance of the priests and, of course, died Catholics. Doctor Milner, in his letters to Doctor Sturges, mentions this matter, and he says, "the answer (of the Protestant parsons) I understand to have been this: —'We are not more afraid, as individuals, to face death than the priests are; but we must not carry poisonous contagion into the bosoms of our families.'" No; to be sure! But then —not to call this the cassock's taking shelter behind the petticoat - in what a dilemma does this place the dean and chapter! Either they neglected their most sacred duty, and left Protestants to flee in their last moments into the arms of "popery"; or that clerical celibacy, against which they have declaimed all their lives and still declaim, and still hold up to us, their flocks, as something both contemptible and wicked, is, after all, necessary to that "care of souls" to which they profess themselves to have been "called" and for which they receive such munificent reward.

It is impossible to talk of the small beer and of the Master of Saint Cross, without thinking of the melancholy change which the "Reformation" has produced in this ancient establishment. Saint Cross, or Holy Cross, situated in a meadow about half a mile from Winchester, is a hospital, or place for hospitality, founded and endowed by a bishop of Winchester about seven hundred years ago. Succeeding bishops added to its endowment, till at last it provided a residence and suitable maintenance for forty-eight decayed gentlemen, with priests, nurses, and other servants and attendants; and, besides this, it made provision for a dinner every day for a hundred of the most indigent men in the city. These met daily in a hall called the "hundred men's hall." Each had a loaf of bread, three quarts of small beer, and "two messes," for his dinner; and they were allowed to carry home that which they did not consume upon the spot. What is seen at the hospital of Holy Cross now? Alas! ten poor creatures creeping about in this noble building, and three out-pensioners; and to those an attorney from Winchester carries or sends, weekly, the few pence, whatever they may be, that are allowed them! But the place of the "Master" is, as I have heard, worth a round sum annually. I do not know exactly what it is; but, the post being a thing given to a son of the bishop, the reader will easily imagine that it is not a trifle. There exists, however, here that which, as Dr. Milner observes, is probably the last remaining vestige of "old English hospitality"; for here any traveller who goes and knocks at the gate and asks for relief receives gratis a pint of good beer and a hunch of good bread.

But (and I had really nearly forgotten it) there is a bishop of Winchester now! And what is he doing? I have not heard that he has founded, or is about to found, any colleges or hospitals. All that I have heard of him in the education way is that in his first charge to his clergy (which he published) he urged them to circulate amongst their flocks the pamphlets of a Society in London, and all I have heard of him in the charity way, is that he is Vice-Patron of a self-created body called the "Hampshire Friendly Society," the object of which is to raise the subscriptions amongst the poor, for "their mutual relief and maintenance", or in other words, to induce the poor labourers to save out of their earnings the means of supporting themselves in sickness or in old age, without coming for relief to the poor rates! Good God! Why, William of Wykham, Bishop Fox, Bishop Wynfleet, Cardinal Beaufort, Henry de Blois, and if you take in all the bishops of Winchester, even back to Saint Swithun himself; never would they have thought of a scheme like this for relieving the poor! Their way of promoting learning was to found and endow colleges and schools; their way of teaching religion was to build and endow churches and chapels; their way of relieving the poor and the ailing was to found and endow hospitals; and all these at their own expense; —out of their own revenues. Never did one of them, in order to obtain an interpretation of "Evangelical truth" for their flocks, dream of referring his clergy to a society. Never did there come into the head of any one of them a thought so bright as that of causing the necessitous to relieve themselves! Ah! but they alas! lived in the "dark ages of monkish ignorance and superstition." No wonder that they could not see that the poor were the fittest persons in the world to relieve the poor. And besides, they had no wives and children! No sweet babes to smile on to soften their hearts. If they had, their conjugal and paternal feelings would have taught them that true charity begins at home; and that it teaches men to sell small beer and not give it away.

Enough now about the celibacy of the clergy; but it is impossible to quit the subject without one word to Parson Malthus. This man is not only a Protestant, but a parson of our Church. Now, he wants to compel the labouring classes to refrain to a great extent from marriage; and Mr.Scarlett actually brought a bill into Parliament, having in one part of it this object avowedly in view; the great end proposed by both being to cause a diminution of the poor-rates. Parson Malthus does not call this recommending celibacy, but "moral restraint." And what is celibacy but moral restraint? So that here are these people reviling the Catholic Church for insisting on vows of celibacy on the part of those who choose to be priests or nuns, and at the same time proposing to compel the labouring classes to live in a state of celibacy or to run the manifest risk of perishing (they and their children) from starvation! Is all this sheer impudence, or is it sheer folly? One or the other it is, greater than ever was before heard from the lips of mortal man. They affect to believe that the clerical vow of celibacy must be nugatory. Like all the other wild schemes and cruel projects relative to the poor, we trace this at once back to the "Reformation," that great source of the poverty and misery and degradation of the main body of the people of this kingdom. The "Reformation" despoiled the working classes of their patrimony; it tore from them that which nature and reason had assigned them; it robbed them of that relief for the necessitous which was theirs by right imprescriptable, and which had been confirmed to them by the law of God and the law of the land. It brought a compulsory, a grudging, an unnatural mode of relief, calculated to make the poor and rich hate each other instead of binding them together as the Catholic mode did, by the bonds of Christian charity. But of all its consequences, that of introducing a married clergy has perhaps been the most prolific in mischief. This has absolutely created an order for the procreation of dependants on the state; for the bringing into the world thousands of persons annually who have no fortunes of their own, and who must be, somehow or other, maintained by burdens imposed upon the people. Places, commissions, sinecures, pensions; something or other must be found for them, some sort of living out of the fruit of the rents of the rich and the wages of labour. If no excuse can be found, no pretence of public service, no corner of the pension list open, then they must come as a direct burden upon the people; and thus it is that we have, within the last twenty years, seen sixteen hundred thousand pounds voted by the parliament out of the taxes, for the "relief of the poor clergy of the Church of England;" and at the very time that this premium on the procreation of idlers was annually being granted, parliament was pestered with projects for compelling the working part of the community to lead a life of celibacy! What that is evil, what that is monstrous, has not grown out of this Protestant "Reformation"!

CHAPTER FIVE

According to Turner in his *History of England*, "No tyranny was ever established that was more unequivocally the creature of popular will, or longer maintained by popular support; in no point did personal interest and public welfare more cordially unite than in the encouragement of monasteries." Again the *Quarterly Review* of December, 1811 writes: "The world has never been so indebted to any body of men as to the illustrious order of the Benedictine monks; but historians, in relating the evil of which they were the occasion, too frequently forget the good which they produced. Even the commonest readers are acquainted with the arch miracle-monger, St. Dunstan, whilst the most learned of our countrymen scarcely remember the names of those admirable men who went from England and became the Apostles of the North. Tinian and Juan Fernandez are not more beautiful spots on the ocean than Malmesbury,

Lindisfarne and Jarrow were in the ages of our heptarchy. A community of pious men, devoted to literature and to the useful arts as well as to religion, seems in those days like a green oasis amid the desert. Like stars on a moonless night, they shine upon us with a tranquil ray. If ever there was a man who could truly be called venerable, it was he to whom the appellation is constantly fixed, Bede, whose life was passed in instructing his own generation and preparing records for posterity. In those days, the Church offered the only asylum from the evils to which every country was exposed —amidst continual wars the Church enjoyed peace —it was regarded as a sacred realm by men who, though they hated one another, believed and feared the same God. Abused as it was by the worldly-minded and ambitious, and disgraced by the artifices of the designing and the follies of the fanatic, it afforded a shelter to those who were better than the world in their youth or weary of it in their age. The wise as well as the timid and gentle fled to this Goshen of God, which enjoyed its own light and calm amidst darkness and storms."

This is a very elegant passage; but as Turner's Protestantism impels him to apply the term "tyranny" to that which honest feeling bids him say was "the creature of the popular will," and was produced and upheld by "a cordial union of personal interest and public welfare," so the Protestantism of the reviewers leads them to talk about "evil" occasioned by an Order to whom "the world is more indebted than to any other body of men;" and it also leads them to repeat the hackneyed charge against St. Dunstan, forgetting, I dare say, that he is one of the saints in our Protestant Church Calendar! However, here is more than enough to serve as an answer to the whole herd of writers who have put forth their venom against the monastic Orders.

To proceed now with our inquiry relative to the effects of the monastic institutions, we may observe that authorities in this case seemed necessary. The lies were of long standing; hypocritical selfishness, backed by every species of violence, tyranny and cruelty, had been at work for ages to delude the people of England. Those who had fattened upon the spoils of the Church and the poor, and who wished still to enjoy the fatness in quiet, naturally laboured to persuade the people that those who had been despoiled were unworthy people; that the institutions which gave them so much property were at least useless; that the possessors were lazy, ignorant and base creatures, spreading darkness over the country instead of light, devouring that which ought to have sustained worthy persons. When the whole press and all the pulpits of a country are leagued for such a purpose, and supported in that purpose by the State; and when the reviled party is, by terrors hardly to be described, reduced to silence; in such a case the assailants must prevail; the mass of the people must believe what they say. Reason, in such a state of things, is out of the question. But truth is immortal; and though she may be silenced for a while, there always, at last, comes something to cause her to claim her due and to triumph over falsehood.

There is now come that which is calculated to give our reasoning faculties fair play. We see the land covered at last with pauperism, fanaticism, and crime. In short, we are now arrived at a point which compels us to inquire into the cause of this monstrous state of things. The immediate cause we find to be the poverty and degradation of the main body of the people; and these, through many stages, we trace back to the "Reformation," one of the effects of which was to destroy those monastic institutions which, as we shall now see, retained the produce of labour in the proper places, and distributed it in a way naturally tending to make the lives of the people easy and happy.

If the monasteries had been the cause of evil, would they have been protected with such care by so many wise and virtuous kings, legislators, and judges? Perhaps Alfred was the greatest man that ever lived. What writer of eminence, whether poet, lawyer, or historian, has not selected him as the object of his highest praises? As king, as soldier, as patriot, as lawgiver, in all his characters he is by all regarded as having been the greatest, wisest, most virtuous of men. And is it reasonable, then, for us to suppose that he, whose whole soul was wrapped up in the hope of making his people free, honest, virtuous, and happy, - is it reasonable to suppose that he would have been, as he was, one of the most munificent founders of monasteries, if those institutions had been vicious in themselves or had tended to evil? We have not these institutions and their effects immediately before our eyes. We do not actually see the monasteries. But we know of them two things; namely, that they were most anxiously cherished by Alfred and his tutor Saint Swithun, and that they were destroyed by the tyrant, Henry the Eighth, and the ruffian, Thomas Cromwell. Upon these two facts alone we might pretty safely decide on the merits of these institutions.

The hospitality and other good things proceeding from the monasteries are not to be forgotten; but we must take a closer view of the subject, in order to do full justice to these calumniated institutions. It is our duty to show that they were founded in great political wisdom as well as in real piety and charity; that they were not, as the malignant and selfish Hume has described them, mere dolers out of bread and meat and beer, but that they were great diffusers of general prosperity, happiness and content; and that one of their natural and necessary effects was to prevent that state of things which sees but two classes of people in a community, masters and slaves, a very few enjoying the extreme of luxury, and millions doomed to the extreme of misery.

From the land all good things come. Somebody must own the land. Those who own it must have the distribution of its revenues. If these revenues be chiefly distributed amongst the people, from whose labour they arise, and in such a way as to afford to them a good maintenance on easy terms, the community must be happy. If the revenues be alienated in very great part, if they be carried away to a great distance, and expended amongst those from whose labour no part of them arises, the main body of the community must be miserable; poor-houses, jails and barracks must arise. Now, one of the greatest advantages attending the monasteries was that they, of necessity, caused the revenues of a large part of the lands of the country to be spent on the spot whence those revenues arose. The hospitals and all other establishments of the kind had the same tendency. There were of the whole, great and small, not less, on an average, than fifty in each county; so that the revenues of the land diffused themselves in great part immediately amongst the people at large. We all well know how the state of a parish becomes instantly changed for the worse, when a noble or other great landowner quits the mansion in it and leaves that mansion shut up. Every one knows the effect which such a shutting up has upon the poor-rates of a parish. It is notorious, that the non-residence of the clergy and of the nobleman and gentlemen is universally complained of as a source of evil to the country. One of the arguments, and a great one it is, in favour of severe game laws, is that the game causes noblemen and gentlemen to reside. What then must have been the effect of twenty rich monasteries in every county, expending constantly a large part of their incomes on the spot? The great cause of the miseries of Ireland is "absenteeship," that is to say, the absence of the landowners, who draw away the revenues of the country and expend them in other countries. If Ireland had still her seven or eight hundred monastic institutions, great and small, she would be as she formerly was, prosperous and happy. There would be no periodical famines and typhus fevers; no need of sunset and sunrise laws; no schemes for getting rid of a "surplus population"; none of that poverty and degradation that threaten to make a desert of the country, or to make it the means of destroying the greatness of England herself.

Somebody must own the lands; and the question is, whether it be best for them to be owned by those who constantly live — and constantly must live — in the country and in the midst of their estates, or by those who always may, and who frequently will and do, live at a great distance from their lands and draw away the revenues of them to be spent elsewhere. The monastics are by many called drones. Bishop Tanner has shown us that this charge is very false; but if it were true, is not a drone in a cowl as good as a drone in a hat and top-boots? By drones are meant those who do not work; and do landowners usually work? The lay landowner and his family spend more of their revenues in a way not useful to the people than the monastics possibly could. But besides this, besides the hospitality and charity of the monastics, and besides, moreover, the lien — the legal lien — which the main body of the people had in many cases to a share, directly or indirectly, in the revenues of the monasteries, we are to look at the monks and nuns in the very important capacity of landlords and landladies. All historians, however Protestant or malignant, agree that they were "easy landlords;" that they let their lands at low rents, and on leases of long terms of years; so that, says even Hume, "the farmers regarded themselves as a species of proprietors, always taking care to renew their leases before they expired." And was there no good in a class of landlords of this sort? Did not they naturally and necessarily create, by slow degrees, men of property? Did they not thus cause a class of yeomen to exist— real yeomen, independent of the aristocracy? And was not this class destroyed by the "Reformation," which made the farmers rack-renters and absolute dependants, as we see them to this day? And was this change favourable, then, to political liberty? Monastics could possess no private property, they could save no money, they could bequeath nothing. They had a life interest in their estate, and no more. They lived, received and expended in common. Historians need not have told us that they were "easy landlords." They must have been such, unless human nature had taken a retrograde march expressly for their accommodation. And was it not happy for the nation that there was such a class of landlords? What a jump for joy would the farmers of England now give, if such a class were to return tomorrow to get them out of the hands of the squandering and needy lord and his grinding land-valuer!

Then look at the monastics as causing, in some of the most important of human affairs, that fixedness which is so much the friend of rectitude in morals, and which so powerfully conduces to prosperity, private and public. The monastery was a proprietor that never died; its tenantry had to do with a deathless landlord; its lands and house never changed owners; its tenants were liable to none of the many of the uncertainties that other tenants were; its oaks had never to tremble at the axe of the squandering heir; its manors had not to dread a change of lords; its villagers had all been born and bred up under its eye and care; their character was of necessity a thing of great value, and, as such, would naturally be an object of great attention. A monastery was the centre of a circle in the country, naturally drawing to it all that were in need of relief, advice and protection, and containing a body of men or of women having no cares of their own, and having wisdom to guide the inexperienced and wealth to relieve the distressed. And was it a good thing then, to plunder and devastate these establishments: was it a reformation to squander estates thus employed upon lay persons, who would not, who could not, and did not, do any part or particle of those benevolent facts and acts of public utility which naturally arose out of the monastic institutions?

Lastly, let us look at the monasteries as a resource for the younger sons and daughters of the aristocracy, and as the means of protecting the government against the injurious effects of their clamorous wants. There cannot exist an aristocracy or body of nobility without the means, in the hands of the government, of preventing that body from falling into that contempt which is, and always must be, inseparable from noble poverty. "Well," some will say, "why need there be any such body?" That is quite another question: for we have it, and have had it for more than a thousand years;

except during a very short interval, at the end of which our ancestors eagerly took it back again. I must, too, though it really has nothing to do with the question before us, repeat my opinion, many times expressed, that we should lose more than we should gain by getting rid of our aristocracy.

However, this has nothing at all to do with the present question: we have the aristocracy, and we must, by a public provision of some sort for the younger branches of it, prevent it from falling into the degradation inseparable from poverty. This provision was, in the times of which we are speaking, made by the monasteries, which received a great number of its monks and nuns from the families of the nobles. This rendered those odious and burdensome things, pensions and sinecures, unnecessary. It of course spared the taxes. It was a provision that was not degrading to the receivers, and it created no grudging and discontent amongst the people, from whom the receivers took nothing. Another great advantage arising from this mode of providing for the younger branches of the nobility was, that it secured the government against the temptation to give offices and to lodge power in unfit hands. Look at our pension and sinecure list; look at the list of those who have commands, and who fill other offices of emolument, and you will at once see the great benefit which must have been derived from institutions which left the government quite free to choose commanders, ambassadors, governors and other persons to exercise power and to be entrusted in the carrying on of the public affairs. These institutions, too, tended to check the increase of the race of nobles; to prevent the persons connected with that order from being multiplied to the extent to which they naturally would otherwise be multiplied. They tended also to make the nobles not so dependent on the Crown, a provision being made for their poor relations without the Crown's assistance; and at the same time they tended to make the people less dependent on the nobles than they otherwise would have been. The monasteries set the example as masters and landlords, an example that others were, in a great degree, compelled to follow. And thus all ranks and degrees were benefited by these institutions which, with malignant historians, have been a subject of endless abuse, and the destruction of which they have recorded with so much delight as being one of the brightest features in the "Reformation"!

Nor must we by any means overlook the effects of those institutions on the mere face of the country. That soul must be low and mean indeed which is insensible to all feeling of pride in the noble edifices of its country. Love of country, that variety of feelings which all together constitute what we properly call patriotism, consists in part of the admiration of and veneration for ancient and magnificent proofs of skill and of opulence. The monastics built as well as wrote for posterity. The never-dying nature of their institutions set aside, in all their undertakings, every calculation as to time and age. Whether they built or planted, they set the generous example of providing for the pleasure, the honour, the wealth and greatness of generations upon generations yet unborn. They executed everything in the very best manner: their gardens, fishponds, farms, in all, in the whole of their economy, they set an example tending to make the country beautiful, to make it an object of pride with the people, and to make the nation truly and permanently great. Go into any county, and survey, even at this day, the ruins of its perhaps twenty abbeys and priories, and then ask yourself, "what have we in exchange for these?" Go to the site of some once opulent convent. Look at the cloister, now become in the hands of a rack-renter the receptacle for dung, fodder and faggot-wood; see the hall, where for ages the widow, the orphan, the aged and the stranger found a table ready spread; see a bit of its walls now helping to make a cattle-shed, the rest having been hauled away to build a workhouse; recognise in the side of a barn a part of the once magnificent chapel; and if, chained to the spot by your melancholy musings, you be admonished of the approach of night by the voice of the screech-owl issuing from those arches which once at the same hour resounded with the vespers of the monk, and which have for seven hundred years been assailed by storms and tempests in vain, — if thus admonished of the necessity of seeking food, shelter and a bed, lift your eyes and look at the white-washed and dry-rotten shell on the hill, called the "gentleman's house," and apprised of the "board wages" and the "spring guns," suddenly turn your head; jog away from the scene of devastation; with "old English hospitality" in your mind reach the nearest inn, and there, in room half-warmed and half-lighted, and the reception precisely proportioned to the presumed length of your purse, sit down and listen to an account of the hypocritical pretences, the base motives, the tyrannical and bloody means under which, from which, and by which that devastation was effected and that hospitality banished for ever from the land.

When men have power to commit and are resolved to commit acts of injustice, they are never at a loss for pretences. We shall presently see what were the pretences under which this devastation of England was begun: but to do the work there required a workman, as to slaughter an ox there requires a butcher. To turn the possessors of so large a part of the estates out of those estates, to destroy establishments venerated by the people from their childhood, to set all law, divine as well as human, at defiance, to violate every principle on which property rested, to rob the poor and helpless of the means of sustenance, to deface the beauty of the country and make it literally a heap of ruins; to do those things there required a suitable agent, and that agent the tyrant found in Thomas Cromwell, whose name, along with that of Cranmer, ought "to stand for aye accursed in the calendar." This Cromwell was the son of a blacksmith of Putney, in Surrey. He had been an underling of some sort in the family of Cardinal Wolsey, and had recommended himself to the King by his sycophancy to him and his treachery to his old master. The King now became head of the Church, and having the supremacy to exercise had very judiciously provided himself with Cranmer as a primate, and to match him he provided himself with Cromwell, who was equal to Cranmer in impiousness and baseness, rather surpassed him in dastardliness, and exceeded him decidedly in quality of ruffian. All nature could not perhaps have afforded another man so fit to be the "Royal Vicegerent and Vicar-general" of the new head of the English Church.

In order to begin the "godly reformation," that is to say, the work of plunder, the "Vicegerent" set on foot a visitation of the monasteries! Dreadful visitation! He, active as he was in wickedness, could not do all the work himself. He, therefore, appointed deputies to assist in making this visitation. The kingdom was divided into districts for this purpose, and two deputies were appointed to visit each district. The object was to obtain grounds of accusation against the monks and nuns. When we consider what the object was, and what was the character of the man to whom the work was committed, we may easily imagine what sort of men these deputies were. They were, in fact, fit to be the subalterns of such a chief. Think of a respectable, peaceful, harmless, and pious family, broken in upon, all of a sudden, by a brace of burglars, with murder written on their scowling brows, demanding an instant production of their title-deeds, money, and jewels: imagine such a scene as this, and you have then some idea of the visitations of these monsters, who came with the threat of the tyrant on their lips, who menaced the victims with charges of high treason, who wrote in their reports, not what was, but what their merciless employers wanted them to write.

The monks and nuns, who had never dreamed of the possibility of such proceedings, who had never had an idea that Magna Charta and all the laws of the land could be set aside in a moment, and whose recluse and peaceful lives rendered them wholly unfit to cope with at once crafty and desperate villainy, fell before these ruffians as chickens fall before the kite. The reports made by these villains met with no contradiction; the accused parties had no means of making a defence; there was no court for them to appear in; they dared not, even if they had had the means, to offer a defence or make a complaint; for they had seen the horrible consequences, the burnings, the rippings up, of all those of their brethren who had ventured to whisper their dissent from any dogma or decree of the tyrant.

However, upon reports thus obtained, an Act of Parliament was passed in March, 1536 — the same year that saw the end of Anne Boleyn — for the suppression, that is to say, confiscation, of three hundred and seventy-six monasteries, and for granting their estates, real and personal, to the King and his heirs! He took plate, jewels, gold

and silver images, and ornaments. This act of monstrous tyranny was, however, base as the Parliament was and full as it was of greedy plunderers, not passed without some opposition. Hume says that "it does not appear that any opposition was made to this important law." He frequently quotes Spelman as an historical authority, but it did not suit him to quote Spelman's *History of Sacrilege*, in which this Protestant historian says that "the bill stuck long in the Lower House and could get no passage, when the king commanded the Commons to attend him in the forenoon in his gallery, where he let them wait till late in the afternoon, and then, coming out of his chamber, walking a turn or two amongst them and looking angrily on them, first on one side and then on the other, at last, 'I hear (saith he) that my bill will not pass, but I will have it pass, or I will have some of your heads,' and without other rhetoric returned to his chamber. Enough was said, the bill passed, and all was given him as he desired."

CHAPTER SIX

The Act was passed in the year 1536, and in the 27th year of the King's reign. The preamble of the Act contains the reasons for its enactments; and as this Act really began the ruin and degradation of the main body of the people of England and Ireland, as it was the first step taken in legal form for robbing the people under pretence of reforming their religion, as it was the precedent on which the future plunderers proceeded until they had completely impoverished the country, as it was the first of that series of deeds of rapine by which this formerly well-fed and well-clothed people have, in the end, been reduced to rags and to a worse than jail-allowance of food, I will insert the lying and villainous preamble at full length. Englishmen in general suppose that there were always poor-laws and paupers in England. They ought to remember that for nine-hundred years, under the Catholic religion, there were neither. They ought, when they hear the parson cry "no popery," to answer him by the cry of "no-pauperism." They ought above all things to endeavour to ascertain how it came to pass that this land of roast beef was changed, all of a sudden, into a land of dry bread or of oatmeal porridge. Let them attend, then, to the base and hypocritical pretences that they will find in the following preamble to this atrocious act of pillage.

"Forasmuch as manifest synne, vicious, carnal

and abominable living is dayly used and committed commonly in such little and small Abbeys, Priories, and other Religious Houses of monks, canons and nuns, where the congregation of such religious persons is under the number of twelve persons, whereby the governors of such Religious Houses, and their Convent, spoyle, destroye, consume, and utterly waste, as well as their churches, monasteries, priories, principal farms, granges, lands, tenements, and hereditaments, as the ornaments of their churches, and their goods and chattels, to the high displeasure of Almighty God, slander of good religion, and to the great infamy of the King's Highness and the realm, if redress should not be had thereof. And albeit that many continual Visitations hath been heretofore had by the space of two hundred years and more, for an honest and charitable reformation of such unthrifty, carnal, and abominable living, yet nevertheless little or none amendment is hitherto had, but their vicious living shamelessly increaseth and augmenteth, and by a cursed custom so rooted and infected, that a great multitude of the religious persons in such small Houses do rather choose to rove abroad in apostacy, than to conform themselves to the observation of good religion; so that without such small Houses be utterly suppressed, and the religious persons therein committed to great and honourable Monasteries of religion in this realm where they may be compelled to live religiously, for reformation of their lives, the same else be no redress nor reformation in that behalf. In consideration whereof the King's most royal Majesty, being supreme Head on Earth, under God, of the Church of England, dayly studying and devysing the increase, advancement and exultation of true doctrine and virtue in the said Church, to the only glory and honour of God, and the total extirpation and destruction of vice and sin, having knowledge that the premises be true, as well as the accompts of his late Visitations, as by sundry credible informations, considering also that divers and great solemn Monasteries of this realm, wherein (thanks be to God)

religion is right well kept and observed, be destitute of such
full number of religious persons as they ought and may
keep, hath thought good that a plain declaration should be
made of the premises, as well to the Lords Spritual and
Temporal, as to other his loving subjects the Commons in
this present Parliament assembled: Whereupon the said
Lords and Commons, by a great deliberation, finally be
resolved that it is and shall be much more to the pleasure of
Almighty God, and for the honour of this his realm, that
the possessions of such small Religious Houses, now being
spent, spoiled, and wasted for increase and maintenance of
sin, should be used and committed to better uses, and the
unthrifty religious persons so spending the same, to be compelled to reform their lives."

This preamble was followed by enactments giving the
whole of the property to the King, his heirs and assigns, "to
do and use therewith according to their own wills, to the
pleasure of Almighty God, and to the honour and profit of
this realm." Besides the lands and houses and stock, this
tyrannical act gave him the household goods, and the gold,
silver, jewels, and every other thing belonging to those
monasteries. Here was a breach of Magna Charta in the first
place, a robbery of the monks and nuns in the next place,
and, in the third place, a robbery of the indigent, the
widow, the orphan and the stranger. The parties robbed,
even the actual possessors of the property, were never heard
in their defence; there was no charge against any particular
convent; the charges were loose and general, and levelled
against all convents whose revenues did not exceed a certain sum. This alone was sufficient to show that the charges
were false; for who will believe that the alleged wickedness
extended to all whose revenues did not exceed a certain
sum, and that, when those revenues got above that point,
the wickedness stopped? It is clear that the reason for stop-
ping at that point was that there was yet something to be
done with the nobles and gentry before a seizure of the
great monasteries could be safely attempted. The weak were

first attacked, but means were very soon found for attacking and sacking the remainder.

The moment the tyrant got possession of this class of the Church estates he began to grant them away to his "assigns," as the act calls them. Great promises had been held out that the King, when in possession of these estates, would never more want taxes from the people, and it is possible that he thought that he should be able to do without taxes; but he soon found that he was not destined to keep the plunder to himself, and that, in short, he must make a sudden stop, if not actually undo all that he had done, unless he divided the spoil with others, who instantly poured in upon him for their share, and they so beset him that he had not a moment's peace. They knew that he had good things, they had taken care to enable him to have "assigns;" and they, as they intended from the first, would give him no rest until he, "to the pleasure of Almighty God and the honour and profit of the realm," made them those "assigns."

Before four years had passed over his head he found himself as poor as if he had never confiscated a single convent, so sharp set were the pious reformers and so eager to "please Almighty God." When complaining to Cromwell of the rapacity of the applicants for grants he exclaimed, "By our Lady! the cormorants, when they have got the garbage, will devour the dish." Cromwell reminded him that there was much more yet to come. "Tut, man," said the King, "my whole realm would not staunch their maws." However, he attempted this very soon after by a seizure of the larger monasteries.

We have seen that the parliament, when they enabled him to confiscate the smaller monasteries, declared that in the "great and solemn monasteries (thanks be to God) religion is right well kept and observed." It seemed, therefore, to be a work of some difficulty to discover (in so short a time after this declaration was made) reasons for the confiscation of these larger monasteries. But tyranny stands in need of no reasons, and in this case no reasons were alleged. Cromwell and his myrmidons beset the heads of these great establishments; they threatened, they promised, they lied, and they bullied. By means the most base that can be conceived they obtained from some few what they called a "voluntary surrender." However, where these unjust and sanguinary men met with sturdy opposition they resorted to false accusations, and procured the murder of the parties under pretence of their having committed high treason. It was under this infamous pretence that the tyrant hanged and ripped up and quartered the abbot of the famous abbey of Glastonbury, whose body was mangled by the executioner, and whose head and limbs were hung up on what is called the Tor, which overlooks the abbey. So that the surrender, wherever it did take place, was precisely of the nature of those "voluntary surrenders" which men make of their purses when the robber's pistol is at their temple or his blood-stained knife at their throat.

After all, however, even to obtain a pretence of voluntary surrender was a work too troublesome for Cromwell and his ruffian visitors, and much too slow for the cormorants who waited for the plunder. Without more ceremony, therefore, an act was passed (31 Henry VIII., Chapter 13) giving all these "surrendered" monasteries to the King, his heirs and assigns, and also all other monasteries, and all hospitals and colleges into the bargain! It is useless to waste our time in uttering exclamations or in venting curses on the memory of the monsters who thus made a general sacking of this then fine, rich, and beautiful country, which, until now, had been for nine hundred years the happiest country, and the greatest country too, that Europe had ever seen.

The carcass being thus laid prostrate, the rapacious vultures who had assisted in the work flew on it and began to tear it in pieces. The people here and there rose in insurrection against the tyrant's satellites; but deprived of their natural leaders, who had for the most part placed themselves on the side of tyranny and plunder, what were the mere common people to do? Hume affects to pity the ignorance of the people (as writers now affect to pity the ignorance of the country people in Spain) in showing their attachment to the monks. Gross ignorance, to be sure, to prefer easy landlords, leases for life, hospitality and plenty; "gross ignorance and superstition" to prefer these to grinding rackrents, buying small beer at bishop's palaces, and living on parish pay! We shall see shortly how soon horrid misery followed these tyrannical proceedings: but we must trace Cromwell and his ruffians in their work of confiscating, plundering, pillaging and devastating.

Tyrants have often committed robberies on their people; but in all cases but this, in England at least, there was always something of legal process observed. In this case there was no such thing. The base parliament who were to share, and who did most largely share, in the plunder, had given not only the lands and houses to the tyrant, or rather, had taken them to themselves, but had disposed, in the same short way, of all the moveable goods, stock on farms, crops and, which was of more consequence, of the gold, silver and jewels. Let the reader judge of the ransackings that now took place. The poorest of the convents had some images, vases, and other things of gold or silver. Many of them possessed a great deal in this way. The altars of their churches were generally enriched with the precious metals, if not with costly jewels; and, which is not to be overlooked, the people in those days were honest enough to suffer all these things to remain in their places without a standing army and without police officers.

Never in all probability since the world began was there so rich a harvest of plunder. The ruffians of Cromwell entered the convents, they tore down the altars to get away the gold and silver, ransacked the chests and drawers of the monks and nuns, tore off the covers of books that were ornamented with the precious metals. These books were all in manuscript. Single books had taken in many cases half a long life-time to compose and to copy out fair. Whole libraries, the getting of which together had taken ages upon ages and had cost immense sums of money, were scattered abroad by these hellish ruffians when they had robbed the covers of their rich ornaments. The ready money in the convents down to the last shilling was seized. In short, the most rapacious and unfeeling soldiery never, in town delivered up to be sacked, proceeded with greediness, shamelessness, and brutality to be at all compared with those of these heroes of the Protestant Reformation; and this, observe, towards persons, women as well as men, who had committed no crime known to the laws, who had had no crime regularly laid to their charge, who had had no hearing in their defence, a large part of whom had within a year been declared by this same parliament to lead most godly and useful lives, the whole of whose possessions were guaranteed to them by the Great Charter as much as the King's crown was to him, and whose estates were enjoyed for the benefit of the poor as well as for that of these plundered possessors themselves.

The tyrant was, of course, the great pocketer of this species of plunder. Cromwell carried, or sent it to him in parcels, twenty ounces of gold at one time, fifty ounces at another; now a parcel of precious stones of one sort, then a parcel of another. Hume, whose main object is to blacken the Catholic religion, takes every possible occasion for saying something or other in praise of its destroyers. He could not, he was too cunning to ascribe justice or humanity to a monster whose very name signifies injustice and cruelty. He therefore speaks of his high spirit, his magnificence and generosity. It was a high-spirited, magnificent and generous King, to be sure, who sat in his palace in London to receive with his own hands the gold, silver, jewels and pieces of money of which his unoffending subjects had been robbed by ruffians sent by himself to commit the robbery. One of the items runs in these words: "Item, Delivered unto the King's royal Majesty, the same day, of the same stuffe, foure chalices of golde, with foure patens of golde to the same, and a spoon of golde, weighing altogether an hundred and six ounces. Received: Henry Rex."

Did subaltern plunderers ever give in just accounts? It is manifest that from this specimen the whole amount of the goods of which the convents were plundered must have been enormous. The reforming gentry ransacked the cathedral churches as well as the convents and their churches. Whatever pile contained the greatest quantity of "the same stuffe" seemed to be the object of their most keen rapacity. Therefore it is by no means surprising that they directed, at a very early stage of their pious and honest progress, their hasty steps towards Canterbury, which, above all other places, had been dipped in the "manifeste synne" of possessing rich altars, tombs, gold and silver images, together with "manifestly synneful" diamonds and other precious stones. The whole of this city, famed as the cradle of English Christianity, was prize; and the "Reformation" people hastened to it with that alacrity and that noise of anticipated enjoyment which we observe in the crows and magpies when flying to the spot where a horse or an ox has accidentally met with its death.

But there were at Canterbury two objects by which the "Reformation" birds of prey were particularly attracted; namely, the monastery of Saint Austin and the tomb of

Thomas à Becket. The former of these renowned men, to whose preaching and whose long life of incessant and most disinterested labour England owed the establishment of Christianity in the land, had for eight or nine centuries been regarded as the Apostle of England. His shrine was in the monastery dedicated to him; and as it was in all respects a work of great magnificence, it offered a plenteous booty to the plunderers, who, if they could have got at the tomb of Jesus Christ Himself, and had found it equally rich, would beyond all question have torn it to pieces. But rich as this prize was, there was a greater in the shrine of Thomas à Becket, in the cathedral church. Becket, who was Archbishop of Canterbury in the reign of Henry II., who resisted that King when the latter was manifestly preparing to rob the Church and to enslave and pillage the people, had been held in the highest veneration all over Christendom for more than three hundred years when the Reformation plunderers assailed his tomb; but especially was his name venerated in England, where the people looked upon him as a martyr to their liberties as well as their religion, he having been barbarously murdered by ruffians sent from the king, and for no other cause than that he persevered in resisting an attempt to violate the Great Charter. Pilgrimages were continually made to his tomb; offerings incessantly poured into it; churches and hospitals and other establishments of piety and charity were dedicated to him, as, for instance, the church of St. Thomas, in the City of London, the monastery of Sende, in Surrey, the hospital of St. Thomas, in the borough of Southwark, and things of this sort, in great numbers, all over the country. The offerings at his shrine had made it exceedingly rich and magnificent. A king of France had given it a diamond supposed to be the most valuable then in Europe. Hume, never losing sight of the double object of maligning the Catholic religion and degrading the English nation, ascribes this sort of half-adoration of Becket to the craft of the priests and to the folly and superstition of the people. He is vexed to death to have to relate that more than a hundred thousand pilgrims to Becket's shrine have been assembled at one time in Canterbury. Indeed! why, then, there must have been some people living in England even in those old times; and those people must have had some wealth too; though, according to the whole tenor of the lying book, which the Scotch call our history, this was, at the time I am now speaking of, a poor, beggarly, scarcely inhabited country. How could they find lodging and entertainment for a hundred thousand grown persons? And this too, observe, at one corner of the island. None but persons of some substance could have performed such a journey. Here is a fact that just slips out sideways, which is of itself much more than enough to make us reflect and inquire before we swallow what the Scotch philosphers are now presenting to us on the subjects of national wealth and population. And then as to the craft and superstition which Hume says produced this concourse of pilgrims. Just as if either were necessary to produce unbounded veneration for the name of a man of whom it was undeniably true that he had sacrificed his life, and that, too, in the most signal manner, for the rights and liberties and religion of his country. Was it "folly and superstition," or was it wisdom and gratitude and real piety to show, by overt acts, veneration for such a man? The bloody tyrant, who had sent More and Fisher to the block, and who of course hated the name of Becket, caused his ashes to be dug up and scattered in the air, and forbade the future insertion of his name in the calendar. We do not, therefore, find it in the calendar in the Common Prayer Book; but, and it is a most curious fact, we find it in Moore's Almanack; in that almanack it is for this very year 1825; and thus, in spite of the ruthless tyrant and in spite of all the liars of the "Reformation," the English nation has always continued to be just and grateful to the memory of this celebrated man.

This tomb of Becket was of wood, most exquisitely wrought, inlaid abundantly with the precious metals, and thickly set with precious stones of all sorts. Here was an object for "Reformation" piety to fix its godly eyes upon! Were such a shrine to be found in one of our churches now, how the swaddlers would cry out for another "Reformation!" The gold, silver and jewels filled two chests, each of which required six or eight men of that day (when the labourers used to have plenty of meat) to move them to the door of the cathedral. How the eyes of Hume's "high-minded, magnificent, and generous prince" must have glistened when the chests were opened! They vied, I dare say, with the diamonds themselves. No robbers of which we have ever had an account equalled these robbers in rapacity, in profligacy, and in insolence. But where is the wonder? The tyrant's proclamations had now the force of laws; he had bribed the people's natural leaders to his side; his will was law; and that will constantly sought plunder and blood.

The monasteries were now plundered, sacked, gutted; for this last is the proper word whereby to describe the deed. As some comfort, and to encourage us to endure the horrid relation, we may here bear in mind that we shall, by-and-by, see the base ruffian, Cromwell, after being the chief instrument in the plunder, laying his miscreant head on the block. But to seize the estates and pillage the churches and apartments of the monasteries was not all. The noble buildings, raised in the view of lasting for countless ages; the beautiful gardens; these ornaments of the country must not be suffered to stand, for they continually reminded the people of the rapacity and cruelty of their tyrant and his fellow-plunderers and partakers in the plunder. How the property in the estates was disposed of we shall see further on, but the buildings must come down. To go to work in the usual way would have been a labour without end, so that in most instances gunpowder was resorted to, and thus, in a few hours, the most magnificent structures, which it had required ages upon ages to bring to perfection, were made heaps of ruins, pretty much such as many of them remain even unto this day. In many cases those who got the estates

were bound to destroy the buildings, or to knock them partly down, so that the people should at once be deprived of
all hope of seeing a revival of what they had lost, and in
order to give them encouragement to take leases under the
new owners.

We have seen how they rifled the tomb of St. Austin at
Canterbury. They tore down the church and the abbey, and
with the materials built a menagerie for wild beasts and a
palace for the tyrant himself. The tomb of Alfred was in an
abbey at Winchester, founded by that king himself. The
abbey and its estates were given by the tyrant to
Wriothesley, who was afterwards made Earl of
Southampton, and who got a pretty good share of the confiscations in Hampshire. One almost sickens at the thought
of a man capable of a deed like the destruction of this
abbey. Where is there one amongst us who has read any
thing at all who has not read of the fame of Alfred? What
book can we open, even for our boyish days, that does not
sound his praise? Poets, moralists, divines, historians,
philosophers, lawyers, legislators, not only of our own country but of all Europe, have cited him, and still cite him, as a
model of virtue, piety, wisdom, valour and patriotism, as
possessing every excellence without a single fault. He, in
spite of difficulties such as no other human being on record
ever encountered, cleared his harassed and half-barbarized
country of horde after horde of cruel invaders, who at one
time had wholly subdued it and compelled him, in order to
escape destruction, to resort to the habit and the life of a
herdsman. From this state of depression he, during a not
long life, raised himself and his people to the highest point
of happiness and of fame. He fought, with his armies and
fleets, more than fifty battles against the enemies of
England. He taught his people by his example as well as by
his precepts, to be sober, industrious, brave and just. He
promoted learning in all the sciences; he planted the
University of Oxford; to him; and not to a late Scotch
lawyer, belongs "Trial by Jury." Blackstone calls him the

founder of the Common Law; the counties, the hundreds, the tithings, the courts of justice, were the work of Alfred. He, in fact, was the founder of all those rights, liberties and laws which made England to be what England has been, which gave her a character above that of other nations, which made her rich and great and happy beyond all her neighbours, and which still give her whatever she possesses of that pre-eminence. If there be a name under heaven to which Englishmen ought to bow with reverence approaching towards adoration it is the name of Alfred. And we are not unjust and ungrateful in this respect at any rate, for, whether Catholics or Protestants, where is there an Englishman to be found who would not gladly make a pilgrimage of a thousand miles to take off his hat at the tomb of this maker of the English name? Alas! that tomb is nowhere to be found. The barbarians spared not even that. It was in the abbey before mentioned, called Hyde Abbey, which had been founded by Alfred himself and intended as the place of his burial. Besides the remains of Alfred this abbey contained those of St. Grimbald, the Benedictine monk, whom Alfred brought into England to begin the teaching at Oxford. But what cared the plunderers for remains of public benefactors? The abbey was knocked down or blown up, the tombs were demolished, the very lead of the coffins was sold, and, which fills one with more indignation than all the rest, the estates were so disposed of as to make the loan-makers, the Barings, at this day the successors of Alfred the Great!

Thus then was the country devastated, sacked and defaced; and I should now proceed to give an account of the commencement of that poverty and degradation which were, as I have pledged myself to show, the consequences of this devastation, and which I shall show, not by bare assertion, nor from what are called "Histories of England," but from Acts of Parliament, and from other sources which every one can refer to, and the correctness of which is beyond all dispute. But before we come to this important matter we must see the end of the ruffian "Vice-gerent," and also the end of the tyrant himself, who was, during the events that we have been speaking of, going on marrying and divorcing or killing his wives, but whose career was, after all, not very long.

After the death of Jane Seymour, who was the mother of Edward VI, and who was the only one of all the tyrant's wives who had the good luck to die a queen and to die in her bed; — after her death, which took place in 1537, he was nearly two years hunting up another wife. None certainly but some very gross and unfeeling woman could be expected to have voluntarily anything to do with a man whose hands were continually steeped in blood. In 1539 he found, however, a mate in Anne, the sister of the Duke of Cleves. When she arrived in England he expressed his dislike of her person; but he found it prudent to marry her. In 1540, about six or seven months after the marriage, he was divorced from her, not daring in this case to set his myrmidons to work to bring her to the block. There was no lawful pretence for the divorce. The husband did not like his wife; that was all, and this was alleged, too, as the ground of the divorce. Cranmer, who had divorced him from two wives before, put his irons into the fire again for this occasion, and produced in a little time as neat a piece of work as ever had come from the shop of the famous "Reformation." Thus the King and Queen were single people again; but the former had another young and handsome wife in his eye. This lady's name was Catherine Howard, a niece of the Duke of Norfolk. This Duke, as well as most of the old nobility, hated Cromwell, and now was an opportunity of inflicting vengeance on him. Cromwell had been the chief cause of the King's marriage with Anne of Cleves; but the fact is his plundering talent was no longer wanted, and it was convenient to the tyrant to get rid of him.

Cromwell had obtained enormous wealth from his several offices, as well as from the plunder of the church and the poor. He had got about thirty of the estates belonging to the monasteries; his house, or rather palace, was gorged with the fruits of the sacking; he had been made Earl of Essex; he had precedence over every one but the King; and, he, in fact, represented the King in the Parliament, where he introduced and defended all his confiscating and murdering laws. He had been barbarous beyond all description towards the unfortunate and unoffending monks and nuns; without such an instrument the plunder never could have been effected: but he was no longer wanted; the ruffian had already lived too long; the very walls of the devastated convents seemed to call for public vengeance on his head. On the morning of the 10th of June, 1540, he was all-powerful; in the evening of the same day he was in prison as a traitor. He lay in prison only a few days before he had to experience the benefit of his own way of administering justice. He had, as we have seen in the last chapter, invented a way of bringing people to the block or the gallows without giving them any form of trial, without giving them even a hearing, but merely by passing a law to put them to death. This was what he had brought about in the case of the Countess of Salisbury; and this was what was now to fall on his own head. He lived only about forty-eight days after his arrest; not half long enough to enable him to expiate, barely to enumerate, the robberies and murders committed under his orders. His time seems, however, to have been spent, not in praying to God to forgive him for these robberies and murders, but in praying to the tyrant to spare his life. Perhaps of all the mean and dastardly wretches that ever died, this was the most mean and dastardly. He who had been the most insolent and cruel of ruffians when he had power, was now the most disgustingly slavish and base. He had, in fact, committed no crime against the King; though charged with heresy and treason, he was no more a heretic than the King was, and as to the charge of treason there was not a shadow of foundation for it. But he was just as guilty of treason as the abbots of Reading, Colchester and Glastonbury, all of whom and many more he had been the chief instrument in putting to death. He put them to death in order to get possession of their property; and I dare say to get at his property, to get the plunder back from him, was one of the motives for bringing him to the block. This very ruffian had superintended the digging up of the ashes of Thomas à Becket and scattering them in the air; and now the people who had witnessed that had to witness the letting of the blood out of his dirty body, to run upon the pavement to be licked up by hogs or dogs. The cowardly creature seems to have had, from the moment of his arrest, no thought about anything but saving his life. He wrote repeatedly to the King in the hope of getting pardoned, but all to no purpose: He had done what was wanted of him, the work of plunder was nearly over, he had, too, got a large share of the plunder which it was not convenient to leave in his hands; and therefore, upon true "Reformation" principles, it was time to take away his life. He in his letters to the King most vehemently protested his innocence. Aye, no doubt of that; but he was not more innocent than were the butchered abbots and monks, he was not more innocent than any one out of those thousands upon thousands whom he had quartered, hanged, burned, or plundered; and amongst all those thousands upon thousands there never was seen one, female or male, so complete a dastard as himself. In these letters to the tyrant he fawned on him in the most disgusting manner; compared his smiles and frowns to those of God; besought him to suffer him "to kiss his balmy hand once more that the fragrance thereof might make him fit for heaven!" The base creature deserved his death, if it had only been for writing these letters. Fox, the "martyr" man, calls this Cromwell the "valiant soldier of the Reformation." Yes, there have been few soldiers to understand sacking better; he was full of valour on foraging parties, and when he had to rifle monks and nuns and to rob altars; a brave fellow when he had to stretch monks and nuns on the rack to make them confess treasonable words or thoughts; but when death began to stare him in the face he was, assuredly, the most cowardly caitiff that ever died. It is hardly necessary to say that this man is a great favourite of Hume, who deeply laments Cromwell's fate, though he has not a word of compassion to bestow upon all the thousands that had been murdered or ruined by him. He, as well as other historians, quotes from the conclusion of one of Cromwell's letters to the King these abject expressions: "I, a most woful prisoner, am ready to submit to death when it shall please God and your Majesty; and yet the frail flesh incites me to call to your grace for mercy and pardon of mine offences. — Written at the Tower with the heavy heart and trembling hand of your Highness's most miserable prisoner and poor slave, Thomas Cromwell. — Most gracious prince, I cry for mercy, mercy, mercy!" That is the language of Fox's "valiant soldier." Fox meant valiant, not in the field or on the scaffold, but in the convent, pulling the rings from women's fingers and tearing the gold clasps from books: that was the Protestant valour of the "Reformation." Hume says that Cromwell "deserved a better fate." Never was fate more just or more appropriate. He had been the willing, the officious, the zealous, the eager agent in the execution of all the tyrannical, sacrilegious, and bloody deeds of his master, and had amongst other things been the very man who first suggested the condemning of people to death without trial. What could be more just than that he should die in the same way? Not a tear was shed at his death, which produced on the spectators an effect such as is produced when the foulest of murderers expiate their crimes on the gallows.

During the seven years that the tyrant himself survived this his cruel and dastardly vice-gerent, he was beset with disappointments, vexations, and torments of all sorts. He discovered at the end of a few months that his new queen had been, and still was, much such another as Anne Boleyn. He with very little ceremony sent her to the block, together with a whole posse of her relations, lovers, and cronies. He raged and foamed like a wild beast, passed laws most bloody to protect himself against lewdness and infidelity in his future wives, and got for his pains the ridicule of the nation and of all Europe. He for the last time took another wife; but this time none would face his laws but a widow, and she very narrowly escaped the fate of the rest. He for some years before he died became, from his gluttony and debaucheries, an unwieldy and disgusting mass of flesh, moved about by means of mechanical inventions. But still he retained all the ferocity and bloody-mindedness of his former days. The principal business of his life was the ordering of accusations, executions, and confiscations. When on his death-bed every one was afraid to intimate his danger to him, lest death to the intimator should be the consequence; and he died before he was well aware of his condition, leaving more than one death-warrant unsigned for want of time.

Thus expired, in the year 1547, in the fifty-sixth year of his age and the thirty-eighth of his reign, the most unjust, hard-hearted, meanest and most sanguinary tyrant that the world had ever beheld, whether Christian or heathen. That England which he found in peace, unity, plenty and happiness, he left torn by factions and schisms, her people wandering about in beggary and misery. He laid the foundations of immorality, dishonesty and pauperism, all which produced an abundant harvest in the reigns of his unhappy, barren, mischievous and miserable children, with whom, at the end of a few years, his house and his name were extinguished for ever. How he disposed of the plunder of the Church and the poor; how his successors completed that work of confiscation which he had carried on so long; how the nation sunk in point of character and of wealth; how pauperism first arose in England; and how were sown the seeds of that system of which we now behold the effects in the impoverishment and degradation of the main body of the people of England and Ireland; all these will be shown in the next chapter, and shown, I trust, in a manner which will leave in the mind of every man of sense no doubt that, of all the scourges that ever

afflicted this country, none is to be put in comparison
with the Protestant "Reformation."

CHAPTER SEVEN

One of Henry's last acts was a will by which he made his
infant son his immediate successor, with remainder, in
case he died without issue, to his daughter Mary, first, and
then in default of issue again, to his daughter Elizabeth,
though, observe, both the daughters had been declared illegitimate by Act of Parliament, and though the latter was
born of Anne Boleyn while the King's first wife, the mother
of Mary, was alive. Parliament had given the king the right
to determine the succession by will.

To carry this will into execution, and to govern the kingdom until Edward, who was then ten years of age, should be
eighteen years of age, there were sixteen executors appointed, amongst whom was Seymour, Earl of Hertford, and the
"honest Cranmer." These sixteen worthies began by taking,
in the most solemn manner, an oath to stand and maintain
the last will of their master. Their second act was to break
that oath by making Hertford, who was a brother of Jane
Seymour, the King's mother, "protector," though the will
gave equal powers to all the executors. Their next step was
to give new peerages to some of themselves. The fourth, to
award to the new peers grants of the public money. The
fifth was to lay aside at the coronation the ancient English
custom of asking the people if they were willing to have
and obey the King. The sixth was "to attend at a solemn
high mass." And the seventh was to begin a series of acts
for the total subversion of all that remained of the Catholic
religion in England, and for the effecting of all that Old
Harry had left unaffected in the way of plunder.

The monasteries were gone; the cream had been taken
off; but there remained the skimmed milk of church altars,

chantries and guilds. The power of the Pope was gotten rid of, the country had been sacked, the poor had been despoiled; but still there were some pickings left. The piety of ages had made every church, however small, contain some gold and silver appertaining to the altar. The altars in

the parish churches, and generally in the cathedrals, had been left as yet untouched; for though the wife-killer had abjured the Pope, whose power he had taken to himself, he still professed to be of the Catholic faith, and he maintained the mass and the sacraments and creeds with fire and faggot. Therefore he had left the church altars unplundered. But they contained gold, silver, and other valuables, and the worthies saw these with longing eyes and itching fingers.

To seize them, however, there required a pretext, and what pretext could there be short of declaring at once that the Catholic religion was false and wicked, and, of course, that there ought to be no altars, and, of course, no gold and silver things appertaining to them! The sixteen worthies, with Hertford at their head and with Cranmer amongst them, had had the King crowned as a Catholic, he as well as they had taken the oaths as Catholics, they had sworn to uphold that religion, they had taken him to a high mass after his coronation: but the altars had good things about them; there was plunder remaining, and to get at this remaining plunder the Catholic religion must be wholly put down. There were doubtless some fanatics, some who imagined that the religion of nine hundred years' standing ought not to be changed, some who had not plunder and plunder only in view; but it is impossible for any man of common sense, of unperverted mind, to look at the history of this transaction, at this open avowal of Protestantism, at this change from the religion of England to that of a part of Germany, without being convinced that the principal authors of it had plunder and plunder only in view.

The old tyrant died in 1547, and by the end of 1549 Cranmer, who had tied so many Protestants to the stake for not being Catholics, had pretty nearly completed a system of Protestant worship. He first prepared a book of homilies and a catechism, in order to pave the way. Next came a law to allow the clergy to have wives, and then, when all things had been prepared, came the book of Common Prayer and Administration of the Sacraments. Gardiner, who was Bishop of Winchester, reproached Cranmer with his duplicity, reminded him of the zeal with which he had upheld the Catholic worship under the late king, and would have made him hang himself or cut his throat if he had had the slightest remains of shame in him.

This new system did not, however, go far enough for the fanatics, and there instantly appeared arrayed against it whole tribes of new lights on the Continent; so that Cranmer, cunning as he was, soon found he had undertaken no easy matter. The Proclamations put forth upon this occasion were disgustingly ridiculous, coming as they did in the name of a king only ten years of age, and expressed in words so solemnly pompous and full of arrogance. However, the chief object was the plunder, and to get at this nothing was spared. There were other things to attract the grasp, but it will be unnecessary to dwell very particularly on anything but the altars and the churches. This was the real "Reformation reign," for it was a reign of robbery and hypocrisy without anything to be compared with them, — anything in any country or in any age. Religion, conscience, was always the pretext; but in one way or another robbery, plunder, was always the end. The people, once so united and so happy, became divided into innumerable sects, no man knowing hardly what to believe, and, indeed, no one knowing what it was lawful for him to say, for it soon became impossible for the common people to know what was heresy and what was not heresy.

That prince of hypocrites, Cranmer, who, during the reign of Henry had condemned people to the flames for not believing in transubstantiation, was now ready to condemn them for believing in it. We have seen that Luther was the beginner of the work of "reformation," but he was soon followed by further reformers on the Continent. These made many attempts to propagate their doctrines in England, but old Henry had kept them down. Now, however, when the churches were to be robbed of what remained in them, and when, to have pretext for that robbery, it was necessary to make a complete change in the form of worship, these sectarians all flocked to England, which became one great scene of religious disputation. Some were for the Common Prayer-Book, others proposed alterations in it, others were for abolishing it altogether; and there now began that division, that multiplicity of hostile opinions, which has continued to the present day. Cranmer employed a part of the resources of the country to feed and fatten those of these religious, or rather impious adventurers who sided with him and who chose the best market for their doctrines. England was overrun by these foreign traders in religion, and this nation, so jealous of foreign influence, was now compelled to bend its haughty neck, not only to foreigners but to foreigners of the most base and infamous character and description. Cranmer could not find Englishmen sufficiently supple to be his tools in executing the work that he had in hand. The Protector, Hertford, who we must now call Somerset (the child-king having made him Duke of Somerset), was the greatest of all "reformers" that had yet appeared in the world, and, as we shall soon see, the great-est and most audacious of all the plunderers that this infa-mous reformation has produced, save and except Henry himself. The total abolition of the Catholic worship was necessary to his projects of plunder, and therefore he was a great encourager of these greedy and villanous foreigners.

The consequences to the morals of the people were such as were naturally to be expected. All historians agree that vice of all sorts and crimes of every kind were never so great and so numerous before. This was confessed by the teachers themselves, and yet the Protestants have extolled this reign as the reign of conscience and religion! It was so manifest that the change was a bad one, that men could not have proceeded in it from error. Its mischiefs were all manifest before the death of the tyrant; that death afforded an opportunity for returning into the right path, but there was plunder remaining, and the plunderers went on. The "Reformation" was not the work of virtue, of fanaticism, of error, of ambition, but of a love of plunder. This was its great animating principle; in this it began, and in this it proceeded till there was nothing left for it to work on.

Henry had, in certain cases, enabled his minions to rob the bishoprics, but now there was a grand sweep at them. The Protector took the lead, and his example was followed by others. They took so much from one, so much from another, and some they wholly suppressed, as that of Westminster, and took their estates to themselves. There were many chantries (private property to all intents and purposes), free chapels (also private property), almshouses, hospitals, guilds or fraternities, the property of which was as much private property as the funds of any friendly society now are. All these became lawful plunder. And yet there are men who pretend that what is now possessed by the Established Church is of so sacred a nature as not to be touched by Act of Parliament! This was the reign in which this our present Established Church was founded, for though the fabric was overset by Mary it was raised again by

Elizabeth. Now it was that it was made. It was made, and
the new worship along with it, by Acts of Parliament. It
had its very birth in division, disunion, discord, and its life
has been worthy of its birth.

The plunder which remained after the seizure of the
monasteries was comparatively small; but still, the very
leavings of the old tyranny, the mere gleanings of the harvest of plunder, were something; and these were not suffered to remain. The plunder of the churches, parochial as
well as collegiate, was preceded by all sorts of antics played
in those churches. Calvin had got an influence opposed to
that of Cranmer; so that there was almost open war
amongst these Protestants, which party should have the
teaching of the people. After due preparation in this way,
the robbery was set about in due form. Every church altar
had, as I have before observed, more or less of gold and silver. A part consisted of images, a part of censers, candlesticks and other things used in celebration of the mass. The
mass was, therefore abolished, and there was no longer to
be an altar, but a table in its stead. The fanatical part of the
reformers amused themselves with quarrelling about the
part of the church where the table was to stand, about the
shape of it, and whether the head of it was to be placed to
the north, the east, the west, or the south, and whether the
people were to stand, kneel or sit at it! The plunderers,
however, thought about other things; they thought about
the value of the images, censers, and the like.

The Protector, Somerset, did not forget himself. Having
plundered four or five of the bishoprics he needed a palace
in London. For the purpose of building this palace, which
was erected in the Strand, London, and which was called
"Somerset House," as the place is called to this day, he took
from three bishops their town houses. He pulled these
down, together with a parish church, in order to get a suitable spot for the erection. The material of these demolished
buildings being insufficient for his purpose, he pulled down
a part of the buildings appertaining to the then cathedral of

Saint Paul; the church of Saint John, near Smithfield, Barking chapel, near the Tower; the college church of Saint Martin-le-Grand; Saint Ewan's church, Newgate; and the parish church of Saint Nicholas. He, besides these, ordered the pulling down of the parish church of Saint Margaret, Westminster; but, says Dr. Heylyn, "the workmen had no sooner advanced their scaffolds when the parishioners gathered together in great multitudes with bows and arrows and staves and clubs, which so terrified the workmen that they ran away in great amazement, and never could be brought again upon that employment."

The *Book of Common Prayer* was to put an end to all dissensions; but its promulgation and the consequent robbery of the churches were followed by open insurrection in many of the counties, by battles, and executions by martial law. The whole kingdom was in commotion, but particularly, to the great honour of those counties, in Devonshire and Norfolk. In the former county the insurgents were superior in force to the hired troops and had besieged Exeter. Lord Russell was sent against them, and at last, reinforced by German troops, he defeated them, executed many by martial law, and most gallantly hanged a priest on the top of the tower of his church! In Norfolk the insurrection was still more formidable, but was finally suppressed by the aid of foreign troops, and was also followed by the most barbarous executions. The people of Devonshire complained of the alterations in religion, "that," as Dr. Heylyn (a Protestant divine) expresses it, "the free-born commonalty was oppressed by a small number of gentry, who glutted themselves with pleasures, while the poor commons, wasted by daily labour like pack-horses, live in extreme slavery; and that holy rites established by antiquity were abolished and a new form of religion obtruded;" and they demanded that the mass and a part of the monasteries should be restored, and that priests should not be allowed to marry. Similar were the complaints and the demands everywhere else; but Cranmer's *Prayer Book* and the Church "by law established," backed by foreign bayonets, finally triumphed, at least for the present, and during the remainder of this hypocritical, base, corrupt and tyrannical reign.

Thus arose the Protestant Church as by law established. Here we see its origin. Thus it was that it commenced its career. How different, alas! from the commencement of that Church of England which arose under St. Austin at Canterbury, which had been cherished so carefully by Alfred the Great, and under the wings of which the people of England had for nine hundred years seen their country the greatest in the world, and had themselves lived in ease and plenty and real freedom, superior to those of all other nations!

Somerset, who had brought his own brother to the block in 1549, chiefly because he had opposed himself to his usurpations (though both were plunderers), was, not long after the commission of the above cruelties on the people, destined to come to that block himself. Dudley, Earl of Warwick, who was his rival in baseness and injustice and his superior in talent, had out-intrigued him in the Council, and at last he brought him to that end which he so well merited. On what grounds this was done is wholly uninteresting. It was a set of most wicked men circumventing and, if necessary, destroying each other; but it is worthy of remark that amongst the crimes alleged against this great culprit was his having brought foreign troops into the kingdom! This was, to be sure, rather ungrateful in the pious reformers, for it was those troops that established for them their new religion. But it was good to see them putting their leader to death, actually cutting off his head, for having caused their projects to succeed. It was, in plain words, a dispute about the plunder. Somerset had got more than his brother plunderers deemed his share. He was building a palace for himself, and if each plunderer could have had a palace it would have been peace amongst them; but as this could not be the rest called him a "traitor," and as the King, the Protestant Edward, had signed the death-warrant of one uncle at the instigation of another uncle, he now signed the death-warrant of that other, he himself being even now only fifteen years of age!

Warwick, who was now become Protector, was made Duke of Northumberland, and got granted to him the immense estates of that ancient house, which had fallen into the hands of the crown. This was, if possible, a more zealous Protestant than the last Protector; that is to say, still more profligate, rapacious and cruel. The work of plundering the Church went on until there remained scarcely anything worthy of the name of clergy. Many parishes were in all parts of the kingdom united in one, and having but one priest amongst them. But indeed there were hardly any persons left worthy of the name of clergy.

The King, who was a poor sickly lad, seems to have had no distinctive characteristic except that of hatred to the Catholics and their religion, in which hatred Cranmer and others had brought him up. His life was not likely to be long, and Northumberland, who was now his keeper, conceived the project of getting the crown into his own family, a project quite worthy of a hero of the "Reformation." In order to carry this project into effect, he married one of his sons, Lord Guilford Dudley, to Lady Jane Grey, who, next after Mary and Elizabeth and Mary Queen of Scotland, was heiress to the throne. Having done this, he got Edward to make a will settling the crown on this Lady Jane, to the exclusion of his two sisters. The advocates of the "Reformation," who of course praise this boy-king, in whose reign the new Church was invented, tell us long stories about the way in which Northumberland persuaded Edward to do this act of injustice; but in all probablity there is not a word of truth in the story. However, what they say is this: that Lady Jane was a sincere Protestant, that the young King knew this, and that his anxiety for the security of the Protestant religion induced him to consent to Northumberland's proposition.

The settlement met with great difficulty when it came to be laid before the lawyers, who somehow or other always contrived to keep their heads out of the halter. Even Henry's judges used, when hard pressed, to refer him to the Parliament for the committing of violations of law. The judges, the lord chancellor, the secretaries of state, the privy council, all were afraid to put their names to this transfer of the crown. The thing was, however, at last accomplished, and with the signature of Cranmer to it; though he, as one of the late king's executors, and the first upon that list, had sworn in the most solemn manner to maintain his will, according to which will the two sisters, in case of no issue by the brother, were to succeed that brother on the throne. Thus, in addition to his fourth act of notorious perjury, this maker of the *Book of Common Prayer* became clearly guilty of high treason. He now at last, in spite of all his craft, had woven his own halter, and that, too, beyond all doubt for the purpose of preserving his bishopric. The Princess Mary was next heir to the throne. He had divorced her mother, he had been the principal agent in that unjust and most wicked transaction; and besides, he knew that Mary was immovably a Catholic, and that of course her accession must be the death of his office and his Church. Therefore he now committed the greatest crime known to the laws, and that, too, from the basest of motives.

The King having made this settlement, and being kept wholly in the hands of Northumberland, who had placed his creatures about him, would naturally, as was said at the time, not live long! In short, he died on the 6th of July, 1553, in the sixteenth year of his age and the seventh of his reign, expiring on the same day of the year that his father had brought Sir Thomas More to the block. These were seven of the most miserable and most inglorious years that England had ever known. Fanaticism and roguery, hypocrisy and plunder, divided the country between them. The people were wretched beyond all description; from the plenty of Catholic times they had been reduced to general beggary; and then, in order to repress this beggary, laws the most ferocious were passed to prevent even starving

creatures from asking alms. Abroad as well as at home the
nation sunk in the eyes of the world. The town of Boulogne
in France, which had been won by Catholic Englishmen,
the base Protestant rulers now, from sheer cowardice, surrendered; and from one end of Europe to the other were
heard jeering and scoffing at this formerly great and lofty
nation. Hume, who finds goodness in every one who was
hostile to the Catholic institutions, says: "All English historians dwell with pleasure on the excellencies of this young
King, whom the flattering promises of hope, joined to many
real virtues, had made an object of the most tender affec-
tions of the public. He possessed mildness of disposition, a
capacity to learn and to judge, and attachment to equity
and justice." Of his mildness we have, I suppose, a proof in
his assenting to the burning of several Protestants who did
not protest in his way; in his signing of the death-warrants
of his two uncles, and in his wish to bring his sister Mary to
trial for not conforming to what she deemed blasphemy,
and from doing which he was deterred only by the menaces
of the Emperor, her cousin. So much for his mildness. As
for his justice, who can doubt of that who thinks of his will
to disinherit his two sisters, even after the judges had unanimously declared to him that it was contrary to law? The
"tender affection" that the people had for him was, doubtless, evinced by their rising in insurrection against his ordi-
nances from one end of the kingdom to the other, and by
their demanding the restoration of that religion which all
his acts tended wholly to extirpate.

The settlement of the crown had been kept a secret from
the people, and so was the death of the king, for three
whole days. In the meanwhile Northumberland, seeing the
death of the young King approaching, had in conjunction,
observe, with Cranmer and the rest of his council, ordered
the two princesses to come near to London, under pretence
that they might be at hand to comfort their brother, but
with the real design of putting them into prison the
moment the breath should be out of his body. Traitors, foul

conspirators, villains of all descriptions have this in common, that they, when necessary to their own interest, are always ready to betray each other. Thus it happened here; for the Earl of Arundel, who was one of the council, and who went with Dudley and others on the tenth of July to kneel before Lady Jane as Queen, had in the night of the sixth sent a secret messenger to Mary, who was no farther off than Hoddesdon, informing her of the death of her brother and of the whole plot against her. Thus warned she set off on horseback, accompanied by only a few servants, to Kenninghall, in Norfolk, whence she proceeded to Framlingham, in Suffolk, and thence issued her commands to the council to proclaim her as their sovereign, hinting at but not positively accusing them with their treasonable designs. They had on the day before proclaimed Lady Jane to be Queen! They had taken all sorts of precautions to ensure their success: army, fleet, treasure, all the powers of government were in their hands. They therefore returned her a most insolent answer, and commanded her to submit, as a dutiful subject, to the lawful queen; at the bottom of which command Cranmer's name stood first.

Honesty and sincerity exult to contemplate the misgivings which, in a few hours afterwards, seized this band of almost unparalleled villains. The nobility and gentry had instantly flocked to the standard of Mary; and the people, even in London, who were most infected with the pestiferous principles of the foreign miscreants that had been brought from the continent to teach them the new religion, had native honesty enough left to make them disapprove of this last and most daring of robberies. Ridley, the Protestant bishop of London, preached at St. Paul's to the Lord Mayor and a numerous assemblage for the purpose of persuading them to take part against Mary, but it was seen that he preached in vain. Northumberland himself marched from London on the 13th of July to attack the Queen. But in a few days she was surrounded by twenty or thirty thousand men, all volunteers in her cause and refusing pay. Before

Northumberland reached Bury St. Edmunds he began to despair; he marched to Cambridge and wrote to his brother conspirators for reinforcements. Amongst these dismay first, and then perfidy, began to appear. In a few days these men, who had been so audacious and who had sworn solemnly to uphold the cause of Queen Jane, sent Northumberland an order to disband his army, while they themselves proclaimed Queen Mary amidst the unbounded applause of the people.

The master-plotter had disbanded his army, or rather, it had deserted him, before the order of the council reached him. This was the age of "reformation" and of baseness. Seeing himself abandoned, he, by the advice of Dr. Sands, the Vice-Chancellor of the University, who only four days before had preached against Mary, went to the market-place of Cambridge and proclaimed her Queen, "tossing," says Stowe, "his cap into the air in token of his joy and satisfaction." In a few hours afterwards he was arrested by the Queen's order, and that, too, by his brother-conspirator the Earl of Arundel, who had been one of the very first to kneel before Lady Jane! No reign, no age, no country ever witnessed rapacity, hypocrisy, meanness, baseness, perfidy such as England witnessed in those who were the destroyers of the Catholic and founders of the Protestant Church. This Dudley, who had for years been a plunderer of the Church, who had been a promoter of every ruffian-like measure against those who had adhered to the religion of his fathers; who had caused a transfer of the crown because, as he alleged, the accession of Mary would endanger the Protestant religion; this very man, when he came to receive justice on the block, confessed his belief in the Catholic faith; and which is more, exhorted the nation to return to it. He, according to Dr. Heylyn (a Protestant, mind) exhorted them "to stand to the religion of their ancestors, rejecting that of later date, which had occasioned all the misery of the fore-going thirty years; and that if they desired to present their souls unspotted before God, and were truly affected to their country, they should expel the preachers of the reformed religion. For himself," he said, "being blinded by ambition, he had made a rack of his conscience by temporising, and so acknowledged the justice of his sentence." Fox, author of the lying *Book of Martyrs*, of whose lies we shall see more by-and-by, asserts that Dudley made this confession in consequence of a promise of pardon. But when he came on the scaffold he knew that he was not to be pardoned; and besides, he himself expressly declared the contrary at his execution, and told the people that he had not been moved by anyone to make it, and had not done it from any hope of saving his life. However, we have yet to see Cranmer himself recant, and to see the whole band of Protestant plunderers on their knees before the Pope's legate, confessing their sins of heresy and sacrilege and receiving absolution for their offences.

Thus ended this reign of "reformation," plunder, wretchedness and disgrace. Three times the form of the new worship was changed, and yet those who adhered to the old worship or who went beyond the new worship were punished with the utmost severity. The nation became every day more and more despised abroad and more and more distracted and miserable at home. The Church "as by law established" arose and was enforced under two protectors or chief ministers, both of whom deservedly suffered death as traitors. Its principal author was a man who had sent both Protestants and Catholics to the stake; who had burnt people for adhering to the Pope, others for not believing in transubstantiation, others for believing in it, and who now burnt others for disbelieving in it for reasons different from his own; a man who now openly professed to disbelieve in that for not believing in which he had burnt many of his fellow-creatures, and who after this most solemnly declared that his own belief was that of these very persons! As this Church "by law established" advanced, all the remains of Christian charity vanished before it. The indigent, whom the Catholic Church had so tenderly gathered under her wings, were now, merely for asking alms, branded with red-hot irons and made slaves, though no provision was made to prevent them from perishing with hunger and cold; and England, so long famed as the land of hospitality, generosity, ease, plenty, and security to person and property, became under a Protestant Church a scene of repulsive selfishness, of pack-horse toil, of pinching want, and of rapacity and plunder and tyranny that made the very names of law and justice a mockery.

CHAPTER EIGHT

We are now entering upon that reign the punishments inflicted during which have furnished such a handle to the calumniators of the Catholic Church, who have left no art untried to exaggerate those punishments in the first place, and in the second place to ascribe them to the Catholic religion, keeping out of sight all the while the thousand times greater mass of cruelty occasioned by Protestants in this kingdom. Of all cruelties I disapprove, I disapprove also of all corporal and pecuniary punishments on the score of religion. Far be it for me, therefore, to defend all the punishments inflicted on this score in the reign of Queen Mary; but it will be my duty to show, first, that the mass of punishments then inflicted on this account has been monstrously exaggerated; secondly, that the circumstances under which they were inflicted found more apology for their severity than the circumstances under which the Protestant punishments were inflicted; thirdly that they were in amount as a single grain of wheat is to a whole bushel, compared with the mass of punishments under the Protestant Church "as by law established;" lastly, that be they what they might, it is a base perversion of reason to ascribe them to the principles of the Catholic religion; and that as to the Queen herself, she was one of the most virtuous of human beings and was rendered miserable, not by her own disposition or misdeeds, but by the misfortune and misery entailed on her by her two immediate predecessors, who had plunged the country into confusion, and who had left no choice but that of making severe examples, or, of being an encourager of and a participator in heresy, plunder, and sacrilege. Her reign our deceivers have taught us to call the reign of "Bloody Queen Mary," while they have taught us to call that of her sister the "Golden Days of Good Queen Bess." They have taken good care never to tell us that for every drop of blood that Mary shed Elizabeth shed a pint; that the former gave up every fragment of the plunder of which the deeds of her predecessors had put her in possession, and that the latter resumed this plunder again, and took from the poor every pittance which had by oversight been left them; that the former never changed her religion, and that the latter changed from Catholic to Protestant, then to Catholic again, and then back again to Protestant; that the former punished people for departing from that religion in which she and they and their fathers had been born, and to which she had always adhered; and that the latter punished people for not departing from the religion of her and their fathers, and which religion, too, she herself professed and openly lived in even at the time of her coronation. Yet we have been taught to call the former "bloody" and the latter "good!" How have we been deceived! And is it not time, then, that this deception, so injurious to our Catholic fellow-subjects and so debasing to ourselves, should cease? It is perhaps too much to hope that I shall be able to make it cease; but towards accomplishing this great and most desirable object I shall do something at any rate, by a plain and true account of the principal transactions of the reign of Mary.

The Queen, who, as we have seen in the last chapter, was at Framlingham in Suffolk, immediately set off for London, where, having been greeted on the road with the strongest demonstrations of joy at her accession, she arrived on the 31st of July, 1553. As she approached London the throngs thickened; Elizabeth, who had kept cautiously silent while the issue was uncertain, went out to meet her, and the two sisters, riding on horseback, entered the city, the houses being decorated, the streets strewed with flowers, and the people dressed in their gayest clothes. She was crowned soon afterwards, in the most splendid manner and after the Catholic ritual, by Gardiner, who had, as we have seen, opposed Cranmer's new Church, and whom she found a prisoner in the Tower, he having been deprived of his bishopric of Winchester, but whom we are to see one of the great actors in restoring the Catholic religion. The joy of the people was boundless. It was a coronation of greater splendour and more universal joy than ever had before been witnessed. This is agreed on all hands. And this fact gives the lie to Hume, who would have us believe that the people did not like the Queen's principles. This fact has reason on its side as well as historical authority, for was it not natural that the people, who only three years before had actually risen in insurrection in all parts of the kingdom against the new Church and its authors, should be half mad with joy at the accession of a queen who they were sure would put down that Church, and put down those who had quelled them by the aid of German troops?

Mary began her reign by acts the most just and benefi- cent. Generously disregarding herself, her ease and means of splendour, she abolished the debased currency which her father had introduced and her brother had made still baser; she paid the debts due by the Crown, and she largely remit- ted taxes at the same time. But that which she had most at heart was the restoration of that religion under the influ- ence of which the kingdom had been so happy and so great for so many ages, and since the abolition of which it had known nothing but discord, disgrace and misery. It is easy to imagine that this same people would hail with joy indescrib- able the prospect of seeing the new Church put down and the ancient one restored, and that, too, under a queen on whose constancy and piety and integrity they could so firmly rely. But the plunder had been so immense, the plunderers were so numerous, they were so powerful, and there were so few men of family of any account who had not participated in deeds one way or another hostile to the Catholic Church, that the enterprise of the Queen was full of difficulty. As to Cranmer's Church "by law established," that was easily disposed of. The gold and silver and cups and candlesticks and other things, of which the altar-robbers of young King Edward's reign had despoiled the churches, could not indeed be restored, but the altars themselves could and speedily were; and the tables which had been put in their stead and the married priests along with them were soon seen no longer to offend the eyes of the people. It is curious to observe how tender-hearted Hume is upon this subject. He says, "Could any notion of law, justice or reason be attended to where superstition predominates, the priests would never have been expelled for their past marriages, which at that time were permitted by the laws of the kingdom." I wonder why it never occurred to him to observe that monks and nuns ought not then to have been expelled! Were not their institutions "permitted by the laws of the kingdom?" Aye, and had been permitted by those laws for nine hundred years, and guaranteed, too, by Magna Charta. He applauds the expelling of them; but this "new thing," though only of three years and a half standing, and though "established" under a boy-king who was under two protectors, each of whom was justly beheaded for high treason, and under a council who were all conspirators against the lawful sovereign, — these married priests, the most of whom had, like Luther, Cranmer, Knox, Hooper, and other great "Reformers," broken their vows of celibacy, and were of course perjurers; no law was to be repealed, however contrary to public good such law might be, if the repeal injured the interests of such men as these! The Queen had, however, too much justice to think thus, and these apostates were expelled, to the great joy of the people, many of whom had been sabred by German troops because they demanded, amongst other things, that priests might not be permitted to marry. The Catholic bishops who had been turned out by Cranmer were restored, and his new bishops were of course turned out. Cranmer himself was in a short time deprived of his ill-gotten see and was in prison, and most justly, as a traitor. The mass was in all parts of the country once more celebrated, the people were no longer burnt with red-hot irons and made slaves merely for asking alms, and they began to hope that England would be England again, and that hospitality and charity would return.

But there were the plunderers to deal with! And now we are about to witness a scene which, were not its existence so well attested, must pass for the wildest of romance. What? That Parliament, who had declared Cranmer's divorce of Catherine to be lawful, and who had enacted that Mary was a bastard, acknowledge that same Mary to be the lawful heir to the throne! That Parliament, which had abolished the Catholic worship and created the Protestant worship on the ground that the former was idolatrous and damnable and the latter agreeable to the will of God, abolish the latter and restore the former! What? Do these things? and that, too, without any force, without being compelled to do them? No, not exactly so; for it had the people to fear, a vast majority of whom were cordially with the Queen so far as related to these matters, respecting which it is surprising what dispatch was made. The late king died only in July, and before the end of the next November all the work of Cranmer, as to the divorce as well as to the worship, was completely overset, and that, too, by Acts of the very Parliament who had confirmed the one and "established" the other. The first of these Acts declared that Henry and Catherine had been lawfully married, and it laid all the blame on Cranmer by name! The second Act called the Protestant Church "as by law established" a "new thing imagined by a few singular opinions," though the Parliament, when it established it, asserted it to have come from "the Holy Ghost." What was now said of it was true enough; but it might have been added, established by German bayonets. The great inventor, Cranmer, who was at last in a fair way of receiving the just reward of his numerous misdeeds, could only hear of the overthrow of his work; for having, though clearly as guilty of high treason as Dudley himself, been as yet only confined to his palace at Lambeth, and hearing that mass had been celebrated in his cathedral church at Canterbury, he put forth a most inflammatory and abusive declaration (which, mind, he afterwards recanted), for which declaration, as well as for his treason, he was committed to the Tower, where he lay at the time when these Acts were passed. But the new Church required no law to abolish it. It was, in fact, abolished by the general feeling of the nation; and, as we shall see in the next chapter, it required rivers of blood to re-establish it in the reign of Elizabeth.

But when the question came, whether the Parliament should restore the Papal Supremacy, the plunder was at stake; for to take the Church property was sacrilege, and if the Pope regained his power in the kingdom he might insist on restitution. The greater part of this property had been seized on eighteen years before. In many cases it had been divided and subdivided, in many the original grantees were dead. The common people, too, had in many cases become dependants on the new proprietors; and besides, they could not so easily trace their connexion between their faith and that supremacy, as they could between their faith and the mass and the sacraments. The Queen, therefore, though she most anxiously wished to avoid giving in any way whatever her sanction to the plunder, was reduced to the necessity of risking a civil war for the Pope's supremacy, to leave her kingdom unreconciled to the Church, and to keep to herself the title of Head of the Church, to her so hateful, or to make a compromise with the plunderers. She was induced to prefer the latter; though it is by no means certain that civil war would not have been better for the country, even if it had ended in the triumph of the plunderers, which, in

all human probablity, it would not. But observe in how for-
lorn a state as to this question she was placed. There was
scarcely a nobleman or gentleman of any note in her kingdom who had not in one way or another soiled his hands
with the plunder. The Catholic bishops, all but Fisher, had
assented to the abolition of the Pope's supremacy. Bishop
Gardiner, who was now her High Chancellor, was one of
these, though he had been deprived of his bishopric and
imprisoned in the Tower because he opposed Cranmer's further projects. These Catholic bishops, and Gardiner especially, must naturally wish to get over this matter as quietly
as possible; for how was he to advise the Queen to risk a
civil war for the restoration of that the abolition of which
he had so fully assented to and so strenuously supported?
And how was she to do anything without councillors of
some sort?

Nevertheless the Queen, whose zeal was equal to her sincerity, was bent on restoration, and therefore a compromise
with the plunderers was adopted. Now then it was fully
proved to all the world, and now this plundered nation,
who had been reduced to the greatest misery by what had
been impudently called the "Reformation," saw, as clearly
as they saw the light of day, that all those who had abetted
the "Reformation," that all the railings against the Pope,
that all the accusations against the monks and nuns, that
all the pretences of abuses in the Catholic Church, that all
the confiscations, sackings and bloodshed, that all these,
from first to last, had proceeded from the love of plunder;
for now the two Houses of Parliament, who had, only about
three or four years before, established Cranmer's Church
and declared it to be "the work of the Holy Ghost," now
these pious "Reformation" men, having first made a firm
bargain to keep the plunder, confessed that they had been
guilty of a most horrible defection from the true Church,
professed their sincere repentance for their past transgres-
sions, and declared their resolution to repeal all laws enacted in prejudice of the Pope's authority!

But this is a matter of too much importance to be dismissed without the mention of some particulars. The Queen had not about her one single man of any eminence who had not in some degree departed from the straight path during one or the other, or both, of the two last reigns. But there was Cardinal Pole, of whom and of the butchery of whose aged and brave mother we have seen an account in Chapter 4. He still remained on the Continent, but now he could with safety return to his native country, on which the fame of his talents and virtues reflected so much honour. The Cardinal was appointed by the Pope to be his legate or representative in England. The Queen had been married on the 25th of July, 1554, to Philip, Prince of Spain, son and heir of the Emperor Charles V., of which marriage I shall speak more fully by-and-by.

In November, the same year, a Parliament was called, and was opened with a most splendid procession of the two Houses, closed by the King and Queen, the first on horseback, the last in a litter, dressed in robes of purple. Their first Act was a repeal of the attainder of Pole, passed in the reign of the cruel Henry VIII. While this was going on, many noblemen and gentlemen had gone to Brussels to conduct Pole to England; and it is worth observing that amongst these was that Sir William Cecil who was afterwards so bitter and cruel an enemy of the Catholics and their religion in the reign of Elizabeth. Pole was received at Dover with every demonstration of public joy and exultation, and before he reached Gravesend, where he took water for Westminster, the gentlemen of the country had flocked to his train to the number of nearly two thousand horsemen. Here is a fact which, amongst thousands of others, shows what the populousness and opulence of England then were.

On the 29th of November the two Houses petitioned the King and Queen. In this petition they expressed their deep regret at having been guilty of defection from the Church, and prayed their Majesties, who had not participated in the sin, to intercede with the Holy Father, the Pope, for their forgiveness and for their re-admission into the fold of Christ. The next day, the Queen being seated on the throne, having the King on her left and Pole, the Pope's legate, on her right, the Lord High Chancellor, Bishop Gardiner, read the petition. The King and Queen then spoke to Pole, and he, at the close of a long speech, gave, in the name of the Pope, to the two Houses and to the whole nation, absolution in the name of the Father, Son and Holy Ghost, at which words the members of the two Houses, being on their knees, made the hall resound with Amen!

Thus was England once more a Catholic country. She was restored to the "fold of Christ;" but the fold had been plundered of its hospitality and charity, and the plunderers before they pronounced the "amen" had taken care that the plunder should not be restored. The Pope had hesitated to consent to this; Cardinal Pole, who was a man full of justice, had hesitated still longer; but, as we have seen before, Gardiner, who was now the Queen's prime minister, and indeed all her council were for the compromise, and therefore these "amen" people, while they confessed that they had sinned by that defection, in virtue of which defection, and of that alone, they got the property of the Church and the poor, while they prayed for absolution for that sin, while they rose from their knees to join the Queen in singing Te Deum in thanksgiving for that absolution, while they were doing these things they enacted that all the holders of Church property should keep it, and that any person who should attempt to molest or disturb them therein should be guilty of praemunire and be punished accordingly!

It doubtless went to the heart of the Queen to assent to this act, which was the very worst deed of her whole reign, the monstrously exaggerated fires of Smithfield not excepted. We have seen how she was situated as to her councillors, and particularly as to Gardiner, who, besides being a most zealous and active minister, was a man of the greatest talents. We have seen that there was scarcely a man of any note who had not first or last partaken of the plunder; but still, great as her difficulty certainly was, she would have done better to follow the dictates of her own mind, insisting upon doing what was right and leaving the consequences to God, as she had so nobly done when Cranmer and the rest of the base council of Edward VI. commanded her to desist from hearing mass and most cruelly took her chaplains from her.

However, she was resolved to keep none of the plunder herself. Henry, as "Head of the Church," had taken to himself the tenths and first fruits, that is to say, the tenth part of the annual worth of each church benefice and the first whole year's income of each. These had of course been kept by King Edward. Then there were some of the Church estates, some of the hospitals and other things, and these amounting to a large sum altogether, that still belonged to the Crown, and of which the Queen was of course the possessor. In November, 1555, she gave up to the Church the tenths and first fruits, which, together with the tithes, which her two immediate predecessors had seized on and kept, were worth about £63,000 a year in money of that day, and were equal to about a million a year of our present money!(c. 1824). Have we ever heard of any other sovereign doing the like? "Good Queen Bess" we shall find taking them back again to herself; and though we shall find Queen Anne giving them up to the Church, we are to bear in mind that in Mary's days the Crown and its officers, ambassadors, judges, pensioners and all employed by it, were supported out of the landed estate of the Crown itself, the remains of which estate we now see in the pitiful rest of "Crown-lands." Taxes were never in those days called for but for wars and other really national purposes, and Mary was queen two years and a half before she imposed upon her people a single farthing of tax in any shape whatever! So that this act of surrendering the tenths and first fruits was the effect of her generosity and piety; and of hers alone, too, for it was done against the remonstrances of her council, and it was not without great opposition that the bill passed in Parliament, where it was naturally feared that this just act of the Queen would awaken the people's hatred of the plunderers. But the Queen persevered, saying that she would be "Defender of the Faith" in reality and not merely in name. This was the woman whom we have been taught to call "the Bloody Queen Mary"!

The Queen did not stop here, but proceeded to restore all the church and abbey lands which were in her possession, being, whatever might be the consequence to her, firmly resolved not to be a possessor of the plunder. Having called some members of her council together she declared her resolution to them, and bade them prepare an account of those lands and possessions, that she might know what measures to adopt for the putting of her intention in execution. Her intention was to apply the revenues, as nearly as possible, to their ancient purposes. She began with Westminster Abbey, which had, in the year 610, been the site of a church immediately after the introduction of Christianity by St. Austin, which church had been destroyed by the Danes, and in 958 restored by King Edgar and St. Dunstan, who placed twelve Benedictine monks in it, and which became, under Edward the Confessor, in 1049, a noble and richly endowed abbey, which, when plundered and suppressed by Henry, had revenues to the amount of £3,977 a year of good old rent in money of that day, and therefore equal to about eighty thousand pounds a year of money of this day! Little of this, however, remained in all probability to the Queen, the estates having in great part been parcelled out amongst the plunderers of the two last reigns. But whatever there remained to her she restored, and Westminster Abbey once more saw a convent of Benedictine monks within its walls. She next restored the Friary at Greenwich, to which had belonged friars Peyto and Elstow, whom we have seen in Chapter 3 so nobly pleading before the tyrant's face the cause of her injured mother, for which they had felt the fury of that ferocious tyrant. She re-established the Black Friars in London. She restored the Nunnery at Sion, near Brentford, on the spot where Sion House now stands. At Sheen she restored the Priory. She restored and liberally endowed the Hospital of St. John, Smithfield. She re-established the hospital in the Savoy for the benefit of the poor, and allotted to it a suitable yearly revenue out of her own purse; and as her example would naturally have great effect, it is, as Dr. Heylyn (a Protestant and a great enemy of her memory) observes, "hard to say how far the nobility and gentry might have done the like if the queen had lived for some few years longer."

These acts were so laudable, so unequivocally good, so clearly the effect of justice, generosity, and charity in the Queen, that coming before us as they do in company with great zeal for the Catholic religion, we are naturally curious to hear what remarks they bring from the unfeeling and malignant Hume. Of her own free will, and even against the wish of very powerful men, she gave up in this way a yearly revenue of probably not less than a million and a half of pounds of our present money. And for what? Because she held it unjustly; because it was plunder; because it had been taken to the Crown in violation of Magna Charta and all the laws and usages of the realm; because she hoped to be able to make a beginning in the restoring of that hospitality and charity which her predecessors had banished from the land; and because her conscience, as she herself declared, forbade her to retain these ill-gotten possessions, valuing, as she did (she told her council), "her conscience more than ten kingdoms." Was there ever a more praiseworthy act? And were there ever motives more excellent? Yet Hume, who exults in the act which the plunderers insisted on to secure their plunder, calls this noble act of the Queen an "impudent" one, and ascribes it solely to the influence of the new Pope, who, he tells us, told her ambassadors that the English would never have the doors of Paradise opened to them unless the whole of the Church property was restored. How false this is, in spite of Hume's authorities, is clear from this undeniable fact, namely, that she gave the tenths and first fruits to the bishops and priests of the Church in England, and not to the Pope, to whom they were formerly paid. This, therefore, is a malignant misrepresentation. Then again, he says that the Pope's remonstrances on this score had "little influence with the nation." With the plunderers, he means; for he has been obliged to confess that in all parts of the country the people, in Edward's reign, demanded a restoration of a part of the monasteries; and is it not clear, then, that they must have greatly rejoiced to see their sovereign make a beginning in that restoration? But it was his business to lessen as much as possible the merit of these generous and pious acts of this basely calumniated queen.

Events soon proved to this just and good but singularly unfortunate queen, that she would have done better to risk a civil war against the plunderers than assent to the Act of Parliament by which was secured to them the quiet possession of their plunder. Her generous example had no effect upon them, but on the contrary made them dislike her, because it exposed them to odium, presenting a contrast with their own conduct so much to their disadvantage. From this cause more than from any other arose those troubles which harassed her during the remainder of her short reign.

She had not been many months on the throne before a rebellion was raised against her, instigated by the "Reformation" preachers who had bawled in favour of Lady Jane Grey, but who now discovered, amongst other things, that it was contrary to God's word to be governed by a woman. The fighting rebels were defeated and the leaders executed, and at the same time the Lady Jane herself, who had been convicted of high treason, who had been kept in prison, but whose life had hitherto been spared, and would evidently still have been spared if it had not manifestly tended to keep alive the hopes of the traitors and disaffected. And as this queen has been called "the bloody," is another instance to be found of so much lenity shown towards one who had been guilty of treason to the extent of actually proclaiming herself the sovereign? There was another rebellion afterwards, which was quelled in like manner, and was followed by the execution of the principal traitors, who had been abetted by a Protestant faction in France if not by the government of that country, which was bitterly hostile towards the Queen on account of her marriage with Philip, the Prince of Spain, which marriage became a great subject of invective and false accusation with the Protestants and disaffected of all sorts.

The Parliament, almost immediately after her accession, advised her to marry, but not to marry a foreigner. How strangely our taste is changed! The English had always a deep-rooted prejudice against foreigners, till, for pure love of the Protestant religion, they looked out for and soon felt the sweets of one who began the work of funding and of making national debts! The Queen, however, after great deliberation, determined to marry Philip, who was son and heir of the Emperor Charles V., and who, though a widower, and having children by his first wife, was still much younger than the Queen, who was now (in July, 1554) in the thirty-ninth year of her age, while Philip was only twenty-seven. Philip arrived at Southampton in July, 1554, escorted by the combined fleets of England, Spain and the Netherlands, and on the 25th of that month the marriage took place in the Cathedral of Winchester, the ceremony being performed by Gardiner, who was the bishop of the see, and being attended by great numbers of nobles from all parts of Christendom. To show how little reliance is to be placed on Hume, I will here notice that he says the marriage took place at Westminster, and to this adds many facts equally false. His account of the whole of this transaction is a mere romance made up from Protestant writers, even whose accounts he has shamefully distorted to the prejudice of the views and character of the Queen.

As things then stood, sound and evident good to England dictated this match. Leaving out Elizabeth, the next heir to the throne was Mary Queen of Scots, and she was betrothed to the Dauphin of France, so that England might fall to the lot of the French king, and as to Elizabeth, even supposing her to survive the Queen, she now stood bastardized by two Acts of Parliament; for the Act which had just been passed declaring Catherine to be the lawful wife of her father made her mother (what, indeed, Cranmer had declared her) an adulteress in law as she was in fact. Besides, if France and Scotland were evidently likely to become the patrimony of one and the same prince, it was necessary that England should take steps for strengthening herself also in the way of preparation.

When the rebels had, at one time, previous to Mary's marriage, advanced even to London, she went to the Guildhall, where she told the citizens that if she thought the marriage were injurious to her people or to the honour of the state she would not assent to it, and that if it should not appear to the Parliament to be for the benefit of the whole kingdom she would never marry at all. "Wherefore," said she, "stand fast against these rebels, your enemies and mine; fear them not, for I assure ye that I fear them nothing at all." Thus she left them, leaving the hall resounding with their acclamations.

When the marriage articles appeared it was shown that on this occasion, as on all others, the Queen had kept her word most religiously, for even Hume is obliged to confess that these articles were "as favourable as possible for the interest and security and even the grandeur of England." What more was wanted, then? And if, as Hume says was the case, "these articles gave no satisfaction to the nation," all that we can say is that the nation was very unreasonable and ungrateful. This is, however, a great falsehood, for what Hume here ascribes to the whole nation he ought to have confined to the plunderers and the fanatics whom, throughout his romance of this reign, he always calls the nation. The articles quoted from Rymer by Hume himself were, that though Philip should have the title of King the administration should be wholly in the Queen; that no foreigner should hold any office in the kingdom; that no change should be made in the English laws, customs, and privileges; that sixty thousand pounds a year (a million of our present money) should be settled on the Queen as her jointure, to be paid by Spain if she outlived him; that the male issue of this marriage should inherit, together with England, both Burgundy and the Low Countries; and that if Don Carlos, Philip's son by his former marriage, should die leaving no issue, the Queen's issue, whether male or female, should inherit Spain, Sicily, Milan, and all the other dominions of Philip. Just before the marriage ceremony was performed, an envoy from the Emperor, Philip's father, delivered to the English Chancellor a deed resigning to his son the kingdom of Naples and the duchy of Milan, the Emperor thinking it beneath the dignity of the Queen of England to marry one that was not a king.

What transaction was ever more honourable to a nation than this transaction was to England? What queen, what sovereign, ever took more care of the glory of a people? Yet the fact appears to be that there was some jealousy in the nation at large as to this foreign connection, and I am not one of those who are disposed to censure this jealousy. But can I have the conscience to commend, or even to abstain from censuring, this jealousy in our Catholic forefathers, without feeling, as a Protestant, my cheeks burn with shame at what has taken place in Protestant times, and even in my own time! When another Mary, a Protestant Mary, was brought to the throne, did the Parliament take care to keep the administration wholly in her and to give her husband the mere title of king? Did they take care then that no foreigners should hold offices in England? Oh, no! That foreign, that Dutch husband, had the administration vested in him; and he brought over whole crowds of foreigners, put them into the highest offices, gave them the highest titles, and heaped upon them large parcels of what was left of the Crown estate, descending to that Crown, in part at least, from the days of Alfred himself! And this transaction is called "glorious," and that, too, by the very men who talk of the "inglorious" reign of Mary! What, then; are sense and truth never to reign in England? Are we to be duped unto all generations?

The traitors and the leading rebels of Mary's reign were all, or affected to be, of the new sects. Though small in number, they made up for that disadvantage by their inde-fatigable malignity, by their incessant efforts to trouble the state, and indeed, to destroy the Queen herself. But I am for rejecting all apologies for her founded in provocations given to her, and also for rejecting all apologies founded on the disposition and influence of her councillors; for if she had been opposed to the burning of heretics, that burning is fairly to be ascribed to her; but as even the malignant Hume gives her credit for sincerity, is it not just to conclude that her motive was to put an end to the propagation amongst her people of errors which she deemed destructive of their souls, and the permission of the propagation of which she deemed destructive of her own? And there is this much to be said in defence of her motive at any rate, that these new lights, into however many sects they might be divided, all agreed in teaching the abominable doctrine of salvation by faith alone without regard to works.

As a preliminary to the punishment of heretics, there was an Act of Parliament passed in December, 1554 (a year and a half after the Queen came to the throne), to restore the ancient statutes relative to heresy. These statutes were first passed against the Lollards in the reigns of Richard II. and Henry IV., and they provided that heretics who were obstinate should be burnt. These statutes were altered in the reign of Henry VIII. in order that he might get the property of heretics, and in that of Edward they were repealed; not out of mercy, however, but because heresy was, according to those statutes, to promulgate opinions contrary to the Catholic faith, and this did, of course, not suit the state of things under the new Church "as by law established." Therefore it was then held that heresy was punishable by common law, and that, in case of obstinacy, heretics might be burnt; and accordingly many were punished and some burnt in that reign by process at common law; and these were, too, Protestants dissenting from Cranmer's Church, who himself condemned them to the flames. Now, however, the Catholic religion being again the religion of the country, it was thought necessary to return to ancient statutes, which accordingly were re-enacted.

The laws being passed were not likely to remain a dead letter. They were put in execution chiefly in consequence of condemnations in the spiritual court by Bonner, Bishop of London. The punishment was inflicted in the usual manner, dragging to the place of execution and then burning to death, the sufferer being tied to a stake in the midst of a pile of faggots, which, when set on fire, consumed him. Bishop Gardiner, the Chancellor, has been by Protestant writers charged with being the adviser of this measure. I can find no grounds for this charge, while all agree that Pole, who was now become Archbishop of Canterbury in the place of Cranmer, disapproved of it. It is also undeniable that a Spanish friar, the confessor of Philip, preaching before the Queen, expressed his disapprobation of it. Now, as the Queen was much more likely to be influenced, if at all, by Pole, and especially by Philip, than by Gardiner, the fair presumption is that it was her own measure. And as to Bonner, on whom so much blame has been thrown on this account, he had indeed been most cruelly used by Cranmer and his Protestants, but there was the council continually accusing all the bishops (and he more than any of the rest) of being too slow in the performance of this part of their duty. Indeed, it is manifest that in this respect the council spoke the almost then universal sentiment; for though the French ceased not to hatch rebellions against the Queen, none of the grounds of the rebels ever were that she punished heretics. Their complaints related almost solely to the connection with Spain, and never to the "flames of

Smithfield," though we of later times have been made to believe that nothing else was thought of; but the fact is, the persons put to death were chiefly of very infamous character, many of them foreigners, almost the whole of them residing in London and called in derision by the people at large the "London Gospellers." Doubtless, out of two hundred and seventy-seven persons (the number stated by Hume on authority of Fox) who were thus punished, some may have been real martyrs to their opinions, and have been sincere and virtuous persons, but in this number of two hundred and seventy-seven many were convicted felons, some clearly traitors, as Ridley and Cranmer.

The real truth about these "Martyrs" is that they were generally a set of most wicked wretches, who sought to destroy the Queen and her government, and, under the pretence of conscience and superior piety, to obtain the means of again preying upon the people. No mild means could reclaim them; those means had been tried: the Queen had to employ vigorous means, or to suffer her people to continue to be torn by the religious factions, created not by her but by her two immediate predecessors, who had been aided and abetted by many of those who now were punished, and who were worthy of ten thousand deaths each if ten thousand deaths could have been endured. They were, without a single exception, apostates, perjurers, or plunderers; and the greater part of them had also been guilty of flagrant high treason against Mary herself, who had spared their lives, but whose lenity they had requited by every effort within their power to overset her authority and her government. To make particular mention of all the ruffians that perished upon this occasion would be a task as irksome as it would be useless; but there were amongst them three of Cranmer's bishops and himself! For now justice at last overtook this most mischievous of all villains, who had justly to go to the same stake that he had unjustly caused so many others to be tied to; the three others were Hooper, Latimer and Ridley, each of whom was, indeed, inferior in villainy to Cranmer, but to few other men that have ever existed.

Hooper was a monk; he broke his vow of celibacy and married a Flandrican; he, being the ready tool of the Protector Somerset, whom he greatly aided in his plunder of the churches, got two bishoprics, though he himself had written against pluralities. He was a co-operator in all the monstrous cruelties inflicted on the people during the reign of Edward, and was particularly active in recommending the use of German troops to bend the necks of the English to the Protestant yoke. Latimer began his career, not only as a Catholic priest, but as a most furious assailant of the Reformation religion. By this he obtained from Henry VIII. the bishopric of Worcester. He next changed his opinions, but he did not give up his Catholic bishopric! Being suspected, he made abjuration of Protestantism; he thus kept his bishopric for twenty years while he inwardly reprobated the principles of the Church, and which bishopric he held in virtue of an oath to oppose to the utmost of his power all dissenters from the Catholic Church. In the reigns of Henry and Edward he sent to the stake Catholics and Protestants for holding opinions which he himself had before held openly, or that he held secretly at the time of his so sending them. Lastly, he was a chief tool in the hands of the tyrannical Protector Somerset in that black and unnatural act of bringing his brother, Lord Thomas Somerset, to the block. Ridley had been a Catholic bishop in the reign of Henry VIII, when he sent to the stake Catholics who denied the King's supremacy and Potestants who denied transubstantiation. In Edward's reign he was a Protestant bishop, and denied transubstantiation himself. He in Edward's reign got the bishopric of London by a most roguish agreement to transfer the greater part of its possessions to the rapacious ministers and courtiers of that day. Lastly, he was guilty of high treason against the Queen, in openly and from the pulpit exhorting the people to stand by the usurper, Lady Jane, and thus endeavouring to produce civil war and the death of his sovereign, in order that he might by treason be enabled to keep that bishopric which he had obtained by simony including perjury.

A pretty trio of Protestant "saints;" quite worthy, however, of Martin Luther, who says in his own works that it was by the arguments of the devil (who, he says, frequently ate, drank and slept with him) that he was induced to turn Protestant; three worthy followers of that Luther who is by his disciple Melancthon called "a brutal man, void of piety and humanity, one more a Jew than a Christian;" three followers altogether worthy of this great founder of that Protestantism which has split the world into contending sects: but black as these are, they bleach the moment Cranmer appears in his true colours. But alas! where is the pen or tongue to give us these colours? Of the sixty-five years that he lived, and of the thirty-five years of his manhood, twenty-nine years were spent in the commission of a series of acts which, for wickedness in their nature and for mischief in their consequences, are absolutely without anything approaching to a parallel in the annals of human infamy. Being a fellow of a college at Cambridge, and having, of course, made an engagement (as the fellows do to this day) not to marry while he was a fellow, he married secretly and still enjoyed his fellowship. While a married man he became a priest and took the oath of celibacy, and going to Germany he married another wife, the daughter of a Protestant "saint," though his oath bound him to have no wife at all. He, as archbishop, enforced the law of celibacy, while he himself secretly kept his German wife in the palace at Canterbury having imported her in a chest. He, as ecclesiastical judge, divorced Henry VIII. from three wives, the grounds of his decision in two of the cases being directly the contrary of those which he himself had laid down when he declared the marriages to be valid; and in the case of Anne Boleyn he, as ecclesiastical judge, pronounced that Anne had never been the king's wife; while as a member of the House of Peers he voted for her death, as having been an adulteress and thereby guilty of treason to her husband.

As archbishop under Henry (which office he entered upon with a premeditated false oath on his lips) he sent men and women to the stake because they were not Catholics, and he sent Catholics to the stake because they would not acknowledge the king's supremacy and thereby perjure themselves as he had so often done. Become openly a Protestant in Edward's reign, and openly professing those very principles for the professing of which he had burnt others, he now punished his fellow Protestants because their grounds for protesting were different from his. As executor of the will of his old master, Henry, which gave the crown (after Edward) to his daughters, Mary and Elizabeth, he conspired with others to rob those two daughters of their right, and to give the crown to Lady Jane, that queen of nine days, whom he with others ordered to be proclaimed. Confined, notwithstanding his many monstrous crimes, merely to the palace at Lambeth, he, in requital of the Queen's lenity plotted with traitors in the pay of France to overset her government. Brought at last to trial and to condemnation as a heretic, he professed himself ready to recant. He was respited for six weeks, during which time he signed six different forms of recantation, each more ample than the former. He declared that the Protestant religion was false; that the Catholic religion was the only true one; that he now believed in all the doctrines of the Catholic Church; that he had been a horrid blasphemer against the Sacrament; that he was unworthy of forgiveness; that he prayed the people, the Queen and the Pope to have pity on and to pray for his wretched soul; and that he had made and signed this declaration without fear and without hope of favour, and for the discharge of his conscience, and as a warning to others. It was a question in the Queen's Council whether he should be pardoned, as other recanters had been; but it was resolved that his crimes were so enormous that it would be unjust to let him escape. Brought, therefore, to the public reading of his recantation on his way to the stake, seeing the pile ready, now finding that he must die, and carrying in his breast all his malignity undiminished, he recanted his recantation, thrust into the fire the hand that had signed it, and thus expired, protesting against that very religion in which, only nine hours before, he had called God to witness that he firmly believed.

And Mary is to be called the "Bloody" because she put to death monsters of iniquity like this! It is surely time to do justice to the memory of this calumniated queen; and not to do it by halves, I must, contrary to my intention, employ part of the next chapter in giving the remainder of her history.

CHAPTER NINE

I now, before I proceed to the "Reformation" works in the reign of Elizabeth, must conclude the reign of Mary. "Few and full of sorrow" were the days of her power. She had innumerable difficulties to struggle with, a most inveterate and wicked faction continually plotting against her, and the state of her health, owing partly to her weak frame and partly to the anxieties of her whole life, rendered her life so uncertain that the unprincipled plunderers, though they had again become Catholics, were continually casting an eye towards her successor, who, though she was now a Catholic, was pretty sure to become Protestant whenever she came to the throne, because it was impossible that the Pope should ever acknowledge her legitimacy.

In the year 1557 the Queen was at war with France, on account of the endeavours of that court to excite rebellion against her in England. Her husband, Philip, whose father, the Emperor, had now retired to a convent, leaving his son to supply his place and possess all his dominions, was also at war with France, the scene of which war was the Netherlands and the north of France. An English army had joined Philip, who penetrated into France and gained a great and important victory over the French. But a French army, under the Duke of Guise, took advantage of the naked state of Calais to possess itself of that important town, which had been in possession of the English for more than two hundred years. It was not Calais alone that England held, but the whole country around for many miles, including Guisnes, Ardres, and other places, together with the whole territory called the county of Oye. Edward III. had taken Calais after a siege of nearly a year. It had always been regarded as very valuable for the purposes of trade; it was deemed a great monument of glory to England, and it was a thorn continually rankling in the side of France. Dr. Heylyn tells us that Monsieur de Cordes, a nobleman who lived in the reign of Louis XI, used to say "that he would be content to lie seven years in hell upon condition that this town were regained from the English."

The Queen felt this blow most severely. It hastened that death which overtook her a few months afterwards; and when her end approached she told her attendants that "if they opened her body they would find Calais at the bottom of her heart." This great misfortune was owing to the neglect if not perfidy of her councillors, joined to the dread of Philip to see Calais and its dependencies in the hands of Mary's successor. Doctor Heylyn (a Protestant, mind) tells us that Philip, "seeing that danger might arise to Calais, advised the Queen of it, and freely offered his assistance for the defence of it; but that the English council, over-wisely jealous of Philip, neglected both his advice and proffer." They left the place with only five hundred men in it, and that they did this intentionally it is hardly possible to doubt. Still, however, if the Queen had lived but a little longer, Calais would have been restored. The war was not yet over. In 1558 Philip and the King of France began negotiations for peace, and one of the conditions of Philip (who was the most powerful, and who had beaten the French) was that Calais should be restored to England; and this condition would unquestionably have been adhered to by

Philip, but in the midst of these negotiations Mary died!

Thus, then, it is to the "Reformation," which had caused the loss of Boulogne in the plundering and cowardly reign of Edward VI, that we, even to this day, owe that we have to lament the loss of Calais, which was at last irretrievably lost by the selfishness and perfidy of Elizabeth. While all historians agree that the loss of Calais preyed most severely upon the Queen and hastened her death, while they all do this great honour to her memory, none of them attempt to say that the loss of Boulogne had even the smallest effect on the spirits of her "Reformation" brother! He was too busy in pulling down altars and in confiscating the property of guilds and fraternities to think much about national honour; or, perhaps, though he, while he was pulling down altars, still called himself "Defender of the Faith," he might think that territory and glory won by Catholics ought not to be retained by Protestants. Be this as it may, we have seen a loss to England much greater than that of Calais; we have seen the half of a continent cut off from the crown of England, and seen it become a most formidable rival on the seas, and we have never heard that it preyed much upon the spirits of the sovereign in whose reign the loss took place.

With the loss of Calais at the bottom of her heart, and with a well-grounded fear that her successor would undo as to religion all that she had done, the unfortunate Mary expired on November 17, 1558, in the forty-second year of her age and in the sixth year of her reign, leaving to her sister and successor the example of fidelity, sincerity, patience, resignation, generosity, gratitude and purity in thought, word and deed; an example, however, which in every particular that sister and successor took special care not to follow.

To the pauper and ripping-up reign we now come. This is the reign of "good Queen Bess." We shall in a short time see how good she was.

Elizabeth during the reign of her brother had been a Protestant, and during the reign of her sister a Catholic. At the time of her sister's death she not only went to mass publicly, but she had a Catholic chapel in her house, and also a confessor. These appearances had not, however, deceived her sister, who to the very last doubted her sincerity. On her death-bed, honest and sincere Mary required from her a frank avowal of her opinions as to religion. Elizabeth, in answer, prayed God that the earth might open and swallow her if she were not a true Roman Catholic. She made the same declaration to the Duke of Feria, the Spanish envoy, whom she so completely deceived that he wrote to Philip that the accession of Elizabeth would make no alteration in matters of religion in England. In spite of all this, it was not long before she began the persecution of her unhappy subjects because they were Roman Catholics.

She was illegitimate by law. The marriage of her mother had been by law, which yet remained unrepealed, declared to be null and void from the beginning. Her accession having been in the usual way notified to foreign powers, that is, that "she had succeeded to the throne by hereditary right and the consent of the nation," the Pope answered that he did not understand the hereditary right of a person not born in lawful wedlock, so that he, of course, could not acknowledge her hereditary right. This was of itself a pretty strong inducement for a lady of so flexible a conscience as she had to resolve to be a Protestant. But there was another and even a stronger motive. Mary, Queen of Scotland, who had married the Dauphin of France, claimed the crown of England as the nearest legitimate descendant of Henry VII; so that Elizabeth ran a manifest risk of losing the crown, unless she became a Protestant and crammed Cranmer's creed down the throats of her people. If she remained a Catholic she must yield submission to the decrees from Rome; and the Pope could have made it a duty with her people to abandon her, or, at the very least, he could have greatly embarrassed her. In short, she saw clearly that if her people remained Catholics she could never reign in perfect safety. She knew that she had no hereditary right; she knew that the law ascribed her birth to adultery. She never could think of reigning quietly over a people the head of whose Church refused to acknowledge her right to the crown; and resolving to wear that crown, she resolved, cost what ruin or blood it might, to compel her people to abandon that very religion, her belief in which she had a few months before declared by praying to "God that the earth might open and swallow her alive if she were not a true Roman Catholic."

The Pope's answer was honest, but it was impolitic, and most unfortunate it was for the English and Irish people, who had now to prepare for sufferings such as they had never known before. The situation of things was extremely favourable to the Protestants. Mary, the Queen of Scots, the real lawful heir to the throne, was, as we have seen, married to the Dauphin of France. If Elizabeth were set aside, or if she died without issue before Mary, England must become an appendage of France. The loss of Calais and of Boulogne had mortified the nation enough, but for England herself to be transferred to France was what no Englishman could think of with patience; so that Elizabeth became strong from the dread that the people had of the consequences of her being put down. It was the betrothing of Mary, Queen of Scots, to the Dauphin which induced Mary, Queen of England, to marry Philip, and thereby to secure an ally for England in case of Scotland becoming a dependence of France. How much more pressing was the danger now, when the Queen of Scots was actually married to the Dauphin (the heir apparent to the French throne), and when, if she were permitted to possess the crown of England, England, in case of her having a son, must become a province of France!

This state of things was therefore most unfortunate for the Catholics. It made many, very many, of themselves cool in opposition to the change which the new queen soon showed her determination to effect; for, however faithful as to their religion, they were Englishmen, and abhorred the thought of being the underlings of Frenchmen. They might hate the Queen for her apostasy and tyranny, but still they could not but desire that England should remain an independent state; and to keep her such the upholding of Elizabeth seemed absolutely necessary. Those who eulogize Henry IV. of France, who became a Catholic expressly and avowedly for the purpose of possessing and keeping the throne of that country, cannot very consistently blame Elizabeth for becoming a Protestant for an exactly similar reason. I do not attempt to justify either of them; but I must confess that if anything would have induced me to uphold Elizabeth, it would have been that she — as far as human foresight could go — was an instrument necessary to preserve England from subjection to France; and beyond all doubt this was the main reason for which, at the outset at least, she was upheld by many of the eminent and powerful men of that day.

But if we admit that she was justified in thus consulting her preservation as a queen and the nation's independence at the expense of religious considerations, if we admit that she had a right to give a preference to Protestants, and to use all gentle means for the totally changing of the religion of her people, if we admit this, — and that is admitting a great deal more than justice demands of us, — who can refrain from being filled with horror at the barbarity which she so unsparingly exercised for the accomplishment of her purpose?

The intention to change the religion of the country became in a short time so manifest that all the bishops but one refused to crown her. She at last found one to do it, but even he would not consent to do the thing without her conformity to the Catholic ritual. Very soon, however, a series of acts were passed which, by degrees, put down the Catholic worship and re-introduced the Protestant, and she found the plunderers and possessors of plunder just as ready to conform to her ecclesiastical sway as they had been to receive absolution from Cardinal Pole in the last reign.

Cranmer's *Book of Common Prayer*, which had been ascribed by the Parliament to the suggestions of the "Holy Ghost," had been altered and amended even in Edward's reign. It was now revived, and altered and amended again, and still it was ascribed to the "dictates of the Holy Ghost!"

If these Acts of Parliament had stopped here they would certainly have been bad and disgraceful enough. But such a change was not to be effected without blood. This Queen was resolved to reign: the blood of her people she deemed necessary to her own safety, and she never scrupled to make it flow. She looked upon the Catholic religion as her mortal enemy; and cost what it might, she was resolved to destroy it if she could, the means being by her those which best answered her end.

With this view statutes the most bloody were passed. All persons were compelled to take the oath of supremacy, on pain of death. To take the oath of supremacy, that is to say, to acknowledge the Queen's supremacy in spiritual matters, was to renounce the Pope and the Catholic religion, or in other words to become an apostate. Thus was a very large part of her people at once condemned to death for adhering to the religion of their fathers, and moreover for adhering to that very religion in which she had openly lived till she became queen, and to her firm belief in which she had sworn at her coronation.

Besides this act of monstrous barbarity, it was made high treason in a priest to say mass, it was made high treason in a priest to come into the kingdom from abroad, it was made high treason to harbour or to relieve a priest. And on these grounds and others of a like nature, hundreds upon hundreds were butchered in the most inhuman manner, being first hung up, then cut down alive, their bowels then ripped up and their bodies chopped into quarters; and this I again beg you, sensible and just Englishmen, to observe, only because the unfortunate persons were too virtuous and sincere to apostatize from that faith which this queen herself had at her coronation, in her coronation oath, solemnly sworn to adhere to and defend!

Having pulled down the altars, set up the tables, having ousted the Catholic priests and worship and put in their stead a set of hungry, beggarly creatures, with Cranmer's *Prayer Book* amended in their hands, having done this, she compelled her Catholic subjects to attend in the churches under enormous penalties, which rose at last to death itself, in case of perseverance in refusal! Thus were all the good, all the sincere, all the conscientious people in the kingdom incessantly harrassed, ruined by enormous fines, brought to the gallows, or compelled to flee from their native country. Thus was this Protestant religion watered with tears and the blood of the people of England. Talk of Catholic persecution and cruelty! Where are you to find persecution and cruelty like this inflicted by Catholic princes? Elizabeth put, in one way or another, more Catholics to death in one year, for not becoming apostates to the religion which she had sworn to be hers, and to be the only true one, than Mary put to death in her whole reign for having apostatized from the religion of her and their fathers, and to which religion she herself had always adhered. Yet the former is called, or has been called, "good Queen Bess," and the latter, "bloody Queen Mary." Even the horrid massacre of St. Bartholomew was nothing when fairly compared with the butcheries and other cruelties of the reign of this Protestant queen of England, — yes, a mere nothing; and yet she put on mourning upon that occasion, and had the consummate hypocrisy to affect horror at the cruelties that the King of France had committed.

At her coming to the throne she found the country at war with France, and Calais in its hands, that fortress and territory having, as we have seen above, been taken by a French army under the Duke of Guise. She almost immediately made peace with France, and that, too, without getting Calais back, as she might have done if she had not preferred her own private interest to the interest and honour of England. The negotiations for peace (England, Spain, and

France being the parties) were carried on at Cateau Cambrésis, in France. All was soon settled with regard to Spain and France; but Philip, (Mary's husband, remember,) faithful to his engagements, refused to sign the treaty until the new Queen of England should be satisfied with regard to Calais; and he even offered to continue the war for six years unless Calais was restored, provided Elizabeth would bind herself not to make a separate peace during that period. She declined this generous offer; she had begun to rip up her subjects, and was afraid of war, and she therefore clandestinely entered into negotiations with France, and it was agreed that the latter should keep Calais for eight years, or pay to England 500,000 crowns! Never was there a baser act than this treaty on the part of England. But this was not all; for the treaty further stipulated that if France committed any act of aggression against England during the eight years, or if England committed any act of aggression against France during that time, the treaty should be void, and that the former should lose the right of retaining and the latter the claim to the restoration of this valuable town and territory.

This treaty was concluded in 1559, and it was a treaty not only of friendship but of alliance between the parties. But before three years out of the eight had passed away, "good Queen Bess," out of pure hatred and fear of the Catholics, from a pure desire to make her tyrannical sway secure, from the sole desire of being still able to fine, imprison, and rip up her unfortunate subjects, forfeited all claim to the restoration of Calais, and that too by a breach of treaty more flagrant and more base than perhaps had ever before been witnessed in the world.

Condé and Coligny, with their Huguenots, had stirred up a formidable civil war in France. "Good Queen Bess's" ambassador at that court stimulated and assisted the rebels to the utmost of his power. At last Vidame, an agent of Condé and Coligny, came secretly over to England to negotiate for military, naval, and pecuniary assistance. They succeeded with "good Bess," who, wholly disregarding the solemn treaties by which she was bound to Charles IX, King of France, entered into a formal treaty with the French rebels to send them an army and money, for the purpose of carrying on war against their sovereign, of whom she was an ally, having bound herself in that character by a solemn oath on the Evangelists! By this treaty she engaged to furnish men, ships, and money; and the traitors, on their part, engaged to put Havre de Grace at once into her hands, as a pledge, not only for the repayment of the money to be advanced, but for the restoration of Calais! This infamous compact richly deserved the consequences that attended it.

The French ambassador in London, when he found that an intercourse was going on between the Queen and the agents of the rebels, went to Cecil, the secretary of state, carrying the treaty of Cateau Cambrésis in his hand, and demanded, agreeably to the stipulations of that treaty, that the agents of the rebels should be delivered up as traitors to their sovereign, and he warned the English government that any act of aggression on its part would annihilate its claim to the recovery of Calais at the end of the eight years. But "good Bess" had caused the civil wars in France; she had, by her bribes and other underhand means, stirred them up, and she believed that the success of the French rebels was necessary to her own security on her throne of doubtful right; and as she hoped to get Calais in this perfidious way, she saw nothing but gain in the perfidy.

The rebels were in possession of Dieppe, Rouen, Havre de Grace, and had extended their power over a considerable part of Normandy. They at once put Havre and Dieppe into the hands of the English. So infamous and treacherous a proceeding roused the Catholics of France, who now became ashamed of that inactivity which had suffered a sect less than a hundredth part of the population to sell their country under the blasphemous plea of a love of the Gospel. "Good Bess," with her usual mixture of hypocrisy and effrontery, sent her proclamations into Normandy, declaring that she meant no hostility against her "good brother," the King of France, but merely to protect his Protestant subjects against the tyranny of the House of Guise; and that her "good brother" ought to be grateful to her for the assistance she was lending! This cool and hypocritical insolence added fury to the flame. All France could not but recollect that it was the skilful, the gallant, the patriotic Duke of Guise, who had, only five years before, ejected the English from Calais, their last hold in France; and they now saw these "sons of the Gospel," as they had the audacity to call themselves, bring those same English back again and put two French seaports into their hands at once! Are we to wonder at the inextinguishable hatred of the people of France against this traitorous sect? Are we to wonder that they felt a desire to extirpate the whole of so infamous a race, who had already sold their country to the utmost of their power?

The French nobility from every province and corner of France flew to the aid of their sovereign, whose army was commanded by the Constable, Montmorency, with the Duke of Guise under him. Condé was at the head of the rebel army, having Coligny as a sort of partner in the concern, and having been joined by the English troops under the Earl of Warwick, nephew of "good Bess's" paramour, Dudley, of whom the Protestant clergymen, Heylyn and Whitaker, will tell us more than enough by-and-by. The first movement of the French against this combined mass of hypocrisy, audacity, perfidy and treason, was the besieging of Rouen, into which Sir Edward Poynings, who had preceded Warwick, had thrown an English reinforcement to assist the faithful "sons of the Gospel." In order to encourage the French, the Queen-Mother (Catherine de Medici), her son the young King Charles (now twelve years of age), and the King of Navarre, were present at the siege. The latter was mortally wounded in the attack, but the Catholics finally took the town by assault and put the whole of the garrison to the sword, including the English reinforcement sent by Elizabeth.

In the meanwhile the brother of Coligny had, by the

money of Elizabeth, collected together a body of German mercenary gospellers and had got them to Orleans, which was then the main hold of the Huguenots, while "good Bess," in order to act her part faithfully, ordered public prayers during three whole days, to implore God's blessing "upon her cause and the cause of the Gospel." Thus reinforced by another body of foreigners brought into their country, the base traitors, Condé and Coligny, first made a feint on the side of Paris; but finding themselves too weak on that side, they took their way towards Normandy, in the hope of there having the aid of the English forces. But the Catholics, still under Montmorency and the Duke of Guise, followed the traitors, overtook them at Dreux, compelled them to fight, took Condé himself prisoner, and though Montmorency was taken prisoner by the rebels, the Duke of Guise took the chief command and drove the rebel Coligny and his army before him, and this too, observe, in spite of "good Bess's" three whole days of prayers.

Nevertheless, Coligny kept the field and pillaged Normandy pretty severely. Elizabeth sent him some money, and offered to be bound for more if he could get any merchants (that is Jews) to lend it him; but she sent him no troops, those under the Earl of Warwick being kept safe and sound in the strong fortress of Havre de Grace, which place honest and "good Bess" intended to keep, let things go which way they might, which honest intention, we shall, however, find defeated in the end. Coligny and his ruffians and German mercenary gospellers cruelly plundered the Normans as far as they could extend their arms. The Catholics, now under the Duke of Guise, laid siege to Orleans. While this siege was going on, one Poltrot, a Huguenot in the pay of Coligny, went under the guise of being a deserter from that inveterate rebel chief, and entered into the service of the army under the Duke of Guise. In a short time this miscreant found the means to assassinate that gallant nobleman and distinguished patriot, instigated and indeed employed for the express purpose by

Coligny, and urged on by Beza, "the famous preacher," as Hume calls him, but really one of the most infamous of all the "reforming" preachers, and perhaps second to none but Luther himself. This atrocious deed met afterwards with retaliation in the massacre of St. Bartholomew, when on Coligny's mangled body there might have been placarded the name of Poltrot. This wretch had been paid by Coligny, and the money had come from honest and sincere "good Queen Bess," whom we shall hereafter find plainly accused by Whitaker (a clergyman of the Church of England) of plotting the assassination of her own cousin and finding no man in her kingdom base enough to perform the deed.

This foul deed seems to have made Condé ashamed of his infamous associate and followers. Ambition had made him a rebel, but he had sense of honour enough left to make him shudder at the thought of being the leader of assassins; and he, with one drop of true blood in him, could not think without horror of such a man as the Duke of Guise, who had rendered such inestimable services to France, being swept from existence by so base a miscreant as that whom his late colleague had hired and paid for that purpose. If the son of the Duke of Guise could have destroyed Coligny and his whole crew, he would have been justified in so doing. And yet the world has been stunned with the Protestant cries of horror at the death of this same Coligny and a small part of his followers.

Condé now sought to get rid of his miscreant associates by proposing, in February, 1563, a pacification, and tendering his submission to his sovereign on condition of an act of oblivion. Coligny was included in the amnesty. The King granted to the Huguenots permission to practise their worship in one town in every bailiwick, and thus were all matters settled between the King and his rebellious subjects. Sad tidings for "good Queen Bess," who, as Whitaker well observes, continually sought her safety in the divisions and misery of others. Condé, in his treaty with her, had stipulated not to conclude any peace without her consent; but had she a right to complain of want of good faith, — she, who had broken her treaty and her oath with Charles IX, and who, in defiance of both, had entered into a treaty with rebels in open arms against their king?

The French King, wishing to get her troops quietly out of Havre de Grace, and finding that she now pretended to hold it as a pledge for the surrender of Calais, at the end of the eight years offered to renew the treaty of Cateau Cambrésis, by which Calais was to be restored to England in 1567. But she rejected this fair and reasonable proposal. She had got Havre, no matter how; and she said that "a bird in hand was worth two in the bush." Finding, however, that all parties in France were now united for the explusion of the English, she reluctantly gave way. She authorised her ambassadors to present a new project of treaty; but by this time the French army, under Montmorency, Condé, Elizabeth's late friend and ally, being serving in the army, was on its way to regain Havre by force of arms, the King of France being well convinced that treaties with Elizabeth were things perfectly vain.

Still, it was not a trifling thing to take Havre out of the hands of the English. A great deal of taxes had been imposed upon this nation (to say nothing of the "prayers"), in order to insure the possession of this place. The Earl of Warwick, instead of sending troops to assist the Queen's allies, had kept his army at Havre; had with six thousand soldiers and seven hundred pioneers rendered the place "impregnable;" had, as soon as he heard that the rebellion was at an end, expelled all the French people from Havre, to their utter ruin and in direct breach of Elizabeth's treaty with Condé and Coligny. But in spite of all this Montmorency was at the end of a short time ready to enter the place by assault, having made his breaches in preparation. The Queen-mother and the King were present in the camp, where they had the indescribable pleasure to see "good Queen Bess's" general humbly propose to surrender the place to its rightful sovereign, without any mention of

Calais and its territory, and on no condition whatever but that of being permitted to return to England with the miserable remnant of his army; and England, after all the treasure and blood expended to gratify the malignity of Elizabeth, and after all the just imputations of perfidy that she had brought upon it, had to receive that remnant, that ratification of disgrace greater than it had had to support from the day when glorious Alfred finally expelled the Danes. And yet this woman is called, or has been called, "Good Queen Bess," and her perfidious and butchering reign has been called glorious!

Great as the mortifications of the Queen now were, and great as were the misfortunes of the country brought upon it by these her proceedings of hitherto unheard-of hypocrisy and breach of faith, we have as yet seen the full measure of neither the one nor the other. For "glorious and good Bess" had now to sue for peace, and with that king with whose rebel subjects she had so recently co-operated. Her ambassadors, going with due passports, were arrested and imprisoned. She stamped and swore, but she swallowed the affront, and took the regular steps to cause them to be received at the French court, who on their part treated her pressing applications with a contemptuous sneer, and suffered many months to pass away before they would listen to any terms of peace. Smith was one of her envoys, and the other was that same Throckmorton who had been her ambassador at Paris, and who had been her agent in stirring up Condé and Coligny to their rebellion. The former was imprisoned at Melun, and the latter at Saint Germain's. Smith was released upon her application, but Throckmorton was detained and was made use of for the following curious and, to "good Bess," most humiliating purpose. The treaty of Cateau Cambrésis, which stipulated for the restoration of Calais in eight years or the forfeiture of 500,000 crowns by the French, contained a stipulation that four French noblemen should be held by Elizabeth as hostages for the fulfilment of the treaty on the part of

France. "Good Bess," by her aiding of the French rebels, had broken this treaty, had lost all just claim to Calais, and ought to have released the hostages; but as the Queen very seldom did what she ought to, — as she might, almost every day of her mischievous life, have with perfect truth repeated that part of the *Prayer Book* "amended" which says, "we have done those things which we ought not to do and have left undone those things which we ought to do," — so this "good" woman had kept the hostages, though she had forfeited all just claim to that for the fulfilment of which they had been put into her hands. Now, however, the French had got a "bird in hand" too. They had got Throckmorton, their old enemy, and he had got a large quantity of the Queen's horrible secrets locked up in his breast! So that, after long discussions, during which Throckmorton gave very significant signs of his determination not to end his days in prison without taking revenge of some sort on his merciless employer, the "good" woman agreed to exchange the four French noblemen for him; and as a quarter of a loaf was better than no bread, to take 125,000 crowns for the relinquishment of Calais to France in perpetuity!

Thus, then, it was "good Queen Bess" after all, glorious and Protestant Bess, that plucked this jewel from the English crown! Nor was this the only signal consequence of her unhallowed and unprincipled treaty and intrigues with the French rebels. The plague, which had got into the garrison of Havre de Grace, and which had left Warwick with only about two thousand out of his seven thousand men, this dreadful disease was brought by that miserable remnant of infected beings to England, where Hume himself allows that it swept off great multitudes, "especially in London, where above twenty thousand persons died of it in one year!" Thus was the nation heavily taxed, afflicted with war, afflicted with pestilence; thus were thousands upon thousands of English people destroyed or ruined or rendered miserable, merely to gratify this proud and malignant woman, who thought that she could never be safe until all

the world joined in her flagrant apostacy. Thus, and merely
for the same reason, was Calais surrendered for ever; Calais,
the proudest possession of England; Calais, one of the two
keys to the northern seas; Calais, that had been won by our
Catholic forefathers two hundred years before; Calais,
which they would have no more thought of yielding to
France than they would have thought of yielding Dover;
Calais, the bare idea of a possibility of losing which had
broken the heart of the honest, the virtuous, the patriotic
and most calumniated Mary!

It is surprising what baseness Hume discovers in treating
of the whole of this important series of transactions; how he
glosses over all the breaches of faith and of oath on the part
of Elizabeth; how he lets pass without censure the flagrant
and malignant treason of the rebels, and even how he
insinuates apologies for them; how he skips by the rare
fidelity of Philip to his engagements; how he praises the
black-hearted Coligny, while he almost censures Condé for
seeking peace after the assassination of the Duke of Guise;
how he wholly suppresses the deep humiliations of England
in the case of Smith and Throckmorton; how he makes the
last bill of sale £220,000, instead of the fourth part of
£500,000; how he passes over the loss of Calais for ever as
nothing in "good Bess," though he had made the temporary
loss of it everything in Mary; but, above all the rest, how he
constantly aims his malignity at that skilful, brave, faithful,
and patriotic nobleman, the Duke of Guise, while he extols
Condé as long as he was a rebel and a traitor engaged in
selling his country, and how he lauds the inveterate and
treacherous Coligny to the last hour of that traitor's life.

Is there any man who does not see the vast importance of
Calais and its territory? Is there any man who does not see
how desirable it would be to us to have it now? Is there an
Englishman who does not lament the loss of it? And is it
not clear as the sun at noonday that it was lost for ever by
"good Bess's" perfidy in joining the rebels of France? If when
those rebels were formidable to their sovereign she had

pressed him to restore Calais at once and to take an equivalent for such anticipated restoration, is it not obvious that he would have consented rather than risk her displeasure at such a moment? And what is the apology that Hume makes for her conduct in joining the rebels? "Elizabeth, besides the general and essential interest of supporting the Protestants and opposing the rapid progress of her enemy, the Duke of Guise" (how was he her enemy?), "had other motives which engaged her to accept this proposal. When she concluded the peace of Cateau Cambrésis she had good reason to foresee that France would never voluntarily fulfil the article with regard to the restitution of Calais, and many subsequent incidents tended to confirm this suspicion. Considerable sums of money had been laid out on the fortifications, long leases had been granted of the lands, and many inhabitants had been encouraged to build and settle there by assurances that Calais would never be restored to the English. The Queen therefore very wisely concluded that, could she get possession of Havre, a place which commanded the mouth of the Seine, and was of much greater importance than Calais, she should easily constrain the French to execute the treaty, and should have the glory of restoring to the crown that ancient possession which was so much the favourite of the nation."

Away then go at once all her professions of desire to defend the "cause of the Gospel;" she is a hypocrite the most profound at once; she breaks faith with the King of France and with the rebels too.

CHAPTER TEN

Though the massacre of Saint Bartholomew took place in France, yet it has formed so fertile a source of calumny against the religion of our fathers, it has served as a pretence with Protestant historians to justify or palliate so many atrocities on the part of their divers sects, and the Queen of England and her ministers had so great a hand in first producing it and then in punishing Catholics under pretence of avenging it, that it is necessary for me to give an account of it.

We have seen that peace had taken place between the French King and his rebellious subjects, but Coligny had all along discovered that his treacherous designs only slept. The King was making a progress through the kingdom about four years after the pacification: a plot was formed by Coligny and his associates to kill or seize him; but by riding fourteen hours without getting off his horse, and without food or drink, he escaped and got safe to Paris. Another civil war soon broke out, followed by another pacification; but such had been the barbarities committed on both sides that there could be, and there was, no real forgiveness. The Protestants had been full as sanguinary as the Catholics; and, which has been remarked even by their own historians, their conduct was frequently, not to say uniformly, characterized by plundering and by hypocrisy and perfidy unknown to their enemies.

During this pacification Coligny had, by the deepest dissimulation, endeavoured to worm himself into favour with the young King; and upon the occasion of a marriage between the King's sister and the young King of Navarre (afterwards the famous Henry IV.), Coligny, who, Condé being now dead, was become the chief of his sect, came to Paris with a company of his Protestant adherents to partake in the celebration, and that, too, at the King's invitation. After he had been there a day or two, some one shot at him in the street with a blunderbuss and wounded him in two or three places, but not dangerously. His partisans ascribed this to the young Duke of Guise, though no proof has ever been produced to support the assertion. They, however, got about their leader and threatened revenge, as was very natural. Taking this for the ground of their justification, the court resolved to anticipate the blow, and on Sunday, August 24,

1572, it being Saint Bartholomew's day, they put their design in execution. There was great difficulty in prevailing upon the young King to give his consent; but at last, by the representations and entreaties of his mother, those of the Duke of Anjou, his brother, and those of the Duke of Guise, he was prevailed upon. The dreadful orders were given, at the appointed moment the signal was made, the Duke of Guise, with a band of followers, rushed to and broke open the house of Coligny, whose dead body was soon thrown out of the window into the street. The people of Paris, who mortally hated the Protestants, and who could not have forgotten Coligny's having put the English in possession of Dieppe and Havre; who could not have forgotten that while the old enemy of France was thus again brought into the country by Coligny and his Protestants, this same traitor and his sect had basely assassinated that brave nobleman, the late Duke of Guise, who had driven the English from their last hold, Calais, and who had been assassinated at the very moment when he was endeavouring to drive this old enemy from Havre, into which this Coligny and his sect had brought that enemy; the people of Paris could not but remember these things, and remembering them they could not but hold Coligny and his sect in detestation indescribable. Besides this there were few of them, some one or more of whose relations had not perished, or suffered in some way or other from the plunderings or butcheries of these marauding and murdering Calvinists, whose creed taught them that good works were unavailing, and that no deeds, however base or bloody, could bar their way to salvation. These "Protestants" as they were called, bore no more resemblance to Protestants of the present day than the wasp bears a resemblance to the bee. That name then was, and it was justly, synonymous with banditti, that is, robber and murderer; and the persons bearing it had been, by becoming the willing tool of every ambitious rebel, a greater scourge to France than foreign war, pestilence and famine united.

Considering these things, and taking into view that the

people, always ready to suspect, even beyond the limits of reason, heard the cry of "treason" on all sides, is it any wonder that they fell upon the followers of Coligny, and that they spared none of the sect that they were able to destroy? When we consider these things, and especially when we see the son of the assassinated Duke of Guise lead the way, is it not a most monstrous violation of truth to ascribe this massacre to the principles of the Catholic religion?

The massacre at Paris very far exceeded the wishes of the court, and orders were instantly despatched to the great towns in the provinces to prevent similar scenes. Such scenes took place, however, in several places; but though by some Protestant writers the whole number of persons killed has been made to amount to a hundred thousand, an account published in 1582, and made up from accounts collected from the ministers in the different towns, made the number, for all France, amount to only 786 persons!

A number truly horrible to think of, but a number not half so great as that of those English Catholics whom the "good Queen Bess" had even at this time (the fourteenth year of her reign) caused to be ripped up, racked till the bones came out of their sockets, or caused to be despatched or to die in prison or in exile; and this, too, observe, not for rebellions, treasons, robberies and assassinations, like those of Coligny and his followers, but simply and solely for adhering to the religion of their and her fathers, which religion she had openly practised for years, and to which religion she had most solemnly sworn that she sincerely belonged! The annals of hypocrisy conjoined with impudence afford nothing to equal her behaviour upon the occasion of the Saint Bartholomew. She was daily racking people nearly to death to get secrets from them, she was daily persecuting women as well as men for saying or hearing that Mass for the celebration of which the churches of England had been erected, she was daily mutilating, racking and butchering her own innocent and conscientious subjects; and yet she and her court women, when the French ambassador came with the King of France's explanation of the cause of the massacre, received him in deep mourning and with all the marks of disapprobation. But when she remonstrated with her "good brother," the King of France, and added her hope that he would be indulgent to his Protestant subjects, her hypocrisy carried her a little too far; for the Queen-mother, in her answer, observed that as to this matter her son could not take a safer guide than his "good sister of England," and that, while like her he forced no man's conscience, like her he was resolved to suffer no man to practise any religion but that which he himself practised. The French Queen-mother was still short of "good Betsy's" mark, for she not only punished the practice of all religions but her own, she, moreover, punished people for not practising her religion, though she herself was a notorious apostate, and that, too, from motives as notoriously selfish.

But there is a tail-piece which most admirably elucidates

"good Betsy's" sincerity upon this memorable occasion, and also that same quality in her which induced her to profess that she wished to live and die a virgin queen. The Parliament and her ministers, anxious for an undisputed succession, and anxious also to keep out the Scotch branch of the royal family, urged her several times to marry. She always rejected their advice. Her amours with Leicester, of whom we shall see enough by-and-by, were open and notorious, and have been most amply detailed by many Protestant historians, some of whom have been clergymen of the Church of England; it is, moreover, well-known that these amours became the subject of a play acted in the reign of Charles II. She was now, at the time of the Saint Bartholomew, in the thirty-ninth year of her age, and she was, as she long had been, leading with Leicester the life that I have alluded to. Ten years afterwards, whether from the advanced age of Leicester or from some other cause, she became bent on wedlock; and being now forty-nine years of age, there was to be sure no time to be lost in providing an hereditary successor to her throne. She had, in the thirteenth year of her reign, assented to an act that was passed, which secured the crown to her "natural issue," by which any offspring that she might have by anybody became heir to the throne; and it was by the same act made high treason to deny that such issue was heir to it. This act, which is still in the Statute-Book, 13 Eliz., chap.1, sec. 2, is a proof of the most hardened profligacy that ever was witnessed in woman; and it is surprising that such a mark of apparent national abjectness and infamy should have been suffered to remain in black and white to this day. However, at forty-nine the queen resolved to lead a married life; and as her father, whom she so much resembled, always looked out for a young wife, so Elizabeth looked out for a young husband; and in order to convince the world of the sincerity of her horror at the massacre of St. Bartholomew, whom should she fix on as a companion for life, whom should she want to take to her arms, but the Duke of Anjou, brother of Charles IX., and one of the perpetrators of those bloody deeds on account of which she and her court ladies had gone into mourning! The Duke was not handsome, but he had what the French call 'la beaute du diable;' he was young, only twenty-eight years of age. Her ministers and the nation, who saw all the dangers of such a match to the independence of their country, protested against it most vehemently, and finally deterred her from it; but a gentleman of Lincoln's Inn, who had written and published a pamphlet against the marriage, was prosecuted and had his right hand chopped off for this public-spirited effort in assisting to save England from the ruin about to be brought upon it for the mere gratification of the appetite of a gross, libidinous, nasty, shameless old woman. It was said of her father, who began the "Reformation," that "he spared no man in his anger and no woman in his lust:" the very same in substance, with a little change of the terms, might be said of his daughter, who completed that "Reformation;" and something approaching to the same degree of wickedness might be justly ascribed to almost every one who acted a conspicuous part in bringing about that, to England, impoverishing and degrading event.

Before we come to the other transactions of her long reign it will be necessary to make ourselves acquainted with the names and characters of some of her principal advisers and co-operators. Leicester was her favourite, both in council and in the field. Doctor Heylyn describes him in these words: "Sir Robert Dudley, the second son of the Duke of Northumberland (the odious traitor executed in the last reign), she made, soon after she came to the throne, Lord Denbigh and Earl of Leicester, having before made him her Master of Horse, Chancellor of the University of Oxford, and a Knight of the Garter; and she now gave him the fair manor of Denbigh, with more gentlemen owing suit and service to it than any other in England in the hands of a subject, adding even to this the goodly castle and manor of Kenilworth. Advanced to this height, he engrossed unto himself the disposing of all offices in court and state and of all preferments in the church; proving, in fine, so unappeasable in his malice and so insatiable in his lusts, so sacriligious in his rapines, so false in promises and so treacherous in point of trust, and finally, so destructive of the lives and properties of particular persons, that his little finger lay far heavier on the English subjects than the loins of all the favourites of the two last kings;" and, mind, those "two kings" were the plundering and confiscating Henry VIII. and Edward VI. "And that his monstrous vices might either be connived at or not complained of, he cloaks them with a seeming zeal for true religion, and made himself the head of the Puritan faction, who spared no pains in setting forth his praises; nor was he wanting to caress them after such manner as he found most agreeable to these holy hypocrites, using no other language in his speech and letters than the pure-Scripture phrase, in which he was as dexterous as if he had received the same inspirations as the sacred penman." We must bear in mind that this character is drawn by a Doctor of the Church of England (Elizabeth's own Church) in a work dedicated by permission to King Charles II. She, beyond all doubt, meant to marry Leicester, who had, as all the world believed, murdered his own wife to make way for the match. She was prevented from marrying him by the reports from her ambassadors of what was said about this odious proceeding in foreign courts, and also by the remonstrances of her other ministers. Yet, after all these things, this man, or rather this monster, continued to possess all his power and his emoluments and all his favour with the Queen to the last day of his life, which ended in 1588, after thirty years of plundering and oppressing the people of England. This was a "reformer" of religion truly worthy of being enrolled with Henry VIII, Cranmer, Thomas Cromwell, and "good Queen Bess."

Sir William Cecil was her next man. He was her Secretary of State, but she afterwards made him a lord, under the title of Burleigh, and also made him Lord Treasurer. He had been a Protestant in the reign of Edward the Sixth, when he was Secretary, first under the Protector Somerset, who, when Dudley overpowered him, was abandoned by Cecil, who took to the latter and was the very man that drew up the treasonable instrument by which

Edward on his death-bed disinherited his sisters, Mary and Elizabeth. Pardoned for his treason by Mary he became a most zealous Catholic, and was, amongst others, a volunteer to go over to Brussels to conduct Cardinal Pole to England. But the wind having changed, he became Protestant again and Secretary of State to Elizabeth, who never cared anything about the character or principles of those she employed, so that they did but answer her selfish ends. This Cecil, who was a man of extraordinary abilities, and of still greater prudence and cunning, was the chief prop of her throne for nearly forty of the forty-three years of her reign. He died in 1598, in the 77th year of his age; and if success in unprincipled artifice, if fertility in cunning devices, if the obtaining of one's ends without any regard to the means, if in this pursuit sincerity be to be set at nought, and truth, law, justice and mercy to be trampled under foot, if, so that you succeed in your end, apostacy, forgery, perjury, and the shedding of innocent blood be thought nothing of, this Cecil was certainly the greatest statesman that ever lived. Above all others he was confided in by the Queen, who, when he grew old and feeble in his limbs, used to make him sit in her presence, saying in her accustomed masculine and emphatical style: "I have you not for your weak legs, but for your strong head."

Francis Walsingham became Secretary of State after Cecil, but he had been employed by the Queen almost from the beginning of her reign. He had been her ambassador at several courts, had negotiated many treaties, was an exceedingly prudent and cunning man, and wholly destitute of all care about means so that he carried his end. He was said to have fifty-three agents and eighteen real spies in foreign courts. He was a most bitter and inflexible persecutor of the Catholics; but before his death, which took place in 1590, he had to feel himself a little of that tyranny and ingratitude and that want of mercy which he had so long mainly assisted to make so many innocent persons feel.

Paulet St. John, Marquis of Winchester. This was not a statesman. He, like many more, was a backer-on. He presided at trials, and did other such-like work. These are unworthy of particular notice here, and Paulet is named merely as a specimen of the character and conduct of the makers and supporters of the famous "Reformation." This Paulet (the first noble of the family) was, at his outset, steward to the bishop of Winchester in the time of Bishop Fox, in the reign of Henry VII. He was by Henry VIII. made treasurer of the king's household, and zealously entering into all the views of that famous "Defender of the Faith," he was made Lord St. John. He was one of those famous executors who were to carry into effect the will of Henry VIII. Though the king had enjoined on these men to maintain his sort of half Catholic religion, Paulet now, in the reign of Edward, became a zealous Protestant and continued to enjoy all his offices and emoluments, besides getting some new grants from the further spoils of the church and poor. Seeing that Dudley was about to supplant Somerset, which he finally did, Paulet joined Dudley, and actually presided at the trial and passed sentence of death on Somerset, "whose very name," says Dr. Milner, "had a little more than two years before caused him to tremble." Dudley made him first Earl of Wiltshire and then Marquis of Winchester, and gave him the palace of the bishop of Winchester at Bishop's Waltham, together with other spoils of that bishopric. When Mary came, which was almost directly afterwards, he became once more a Catholic, and continued to hold and enjoy all his offices and emoluments. Not only a Catholic, but a most furious Catholic, and the most active and vigorous of all the persecutors of those very Protestants with whom he had made it his boast to join in communion only about two years before! We have heard a great deal about the cruelties of the "bloody Bishop Bonner," but nobody ever tells us that this Marquis of Winchester, as president of the council, repeatedly reprimanded Bonner in very severe terms for want of zeal and diligence in sending Protestants to the stake! Fox says that "of the council, the most active in these prosecutions was the Marquis of Winchester." But now, Mary being dead and Elizabeth being resolved to extirpate the Catholics, Paulet instantly became a Protestant again, a most cruel persecutor of the Catholics, president on several commissions for condemning them to death, and he was in such high favour with "good Bess" that she said were he not so very old as he was she would prefer him as a husband to any man in her dominions. He died in the thirteenth year of her reign, at the age of 97, having kept in place during the reigns of five sovereigns, and having made four changes in his religion to correspond with the changes made by four out of the five. A French historian says that Paulet, being asked how he had been able to get through so many storms, not only unhurt but rising all the while, answered: "En étant un saule et non pas un chêne," "by being a willow and not an oak."

Such were the tools with which Elizabeth had to work; and we have now to see in what manner they all worked with regard to Mary Stuart, the celebrated and unfortunate Queen of the Scotch. Without going into her history it is impossible to make it clearly appear how Elizabeth was able to establish the Protestant religion in England in spite of the people of England, for it was, in fact, in spite of almost the whole of the people of all ranks and degrees. She actually butchered some hundreds of them, she put many and many hundreds of them to the rack, she killed in various ways many thousands, and she reduced to absolute beggary as many as made the population of one of the smaller counties of England, to say nothing at present of that great slaughter-house, Ireland. It is impossible for us to see how she came to be able to do this; how she came to be able to get the Parliament to do the many monstrous things that they did; how they, without any force, indeed, came to do such barefaced things as to provide that any offspring she might have should inherit the throne, and to make it high treason to deny that such offspring was rightful heir to the throne. It is impossible to account for her being able to exist in England after that act of indelible infamy, the murder of Mary Stuart. It is impossible for us to see these things in their causes unless we make ourselves acquainted with the history of Mary, and thereby show how the English were influenced at this most interesting period the transactions of which were so decisive as to the fate of the Catholic religion in England.

Mary Stuart, born in 1542 (nine years after the birth of Elizabeth), was daughter of James V, king of Scotland, and of Mary of Lorraine, sister of that brave and patriotic nobleman the Duke of Guise, who, as we have seen, was so basely murdered by the vile traitor Coligny. Mary Stuart's father died when she was only eight days old, so that she became the reigning queen of Scotland while in the cradle. Her father (James V.) was the son of James IV. and Margaret, the eldest sister of Henry VIII. This "Defender of the Faith" wished Mary Stuart to be betrothed to his son Edward, and by that means to add Scotland to the dominions of England. The family of Guise were too deep for the old "Defender." Mary Stuart (a regency having been settled in Scotland) was taken to France, where she had her education, and where her heart seemed to remain all her life. The French, in order to secure Scotland to themselves as a constant ally against England, got Mary to be betrothed to Francis, Dauphin of France, son and successor of Henry II., King of France. She, at the age of seventeen years, was married to him, who was two years younger than herself, in 1558, the very year that Elizabeth mounted the throne of England.

That very thing now took place which Henry had been so much afraid of, and which, indeed, had been the dread of his councillors and his people. Edward was dead. Queen Mary was dead; and as Elizabeth was a bastard, both in law and in fact, Mary Stuart was the heiress to the throne of England, and she was now the wife of the immediate heir to the king of France. Nothing could be so fortunate for

Elizabeth. The nation had no choice but one; to take her and uphold her, or to become a great province of France. If Elizabeth had died at this time, or had died before her sister Mary, England must have been degraded thus, or it must have created a new dynasty or become a republic. Therefore it was that all men, whether Catholics or Protestants, were for the placing and supporting of Elizabeth on the throne, and for setting aside Mary Stuart, though unquestionably she was the lawful heiress to the crown of England.

As if purposely to add to the weight of this motive, of itself weighty enough, Henry II, King of France, died in eight months after Elizabeth's accession; so that Mary Stuart was now, 1559, Queen-consort of France, Queen of Scotland, and called herself Queen of England; she and her husband bore the arms of England along with those of France and Scotland, and the Pope had refused to acknowledge the right of Elizabeth to the English throne. Thus, as Henry VIII. had foreseen when he made his will setting aside the Scotch branch of his family, was England actually transferred to the dominion of France, unless the nation set at nought the decision of the Pope and supported Elizabeth.

This was the real cause of Elizabeth's success in her work of extirpating the Catholic religion. According to the decision of the head of the Catholic Church Elizabeth was an usurper; if she were an usurper she ought to be set aside; if she were set aside, Mary Stuart and the King of France became Queen and King of England; if they became Queen and King of England, England became a mere province ruled by Scotchmen and Frenchmen, the bare idea of which was quite sufficient to put every drop of English blood in motion. All men, therefore, of all ranks in life, whether Protestants or Catholics, were for Elizabeth. To preserve her life became an object dear to all her people; and though her cruelties did, in one or two instances, arm Catholics against her life, as a body, they were as loyal to her as her Protestant subjects, and even when she was executing them they, without a single exception, declared her to be their lawful queen. Therefore, though the decision of the Pope was perfectly honest and just in itself, that decision was, in its obvious and inevitable consequences, rendered, by a combination of circumstances, so hostile to the greatness, the laws, the liberties and the laudable pride of Englishmen, that they were reduced to the absolute necessity of setting his decision at nought or of surrendering their very name as a nation. But observe, by-the-by, this dilemma and all the dangers and sufferings that it produced arose entirely out of the "Reformation." Had Henry VIII. listened to Sir Thomas More and Bishop Fisher, there would have been no obstacle to the marrying of his son with Mary Stuart; and besides, he would have had no children whose legitimacy could have been disputed, and in all human probability several children to be in lawful succession heirs to the throne of England.

Here we have the great, and indeed, the only cause of Elizabeth's success in rooting out the Catholic religion. Her people were ninety-nine hundredths of them Catholics. They had shown this clearly at the accession of her sister Mary. Elizabeth was as great a tyrant as ever lived, she was the most cruel of women, her disgusting amours were notorious, yet she was the most popular sovereign that had ever reigned since the days of Alfred, and we have thousands of proofs that her people of all ranks and degrees felt a most anxious interest in every-thing affecting her life or her health. Effects like this do not come from ordinary causes. Her treatment of great masses of her people, her almost unparalleled cruelties, her flagrant falsehoods, her haughtiness, her insolence, and her lewd life, were naturally calculated to make her detested and to make her people pray for anything that might rid them of her. But they saw nothing but her between them and subjection to foreigners, a thing which they had always most laudably held in the greatest abhorrence. Hence it was that the Parliament, when they could not prevail upon her to marry, passed an act to make any offspring ("natural issue") of hers lawful heir to the throne. Whitaker (a clergyman of the Church of England) calls this a most infamous act. It was, in itself, an infamous act; but that abjectness in the nation which it now, at first sight, appears to denote, disappears when we consider well what I have stated above. To be preserved from Mary Stuart, from the mastership of the Scotch and the French, was at that time the great object of anxiety with the English nation.

Mary Stuart was in the year 1559, as we have seen above, on the highest pinnacle of earthly glory, Queen-consort of France, Queen-regnant of Scotland, Queen in lawful right of England, and was besides deemed one of the most beautiful women in the whole world. Never was fall like that of this queen. Her husband, Francis II, died seventeen months after his accession, and was succeeded by Charles IX, then not more than three years old. Her husband's mother, Catherine de Medici, soon convinced her that to be any thing she must return to Scotland. To Scotland she returned with a heavy heart, anticipating very little quiet in a country which was plunged in all the horrors of the "Reformation" even more deeply than England had been. Her long minority, together with her absence from her dominions, had given rise to contending factions of nobles, who alternately triumphed over each other, and who kept the country in a state of almost incessant civil war, accompanied with deeds of perfidy and ferocity of which there is scarcely any parallel to be found in history, ancient or modern. Added to this was the work of the new saints, who carried the work of "reformation" much further than in England. The famous John Knox, an apostate monk, whom Dr. Johnson calls the "Ruffian of the Reformation," was leader of the "holy hypocrites" (as Dr. Heylyn calls them) in Scotland. Mary, who had been bred a Catholic, and who had almost been deified in the court of France, was not likely to lead a happy life amongst people like these.

All this, however, Elizabeth and her ministers and (for let us have no disguise) the English people saw with great and ungenerous satisfaction. There was, for the present at least, an end to the danger from the union of Scotland with France. But Mary Stuart might marry again. There were the powerful family of Guise, her near relations; and she was still a formidable person, especially to Elizabeth. If Mary had been a man Elizabeth would certainly have married her; but here was a difficulty too great even for Cecil to overcome. The English Queen soon began to stir up factions and rebellions against her cousin; and, indeed, by her intrigues with the religious factions and with the aspiring nobles, she became in a short time, with the aid of money (a drug of infallible effect with the Scotch reformers), more the real ruler of Scotland than poor Mary was. She had for the greater part of her whole reign always a band of one faction or the other at or about her court. Her object was to keep Mary from possessing any real power, and to destroy her if by any means short of detectable murder she could effect that purpose.

In 1565, about three years after the return of Mary to Scotland, she was married to Henry Stuart, Earl of Darnley, her cousin, in which she overreached the Queen of England, who, fearing that a visible heir to her own throne (as it actually happened) might come from this marriage, took desperate measures to prevent it; but those measures came too late. Darnley, though young and handsome, proved to be a very foolish and disagreeable husband, and he was a Protestant into the bargain. Mary soon treated him with great contempt, suffered him to have no real authority, and, in fact, as good as banished him from her court and disowned him. Darnley sought revenge. He ascribed his ill-treatment to Mary's being under the advice and control of her Catholic favourites, particularly to the advice of Rizzio, a foreigner, her private secretary. Several malcontent "reformed" nobles joined with Darnley in agreeing to assist him in the assassinating of Rizzio, taking a bond from him to protect them against evil consequences. Mary was sitting at supper with some ladies of her court,

Rizzio and other servants being in waiting, when the conspirators rushed in. Darnley went to the back of the Queen's chair; Rizzio, seeing their object, ran to the Queen for protection; she, who was in the sixth month of her pregnancy, endeavoured by entreaties and screams to save his life. The ruffians stabbed him at her feet, and then dragged him out and covered his body with wounds.

This black and bloody transaction, for which not one of the assistants of Darnley was ever punished, was in all probability the cause, the chief cause, of the just, though illegal, killing of Darnley himself. The next year after the murder of Rizzio, 1567, Mary having in the meanwhile brought forth a son (afterwards our James I., of half Pope and half Puritanical memory), Darnley was taken ill at Glasgow. The Queen went to visit him, treated him with great kindness, and, when he became better in health, brought him back to Edinburgh; but for the sake of better air lodged him in a house at some distance from other houses, out of the town, where she visited him daily, and where in a room immediately under his he slept every night. But on the night of the 10th of February (1567) she, having notified it to him, slept at her palace, having promised to be present at the marriage of two of the attendants of her court, which marriage took place and at which she was present: on this very night the king's lodging-house was blown up by powder, and his dead body cast into an adjoining piece of ground! If the powder had given this base and bloody man time for thought, he would, perhaps, have reflected on the stabs he had given Rizzio in spite of the screams of a swooning and pregnant wife.

Now it was that the great and life-long calamities of this unfortunate queen began. She had been repeatedly insulted, and even imprisoned, by the different factions, who, aided and abetted by the English Queen, alternately oppressed both her and her people; but she was now to lead the life and die the death of a malefactor. It has been proved beyond all doubt that the Earl of Bothwell, with other associates, bound in a "bloody bond," murdered Darnley. This was openly alleged, and in placards about the streets it was averred that Mary was in the plot. No positive proof has ever been produced to make good this charge, but the subsequent conduct of the Queen was of a nature very suspicious. I shall simply state such facts as are admitted on all hands; namely, that Bothwell had before the murder been in great favour with the Queen and possessed power that his talents and character did not entitle him to; that after the murder he was acquitted of it by a mock trial, which she might have prevented; that on the 24th of April (fifty-three days after the murder) she was, on her return from a visit to her infant son, seized by Bothwell at the head of 3,000 horsemen and carried to his castle at Dunbar; that before she left the castle, on the 3rd of May, she agreed to marry him; that he had a wife then alive; that a divorce, both Protestant and Catholic, in one court for adultery and in the other for consanguinity, took place between Bothwell and his wife in the space of six days; that on the 12th of May Bothwell led the Queen to the Sessions-house, where, in the presence of the judges, she pardoned him for the violence committed on her person; that on the 15th of May she openly married him; that the French ambassador refused to appear at the ceremony, and that Mary refused, in this case, to listen to the entreaties of the family of Guise.

Scores of volumes have been written, some in support of the assertion that Mary was consenting to the murder of her husband, and others in support of the negative of that proposition. But nobody can deny the above-stated facts; nobody can deny that she was carried off by Bothwell, that she, being at perfect liberty, pardoned him for that, and that she immediately married him, though it excited horror in the family of Guise, whom she had always theretofore listened to with the docility of a dutiful daughter.

This gross conduct, almost equal, in power of exciting odium, to the murder of such a wretch as Darnley, was speedily followed by tremendous punishment. A part of her subjects armed against her and defeated Bothwell, who was compelled to flee the country, and who in a few years afterwards died in prison in Denmark. She herself became a prisoner in the hands of her own subjects, and she escaped from their prison walls only to come and end her life within those of Elizabeth, her wily and deadly enemy.

Her prison was, indeed, changed two or three times, but a prisoner she remained for nineteen long years, and was at last most savagely murdered for an imputed crime, which she neither did nor could commit. During these nineteen years Elizabeth was intriguing with Mary's rebellious subjects, tearing Scotland to pieces by means of her corruption spread amongst the different bands of traitors, and inflicting on a people who had never offended her every species of evil that a nation can possibly endure. At last, in 1587, she brought her long-suffering victim to the block! Those means of dividing and destroying which she had all her life long been employing against others, began now to be employed against herself, and she saw her life in constant danger. She thought, and perhaps rightly, that these machinations against her arose from a desire in the Catholics (and a very natural desire it was) to rid the world of her and her horrid barbarities and to make way for her Catholic lawful successor, Mary, so that now nothing short of the death of this queen seemed to her a competent guarantee for her own life. In order to open the way for the foul deed that had been resolved on, an Act of Parliament was passed, making it death for any one who was within the realm to conspire with others for the purpose of invading it or for the purpose of procuring the death of the Queen. A seizure was made of of Mary's papers. What was wanting in reality was, as Whitaker has proved, supplied by forgery, "a crime," says he, "which, with shame to us, it must be confessed, belonged peculiarly to the Protestants."

When the mode of getting rid of Mary was debated in Elizabeth's council, Leicester was for poison, others were for hardening her imprisonment and killing her in that way; but Walsingham was for death by means of a trial, a legal proceeding being the only one that would silence the tongues of the world. A commission was accordingly appointed, and Mary was tried and condemned, and that, too, on the evidence of papers, a part, at least, of which were barefaced forgeries, all of which were copies, and the originals of none of which were attempted to be produced! The sentence of death was pronounced in October. For four months the savage Elizabeth was employed in devising plans for causing her victim to be assassinated, in order to avoid the odium of being herself the murderer! This is proved by Whitaker beyond all possibility of doubt; but though she had entrusted the keeping of Mary to two men, mortal enemies of the Catholics, they, though repeatedly applied to for the purpose, perseveringly refused. Having ordered her secretary, Davison, to write to them on the subject, Sir Amias Paulet, one of the keepers, returned for answer that he "was grieved at the motion made to him, that he offered his life and his property to the disposal of her Majesty, but absolutely refused to be concerned in the assassination of Mary." The other keeper, Sir Drue Drury, did the same. When she read this answer she broke out into reproaches against them, complained of the "daintiness of their consciences," talked scornfully of "the niceness of such precise fellows," and swore that she would "have it done without their assistance." At the end, however, of four months of unavailing efforts to find men base and bloody enough to do the deed, she resorted to her last shift, the legal murder, which was committed on her hapless victim on the 8th of February, 1587, a day of everlasting infamy to the memory of the English queen, "who," says Whitaker, "had no sensibilities of tenderness and no sentiments of generosity; who looked not forward to the awful verdict of history, and who shuddered not at the infinitely more awful doom of God."

CHAPTER ELEVEN

Detestably base as was the conduct of "good Queen Bess" in the act of murdering her unfortunate cousin, her subsequent hypocrisy was still more detestable. She affected the deepest sorrow for the act that had been committed, pretended that it had been done against her wish, and had the superlative injustice and baseness to imprison her secretary, Davison, for having despatched the warrant for the execution, though she, observe, had signed that warrant, and though, as Whitaker has fully proved, she had reviled Davison for not having despatched it after she had in vain used all the means in her power to induce him to employ assassins to do the deed. She had, by a series of perfidies and cruelties wholly without a parallel, brought her hapless victim to the block in that very country to which she had invited her to seek safety; she had, in the last sad and awful moments of that victim, had the barbarity to refuse her the consolations of a divine of her own communion; she had pursued her with hatred and malice that remained unglutted even when she saw her prostrate under the common hangman and when she saw the blood gushing from her severed neck; unsated with the destruction of her body, she, Satan-like, had sought the everlasting destruction of her soul; and yet, the deed being done, she had the hypocrisy to affect to weep for the untimely end of her "dear cousin," and, which was still more diabolical, to make use of her despotic power to crush her humane secretary under pretence that he had been the cause of the sad catastophe. All expressions of detestation and horror fall short of our feeling, and our only consolation is that we are to see her own end ten thousand times more dreadful than that of her victim.

Yet such were the peculiar circumstance of the times, that this wicked woman escaped, not only for the present but throughout her long reign, that general hatred from her subjects which her character and deeds so well merited; nay, it perversely happened that immediately after this foul deed there took place an event which rallied all her people round her, and made her life more than ever an object of their solicitude.

Philip II, King of Spain, who was also sovereign of the Low Countries, resolved on an invasion of England, with a fleet from Spain and with an army from Flanders. She had given him quite provocation enough: she had fomented rebellions against him, as she long had in France against the king of that country. Philip was the most powerful monarch in Europe: he had fleets and armies vastly superior to hers; the danger to England was really great; but though these dangers had been brought upon it solely by her malignity, bad faith, and perfidy, England was still England to her people, and they unanimously rallied round her. On this occasion, and indeed, on all others where love of country was brought to the test, the Catholics proved that no degree of oppression could make them forget their duty as citizens or as subjects. Even from Hume it is extorted that the Catholic gentlemen, though her laws excluded them from all trust and authority, "entered as volunteers in her fleet or army; some equipped ships at their own charge and gave command of them to Protestants; others were active in animating their tenants and vassals and neighbours to the defence of their country; and every rank of men, burying for the present all party distinctions, seemed to prepare themselves with order as well as vigour to resist these invaders." Charles I, James II, George I, and George II, and even George III, all saw the time when they might have lamented the want of similar loyalty in Protestants. The first lost his head, the second his throne, the third and fourth were exposed to great danger of a similar loss, and the fifth lost America; and all by the doings of Protestants.

As to Ireland, where the estates of the convents and where the church property had been confiscated in the same way as in England, and where the greater distance of the people from the focus of power, and apostacy and fanaticism, had rendered it more difficult to effect their "conversion" at the point of the bayonet, or by the halter or the rack,—as to this portion of her dominions, Elizabeth's reign was almost one unbroken series of robberies and butcheries. One greedy and merciless minion after another was sent to goad that devoted people into acts of desperation, and that, too, not only for the obvious purpose, but for the avowed purpose, of obtaining a pretence for new confiscations. The "Reformation" had from its very outset had plunder written on its front, but as to Ireland it was all plunder from the crown of its head to the sole of its foot. This horrible lynx-like she-tyrant could not watch each movement of the Catholics there as she did in England; she could not so harass them in detail; she could find there no means of executing her dreadful policy; and therefore she murdered them in masses. She sent over those parsons whose successors are there to the present day. The ever blood-stained sword secured them the tithes and the church lands; but even that blood-stained sword could not then and never did, though at one time wielded by the unsparing and double-distilled Protestant Cromwell, obtain them congregations. However, she planted, she watered with rivers of blood, and her long reign saw take fast root in the land that tree the fruit of which the unfortunate Irish taste to this hour, and which will, unless prevented by more wise and more just measures than appear to have been yet suggested, finally prove the overthrow of England herself.

I am to speak further on of the monstrous immoralities produced in England by the "Reformation," and also of the poverty and misery that it produced; and then I shall have to trace (through Acts of Parliament) this poverty and misery up to the "Reformation:" yes, for therein we shall see, clearly as we see the rivulet bubbling out of the bed of the spring, the bread and water of England and the potatoes of Ireland; but even in this place it is necessary to state the cause of the greater poverty and degradation of the Irish people. For ages that ill-treated people have, in point of clothing and food, formed a contrast with the English. Dr. Franklin, in speaking of Ireland, says that "one would think that the cast-off clothes of the working-people of England were sent over to be worn by the working-people here."

Whence comes it that this contrast has so long existed? The soil and the climate of Ireland are as good as those of England. The islands are but a few miles assunder. Both are surrounded by the same sea. The people of the former are as able and as willing to labour as those of the latter; and of this they have given proof in all parts of the world to which they have migrated, not to carry packs to cheat fools out of their money, not to carry the lash to make others work, but to share themselves, and cheerfully to share, in the hardest labours of those amongst whom they have sought shelter from the rod of unrelenting oppression. Whence comes it, then, that this contrast, so unfavourable to Ireland, has so long existed? The answer to this interesting question we shall find by attending to the different measures dealt out to the two people during the long and cruel reign of which we are now speaking; and we at the same time trace all the miseries of Ireland back at once to that "Reformation" the blessings of which have, with such persevering falsehood and hypocrisy, been dinned in our ears for ages.

We have seen in Chapter 2 of this little work that the Catholic Church was not and is not an affair of mere abstract faith; that it was not so very spiritual a concern as to scorn all cares relative to the bodies of the people; that one part, and that a capital part, of its business was to cause works of charity to be performed; that this charity was not of so very spiritual a nature as not to be at all tangible or obvious to the vulgar sense; that it showed itself in good works done to the needy and suffering; that the tithes and offerings and income from real property of the Catholic Church went in great part to feed the hungry, to clothe the naked, to lodge and feed the stranger, to sustain the widow and the orphan, and to heal the wounded and the sick; that, in short, a great part and, indeed, one of the chief parts of the business of this Church was to take care that no person, however low in life, should suffer from want either of sustenance or care; and that the priests of this Church should have as few selfish cares as possible to withdraw them from this important part of their duty, they were forbidden to marry.

But when the Protestant religion came, and along with it a married priesthood, the poorer classes were plundered of their birthright and thrown out to prowl about for what they could beg or steal. Luther and his followers wholly rejected the doctrine that good works were necessary to salvation. They held that faith, and faith alone, was necessary. They expunged from their Bible the Epistle of St. James, because it recommends and insists on the necessity of good works, which Epistle Luther called "an Epistle of straw."

The Douay Catechism, which the Protestant parsons so much abuse, says that "the first fruit of the Holy Ghost is charity." And then it tells us what charity is, namely, "to feed the hungry, to give drink to the thirsty, to clothe the naked, to visit and ransom captives, to harbour the harbourless, to visit the sick, to bury the dead." Can you guess, my friends, why fat Protestant parsons rail so loudly against this wicked Douay Catechism?

However, although this terrible she-tyrant spared neither racks nor halters, though she was continually reproving the executors of her bloody laws for their remissness, while they were strewing the country with carcasses of malefactors or alleged malefactors, all would not do; that hunger which breaks through stone walls set even her terrors and torments at defiance. At last it was found to be absolutely necessary to make some general and permanent and solid provision for the poor, and in the forty-third year of her reign was passed that act which is in force to this day, and which provides a maintenance for indigent persons, which maintenance is to come from the land, assessed and collected by overseers, and the payment enforced by process the most effectual and most summary. And here we have the great, the prominent, the staring, the horrible and ever durable consequence of the "Reformation;" that is to say, pauperism established by law.

Yet this was necessary. The choice that the plunderers had in England was this, — legal pauperism or extermination; and this last they could not effect, and if they could it would not have suited them. They did not possess power sufficient to make the people live in a state of three-fourths starvation, therefore they made a legal provision for the poor; not, however, till they had tried in vain all other methods of obtaining a something to supply the place of Catholic charity. They attempted at first to cause the object to be effected by voluntary collections at the churches; but alas! those who now entered those churches looked upon Luther as the great teacher, and he considered St. James's Epistle as an "epistle of straw." Every attempt of this sort having failed, as it necessarily must when the parsons who were to exhort others to charity had enough to do to rake together all they could for their own wives and children,

every act (and there were many passed) short of a compulsory tax, enforced by distraint of goods and imprisonment of person, having failed, to this "glorious Bess" and her "Reformation" Parliament at last came; and here we have it

to this day, filling the country with endless quarrels and liti-
gation, setting parish against parish, man against master,
rich against poor, and producing, from a desire of the rich
to shuffle out of its provisions, a mass of hypocrisy, idleness,
fraud, oppression and cruelty, such as was, except in the
deeds of the original "Reformers," never before witnessed in
the world.

Nevertheless it was, as far as it went, an act of justice. It
was taking from the land and giving to the poor a part at
least of what they had been robbed of by the
"Reformation." It was doing in a hard and odious way a part
of that which had been done in the most gentle and amiable way by the Church of our fathers. It was, indeed, feed-
ing the poor like dogs, instead of like one's children; but it
was feeding them.

We have seen how absolute necessity compelled the
Queen and her plunderers to make a legal provision for the
relief of the indigent in England; we have seen that it was
only restoring to them a part of that of which they had
been plundered; and upon what principle was it that they
did not do the same with regard to the people of Ireland?
These had been plundered in precisely the same manner
that the former had; they had been plunged into misery by
precisely the same means, used under precisely the same
hypocritical pretences; why were not they to be relieved
from that misery in the same manner, and why was not the
poor-law to be extended to Ireland?

Thus it was that Ireland was pillaged without the smallest chance of even the restoration which the English have
obtained; and thus have they, down unto this our day, been
a sort of outcasts in their own country, being stripped of all
the worldly goods that God and nature allotted them and
having recieved not the smallest pittance in return.

Why is Ireland to be the only civilised country upon the
face of the earth where no sort of settled legal provision is
made for the indigent, and where the pastors are at the
same time total strangers to the flocks, except in the season

of shearing? Let us at least, as long as this state of things shall be suffered to exist, have the decency not to cry out quite so loudly against the "outrages of the Irish."

I must now return from this digression (into which the mention of Elizabeth's barbarous treatment of Ireland has led me) in order to proceed with my account of her "reforming" projects. She gave what she called a commission to certain bishops and others, whose power extended over the whole kingdom and over all ranks and degrees of the people. They were empowered to have an absolute control over the opinions of all men, and to punish all men according to their discretion, short of death. They might proceed legally if they chose, in the obtaining of evidence against parties; but if they chose they were to employ imprisonment, the rack, or torture of any sort, for this purpose. If their suspicions alighted upon any man, no matter respecting what, and they had no evidence nor any even hearsay against him, they might administer an oath called ex-officio to him, by which he was bound, if called upon, to reveal his thoughts and to accuse himself, his friend, his brother or his father, upon pain of death.

It is hardly necessary to attempt to describe the sufferings that the Catholics had to endure during this murderous reign. No tongue, no pen is adequate to the task. To hear mass, to harbour a priest, to admit the supremacy of the Pope, to deny this horrid virago's spiritual supremacy, and many other things which an honourable Catholic could scarcely avoid, consigned him to the scaffold and to the bowel ripping knife. But the most cruel of her acts, even more cruel than her butcheries because of far more extensive effect and far more productive of suffering in the end, were the penal laws inflicting fines for recusancy, that is to say, for not going to her new-fangled Protestant Church.

The fines were so heavy and were exacted with such unrelenting rigour, and for the offence of recusancy alone the sums were so enormous, that the whole of the conscientious Catholics were menaced with utter ruin. The priests who had never been out of England, and who were priests before the reign of this horrible woman, were by the twentieth year of her reign few in number, for the laws forbade the making of any new ones on pain of death, and indeed, none could be made in England, where there was no clerical authority to ordain them, the surviving Catholic bishops being forbidden to do it on pain of death. Then she harassed the remainder of the old priests in such a way that they were, by the twentieth year of her reign, nearly exterminated; and as it was death for a priest to come from abroad, death to harbour him, death for him to perform his functions in England, death to confess to him, there appeared to be an impossibility of preventing her from extirpating, totally extirpating from the land that religion under which England had been so great and so happy for ages so numerous, — that religion of charity and hospitality, that religion which made the name of pauper unknown, that religion which had built the churches and cathedrals, which had planted and reared the Universities, whose professors had made Magna Charta and the Common Law, and who had performed all those glorious deeds in legislation and in arms which had made England really "the envy of surrounding nations and the admiration of the world;" there now appeared to be an impossibility, and especially if the termagant tyrant should live for another twenty years (which she did), to prevent her from effecting this total extirpation. From accomplishing this object she was prevented by the zeal and talents of William Allen, an English gentleman, now a priest, and who had before been of the University of Oxford. In order to defeat the she-tyrant's schemes for rooting out the Catholic religion, he formed a seminary at Douay, in Flanders, for the education of English priests. He was joined by many other learned men; and from this depot, though at the manifest hazard of their lives, priests came into England, and thereby the malignity of this inexorable apostate was defeated. There was the sea between her and Allen, but while he safely defied her death-dealing power she could not defy his, for she could not erect a wall round the island, and into it priests would come and did come; and in spite of her hundreds of spies and her thousands of "pursuivants," as were called the myrmidons who executed her tormenting and bloody behests, the race of English priests was kept in existence, and the religion of their fathers along with it. In order to break up the seminary of Allen, who was afterwards made a cardinal, and whose name can never be pronounced but with feelings of admiration, she resorted to all sorts of schemes, and at last, by perfidiously excluding from her ports the fleet of the Dutch and Flemish insurgents, to whom she stood pledged to give protection, she obtained from the Spanish Governor a dissolution of Allen's college; but he found protection in France from the House of Guise, by whom he and his college were, in spite of most bitter remonstrances from Elizabeth to the King of France, re-established at Rheims.

Thus defeated in all her projects for destroying the missionary trunk, she fell with more fury than ever on the branches and on the fruit. To say mass, to hear mass, to make confession, to hear confession, to teach the Catholic religion, to be taught it, to keep from her church service, these were all great crimes, and all punished with a greater or less degree of severity; so that the gallows and gibbets and racks were in constant use, and the gaols and dungeons choking with the victims. See a gentleman of perhaps sixty years of age or more, see him, born and bred a Catholic, compelled to make himself and his children beggars, actual beggars, or to commit what he deemed an act of apostasy and blasphemy.

In the enforcing of these horrible edicts every insult that base minds could devise was resorted to and in constant use. No Catholic or reputed Catholic had a moment's security or peace. At all hours, but generally in the night-time, the ruffians entered his house by breaking it open, rushed in different divisions into the rooms, broke open closets, chests and drawers, rummaged beds and pockets, in short, searched every place and thing for priests, books, crosses, vestments or any person or thing appertaining to the Catholic worship. In order to pay the fines gentlemen were compelled to sell their estates piece by piece; when they were in arrear the tyrant was by law authorised to seize all their personal property, and two-thirds of their real estate every six months, and they were in some cases suffered, as a great indulgence, to pay an annual composition for the liberty of abstaining from what they deemed apostasy and blasphemy. Yet whenever she took it into her suspicious head that her life was in danger, from whatever cause or causes, and just cause enough there always was, she had no consideration for them on account of the fines or the composition. She imprisoned them either in gaol or in the houses of Protestants — kept them banished from their own homes for years. The Catholic gentleman's own house afforded him no security; the indiscretion of children or friends, the malice of enemies, the dishonesty or revenge of tenants or servants, the hasty conclusions of false suspicion, the deadly wickedness of those ready to commit perjury for gain's sake, the rapacity and corruption of constables, sheriffs and magistrates, the virulent prejudice of fanaticism, — to every passion hostile to justice, happiness and peace, to every evil against which it is the object of just laws to protect a man, the conscientious Catholic gentleman lived continually exposed, and that, too, in that land which had become renowned throughout the world by those deeds of valour and those laws of freedom which had been performed and framed by his Catholic ancestors.

As to the poor conscientious "recusants," that is to say, keepers away from the tyrant's church, they who had no money to pay fines with were crammed into prison until the gaols could (which was very soon) hold no more, and until the counties petitioned to be relieved from the charge of keeping them. They were then discharged, being first publicly whipped, or having their ears bored with a hot iron. This not answering the purpose, an act was passed to compel all "recusants" not worth twenty marks a year to quit the country in three months after conviction, and to punish them with death in case of their return. The old "good Bess" defeated herself here, for it was found impossible to cause the law to be executed, in spite of all her menaces against the justices and sheriffs who could not be brought up to her standard of ferociousness; and they, therefore, in order to punish the poor Catholics, levied sums on them at their pleasure, as a composition for the crime of abstaining from apostacy and profanation.

The Catholics at one time entertained a hope that, by a declaration of their loyalty, they should obtain from the Queen some mitigation, at least, of their sufferings. With this view they drew up a very able and most dutiful petition, containing an expression of their principles, their sufferings and their prayers. Alas! they appealed to her to whom truth and justice and mercy were all alike wholly unknown. The petition being prepared, all trembled at the thought of the danger of presenting it to her. At last Richard Shelley, of Michael Grove, Sussex, assumed the perilous charge. She had the (as it would have been in any other human being) incomparable baseness to refer him for an answer to the gloomy echoes of a pestiferous prison, where he expired, a victim to his own virtue and to her implacable cruelty.

It is to inflict most painful feelings on Protestants, to be sure; but justice demands that I describe one or two of her instruments of torture, because in them we see some of the most powerful of those means which she made use of for establishing her Protestant Church: and here I thank Dr. Lingard for having enabled me to give this description. One kind of torture which was called "the Scavenger's Daughter, was a broad hoop of iron, consisting of two parts fastened by a hinge. The prisoner was made to kneel on the pavement and to contract himself into as small a compass as he could. Then the executioner, kneeling on his shoulders, and having introduced the hoop under his legs, compressed the victim close together till he was able to fasten the feet and hands together over the small of the back. The time allotted to this kind of torture was an hour and a half, during which time the blood gushed from the nostrils, and sometimes from the hands and feet." There were several other kinds of arguments of conversion that gentle Betsy made use of to eradicate the "damnable errors" of popery, but her great argument was the rack. This "was a large open frame of oak raised three feet from the ground. The prisoner was laid under it on his back on the floor; his wrists and ankles were attached by cords to two rollers at the ends of the frame; these were moved by levers in opposite directions, till the body rose to a level with the frame. Questions were then put; and if the answers did not prove satisfactory, the sufferer was stretched more and more till the bones started from their sockets."

The other deeds and events of the reign of this ferocious woman are now of little interest, and indeed do not belong to my subject; but seeing that the pensioned poet, Thompson, in that sickly stuff of his which no man of sense ever can endure after he gets to the age of twenty, has told us about "the glories of the maiden reign," it may not be amiss, before I take my leave of this "good" creature, to observe that her "glories" consisted in having broken innumerable solemn treaties and compacts, in having been continually bribing rebel subjects to annoy their sovereigns, in having had a navy of freebooters, in having had an army of plunderers, in having bartered for a little money the important town of Calais, and in never having added even one single leaf of laurel to that ample branch which had for ages been seated on the brows of England; and that as to her maiden virtues, Whitaker (a Protestant clergyman, mind,) says that "her life was stained with gross licentiousness, and she had many gallants, while she called herself a maiden queen." Her life, as he truly says, was a life of "mischief and of misery," and in her death (which took place in the year 1603, the seventieth of her age and the forty-fifth of her reign) she did all the mischief that it remained in her power to do by sulkily refusing to name her successor, and thus leaving to a people whom she had been pillaging and scourging for forty-five years a probable civil war, as "a legacy of mischief after her death." Historians have been divided in opinion as to which was the worst man that England ever produced, her father or Cranmer; but all mankind must agree that this was the worst woman that ever existed in England, or in the whole world, Jezebel herself not excepted.

CHAPTER TWELVE

The "good and glorious" Queen Elizabeth, who, amongst her other "godly" deeds, granted to her minions, to whom there was no longer church plunder to give, monopolies of almost all the necessaries of life, so that salt, for instance, which used to be about 2d. a bushel was raised to 15s., or about £7 of our present money; the Queen, who had, as Whitaker says, expired in sulky silence as to her successor, and had thus left a probable civil war as a legacy of mischief, was, however, peaceably succeeded by James I, that very child of whom poor Mary Stuart was pregnant when his father, Henry Stuart, Earl of Darnley, and associates murdered Rizzio in her presence, as we have seen in Chapter 10, and which child, when he came to man's estate, was a Presbyterian, was generally a pensioner of Elizabeth, abandoned his mother to that queen's wrath, and amongst his first acts in England took by the hand, confided in, and promoted that Cecil who was the son of the old Cecil, who did, indeed, inherit the great talents of his father, but who had also been, as all the world knew, the deadly enemy of this new king's unfortunate mother.

James, like all the Stuarts except the last, was at once prodigal and mean, conceited and foolish, tyrannical and

weak; but the staring feature of his character was insinceri-
ty. It would be useless to dwell in the detail on the measures
of this contemptible reign, the prodigalities and
debaucheries and silliness of which did, however, prepare
the way for that rebellion and that revolution which took
place in the next, when the "double-distilled Reformers"
did at last provide a "martyr" for the hitherto naked pages
of the Protestant calendar. Indeed, this reign would, as far
as my purposes extend, be a complete blank, were it not for
that "gunpowder plot" which alone has caused this Stuart
to be remembered, and of which, seeing that it has been
and is yet made a source of great and general delusion, I
shall take much more notice than it would otherwise be
entitled to.

That there was a plot in the year 1605 (the second year
after James came to the throne), the object of which was to
blow up the King and both Houses of Parliament on the
first day of the session, that Catholics and none but
Catholics were parties to this plot, that the conspirators
were ready to execute the deed, and that they all avowed
this to the last, are facts which no man has ever attempted
to deny.

However, these conspirators had provocation, and now
let us see what that provocation was. The King, before he
came to the throne, had promised to mitigate the penal
laws which, as we have seen, made their lives a burden.
Instead of this those laws were rendered even more severe
than they had been in the former reign. Every species of
insult as well as injury, which the Catholics had had to
endure under the persecutions of the Established Church,
was now heightened by that leaven of Presbyterian malignity and ferocity which England had now imported from the
north, which had then poured forth upon this devoted
country endless hordes of the most greedy and rapacious
and insolent wretches that God had ever permitted to
infest and scourge the earth. We have seen in the last
Chapter how the houses of conscientious Catholic gentle-

men were rifled, how they were rummaged, in what constant dread these unhappy men lived, how they were robbed of their estates as a punishment for recusancy and other things called crimes; we have seen that by the fines imposed on these accounts the ancient gentry of England, whose families had for ages inhabited the same mansions and had been venerated and beloved for their hospitality and charity, we have seen how all these were gradually sinking into absolute beggary in consequence of these exorbitant extortions: but what was their lot now? The fines, as had been the practice, had been suffered to fall in arrear in order to make the fined party more completely at the mercy of the crown; and James, whose prodigality left him not the means of gratifying the greediness of his Scotch minions out of his own exchequer, delivered over the English Catholic gentry to these rapacious minions, who, thus clad with royal authority, fell with all their well-known hardness of heart upon the devoted victims as the kite falls upon the defenceless dove. They entered their mansions, ransacked their closets, drawers and beds, seized their rent-rolls, in numerous instances drove their wives and children from their doors, and with all their native upstart insolence made a mockery of the ruin and misery of the unoffending persons whom they had despoiled.

Human nature gave the lie to all preachings of longer passive obedience, and at last one of these oppressed and insulted English gentlemen, Robert Catesby, of Northamptonshire, resolved on making an attempt to deliver himself and his suffering brethren from this almost infernal scourge. But how was he to obtain the means? From abroad, such was the state of things, no aid could possibly be hoped for. Internal insurrection was, as long as the makers and executors of the barbarous laws remained, equally hopeless. Hence he came to the conclusion, that to destroy the whole of them afforded the only hope of deliverance; and to effect this there appeared to him no other way than that of blowing up the Parliament House when, on the first day of the session, all should be assembled together. He soon obtained associates; but in the whole they amounted to only about thirteen, and all except three or four in rather obscure situations in life, amongst whom was Guy Fawkes, a Yorkshireman, who had served as an officer in the Flemish wars. He it was who undertook to set fire to the magazine, consisting of two hogsheads and thirty-two barrels of gunpowder; he it was who, if not otherwise to be accomplished, had resolved to blow himself up along with the persecutors of his brethren; he it was who, on the 5th of November, 1605, a few hours only before the Parliament was to meet, was seized in the vault with two matches in his pocket and a dark lantern by his side, ready to effect his tremendous purpose; he it was who, when brought before King and Council, replied to all their questions with defiance; he it was who, when asked by a Scotch Lord of the Council why he had collected so many barrels of gunpowder, answered, "to blow you Scotch beggars back to your native mountains," and in this answer proclaimed to the world the true immediate cause of this memorable conspiracy; an answer which, in common justice, ought to be put into the mouth of those effigies of him which crafty knaves induce foolish boys still to burn on the 5th of November. James (whose silly conceit made him an author) was just in one respect at any rate. In his works he calls Fawkes "the English Scaevola," and history tells us that that famous Roman, having missed his mark in endeavouring to kill a tyrant who had doomed his country to slavery, thrust his offending hand into a hot fire, and let it burn while he looked defiance at the tyrant.

Catesby and the other conspirators were pursued; he and three of his associates died with arms in their hands, fighting against their pursuers. The rest of them (except Tresham, who was poisoned in prison) were executed, and also the famous Jesuit, Garnet, who was wholly innocent of any crime connected with the conspiracy, and who, having come to a knowledge of it through the channel of confession, had, on the contrary, done everything in his power to prevent the perpetrating of its object. The conspirators could not give warning to the Catholics without exciting suspicions. They did give such warning where they could, and this led to the timely detection, otherwise the whole of the two Houses, and the King along with them, would have been blown to atoms; for though Cecil evidently knew of the plot long before the time of intended execution; though he took care to nurse it till the moment of advantageous discovery arrived; though he was, in all probability, the author of a warning letter which, being sent anonymously to a Catholic nobleman and communicated by him to the government, became the ostensible cause of the timely discovery; notwithstanding these well-attested facts, it by no means appears that the plot originated with him, or, indeed, with anybody but Catesby, of whose conduct men will judge differently according to the difference in their notions about passive obedience and non-resistance.

This would be enough of the famous gunpowder plot; but since it has been ascribed to bloody-mindedness as the natural fruit of the Catholic religion, since in our Common Prayer-Book we are taught, in addressing God, to call Catholics indiscriminately "our cruel and blood-thirsty enemies," let us see a little what Protestants have attempted and done in this blowing-up way. This King James, as he himself averred, was nearly being assassinated by his Scotch Protestant subjects, Earl Gowrie and his associates; and after that narrowly escaped being blown up with all his attendants by the furious Protestant burghers of Perth by gunpowder and thereby killed. Then, again, the Protestants in the Netherlands formed a plot to blow up their Governor, the Prince of Parma, with all the nobility and magistrates of those countries, when assembled in the city of Antwerp. But the Protestants did not always fail in their plots, nor were those engaged in them obscure individuals. For, as we have seen, this very King James's father, the king of Scotland, was, in 1567, blown up and thereby killed.

This was doing the thing effectually. Here was no warning given to anybody; and all the attendants and servants, of whatever religion and of both sexes, except such as escaped by mere accident, were remorsely murdered along with their master. And who was this done by? "By bloodthirsty Catholics?" No; but by the loves of the "Avangel" as the wretches called themselves, the followers of that Knox to whom a monument had been erected at Glasgow. The conspirators on this occasion were not thirteen obscure men, and those too, who had received provocation enough to make men mad, but a body of noblemen and gentlemen who really had received no provocation at all from Mary Stuart, to destroy whom was more the object than it was to destroy her husband.

Let us take account of these conspirators in the words of Whitaker; and let the reader recollect that Whitaker, who published his book in 1787, was a parson of the Church of England, rector of Ruhan-Lanyhorne, in Cornwall, and that he was amongst those clergymen who were most strenuously opposed to the rites and ceremonies and tenets of the Catholic Church; but he was a truly honest man, a most zealous lover of truth and hater of injustice. Hear this staunch Church parson, then, upon the subject of this Protestant gunpowder plot, concerning which he had made the fullest inquiry and collected together the clearest evidence. He says, in speaking of the plot, "the guilt of this wretched woman, Elizabeth, and the guilt of that wretched man, Cecil, appear too evident at last upon the face of the whole. Indeed, as far as we can judge of the matter, the whole disposition of the murderous drama was this: the whole was originally planned and devised between Elizabeth, Cecil, Morton and Murray, and the execution committed to Lethington, Bothwell and Balfour; and Elizabeth, we may be certain, was to defend the original and more iniquitous part of the conspirators, Morton and Murray, in charging their own murder upon the innocent Mary." Did hell itself, did the devil, who was, as Luther himself says, so long the companion and so often the bed-fellow of this first "Reformer," ever devise wickedness equal to this Protestant plot? Let us hear no more, then, about the blood-thirstiness of the Catholic religion; and if we must still have our 5th of November, let the "moral" disciples of Knox, the inhabitants of "Modern Athens," have their 10th of February. Let them, too (for it was Protestants that did the deed), have their 30th of January, the anniversary of the killing of the son of this same King James. Nobody knew better than James himself the history of his father's and his mother's end. He knew that they had both been murdered by Protestants, and that, too, with circumstances of atrocity quite unequalled in the annals of human infamy, and therefore he himself was not for vigorous measures against the Catholics in general on account of the plot; but love of plunder in his minions prevailed over him, and now began to blaze with fresh fury that Protestant reformation spirit which at last gave him a murdered son and successor, as it had already given him a murdered father and mother.

Charles I, who came to the throne on the death of his father in 1625, with no more sense and with a stronger tincture of haughtiness and tyranny than his father, seemed to wish to go back in church matters towards the Catholic rites and ceremonies, while his parliaments and people were every day becoming more and more puritanical. Divers were the grounds of quarrel between them, but the great ground was that of religion. The Catholics were suffering all the while, and especially those in Ireland, who were plundered and murdered by whole districts, and especially under Wentworth, who committed more injustice than ever had before been committed even in that unhappy country. But all this was not enough to satisfy the Puritans; and Laud, the Primate of the Established Church, having done a great many things to exalt that Church in point of power and dignity, the purer Protestants called for "another Reformation," and what they called a "thorough godly Reformation."

Now, then, this Protestant Church and Protestant King had to learn that "Reformations," like comets, have tails. There was no longer the iron police of Elizabeth to watch and to crush all gainsayers. The Puritans artfully connected political grievances, which were real and numerous, with religious principles and ceremonies, and having the main body of the people with them as to the former, while these were, in consequence of the endless change of creeds, become indifferent as to the latter, they soon became, under the name of "The Parliament," the sole rulers of the country; they abolished the Church and the House of Lords, and finally brought, in 1649, during the progress of their "thorough godly Reformation," the unfortunate King himself to trial and to the block!

All very bad, to be sure; but all very natural, seeing what had gone before. If "some such man as Henry VIII." were, as Burnet says he was, necessary to begin a "Reformation," why not "some such man" as Cromwell to complete it? If it were right to put to death More, Fisher, and thousands of others, not forgetting the grandmother of Charles, on a charge of treason, why was Charles's head to be so very sacred? If it were right to confiscate the estates of the mona-teries and to turn adrift or put to death the abbots, priors, monks, friars and nuns, after having plundered the latter of even their ear-rings and silver thimbles, could it be so very wrong to take away merely the titles of those who possessed the plundered property? And as to the Protestant Church, if it were right to establish it on the ruins of the ancient Church by German bayonets, by fines, gallows and racks, could it be so very wrong to establish another newer one on its ruins by means a great deal milder? If, at the time we are now speaking of, one of Elizabeth's parsons, who had ousted a priest of Queen Mary, had been alive, and had been made to fly out of his parsonage-house, not with one of Bess's bay-onets at his back, but on the easy toe of one of Cromwell's godly Bible-reading soldiers, could that parson have reason-ably complained?

Cromwell (whose reign we may consider as having lasted from 1649 to 1659), therefore, though he soon made the Parliament a mere instrument in his hands, though he was tyrannical and bloody, though he ruled with a rod of iron, though he was a real tyrant, was nothing more than the "natural issue," as Elizabeth would have called him, of the "body" of the "Reformation." He was cruel towards the Irish ·— he killed them without mercy; but, except in the act of selling 20,000 of them to the West Indies as slaves, in what did he treat them worse than Charles, to whom and to whose descendants they were loyal from first to last?

As if to make "Reformation" the second as much as possible like "Reformation" the first, there was now a change of religion made by laymen only. The Church clergy were calumniated just as the Catholic clergy had been, the bishops were shut out of Parliament as the abbots and Catholic bishops had been, the cathedrals and churches were again ransacked, Cranmer's tables (put in place of the altars) were now knocked to pieces, there was a general crusade against crosses, portraits of Christ, religious pictures, paintings on church windows, images on the outside of cathedrals, tombs in these and the churches. As the mass-books had been destroyed in "Reformation" the first, the church books were destroyed in "Reformation" the second, and a new book called the "Directory" ordered to be used in its place, a step which was no more than an imitation of Henry VIII.'s "Christian Man" and Cranmer's "Prayer book." And why not this "Directory"?

The heroes of "Reformation" the second were great Bible-readers, and almost every man became at times a preacher. The soldiers were uncommonly gifted in this way, and they claimed a right to preach as one of the conditions upon which they bore arms against the king. Everyone interpreted the Bible in his own way; they were all for the Bible without note or comment. Roger North (a Protestant), in his Examen, gives an account of all sorts of blasphemies and of horrors committed by these people, who had poisoned the minds of nearly the whole of the community. At Dover a woman cut off the head of her child, alleging that, like Abraham, she had had a particular command from God. A woman was executed at York for crucifying her mother; she had at the same time sacrificed a calf and a cock. These are only amongst the horrors of that "thoroughly godly Reformation;" only a specimen. And why not these horrors? We read of killings in the Bible; and if every man be to be his own interpreter of that book, who is to say that he acts contrary to his own interpretation? Why not all these new monstrous sects? If there could be one new religion, one new creed made, why not a thousand? What right had Luther to make a new religion, and then Calvin another new one, and Cranmer one differing from both these, and then Elizabeth to make an improvement upon Cranmer's? Were all these to make new religions, and were the enlightened soldiers of Cromwell's army to be deprived of this right? The former all alleged as their authority the "inspiration of the Holy Ghost." What, then? Were Cromwell and his soldiers to be deprived of the benefit of this allegation? Poor "godly" fellows, why were they to be the only people in the world not qualified for choosing a religion for themselves and for those whom they had at the point of their bayonets? One of Cromwell's "godly" men went, as North relates, into the church of Walton-upon-Thames with a lantern and five candles, telling the people

that he had a message to them from God, and that they would be damned if they did not listen to him. He put out one light as a mark of the abolition of the Sabbath, the second as a mark of the abolition of all tithes and church dues, the third as a mark of the abolition of all ministers and magistrates; and then the fourth light he applied to setting fire to a Bible, declaring that that also was abolished! These were pretty pranks to play; but they were the natural, the inevitable consequence of "Reformation" the first.

In one respect, however, these new reformers differed from the old ones. They did, indeed, make a new religion and command people to follow it, and they inflicted punishments on the refractory; but those punishments were beds of down compared with oak planks, when viewed by the side of those inflicted by Elizabeth and her Church. They forbade the use of the Common Prayer Book in all churches and also in private families; but they punished the disobedient with a penalty of five pounds for the first offence, ten pounds for the second, and with three years' imprisonment for the third, and did not hang them, as the Church of England sovereigns had done by those who said or heard mass. Bad as these fanatics were, wicked and outrageous as were their deeds, they never persecuted nor attempted to persecute with a hundredth part of the cruelty that the Church of England had done, —aye, and that it did again the moment it regained its power after the restoration of Charles II., when it became more cruel to the Catholics even than it had been in the reign of Queen Elizabeth, and that, too, notwithstanding that the Catholics of all ranks and degrees had signalised themselves during the civil war in every way in which it was possible for them to aid the royal cause.

This at first sight seems out of nature; but if we consider that this Church of England felt conscious that its possessions did once belong to the Catholics, that the cathedrals and churches and the colleges were all the work of Catholic piety, learning and disinterestedness; when we consider this, can we be surprised that these new possessors, who had got possession by such means, too, as we have seen in the course of this work, — when we consider this are we to be surprised that they should do everything in their power to prevent the people from seeing, hearing, and contracting a respect for those whom these new possessors had ousted? Here we have the true cause of all the hostility of the Church of England clergy towards the Catholics. Take away the possessions, and the hostility would cease tomorrow; though there is, besides that, a wide and, on their side, a very disadvantageous difference between a married clergy and one not married. The former will never have an influence with the people anything like approaching that of the latter. There is, too, the well-known superiority of learning on the side of the Catholic clergy, to which may be added the notorious fact that in fair controversy the Catholics have always triumphed. Hence the deep-rooted, the inflexible, the persevering and absolutely implacable hostility of this established Church to the Catholics, not as men, but as Catholics. To what else are we to ascribe that, to this day, the Catholics are forbidden to have steeples or bells to their chapels? They whose religion gave us our steeples and bells! To what else are we to ascribe that their priests are, even now, forbidden to appear in the streets, or in private houses, in their clerical habiliments, and even when performing their functions at funerals? Why all this anxious pains to keep the Catholic religion out of sight? Men may pretend what they will, but these pains argue anything but consciousness of being right on the part of those who take those pains. Why, when the English nuns came over to England during the French Revolution and settled at Winchester, get a bill brought into Parliament (as the Church clergy did) to prevent them from taking Protestant scholars, and give up the bill only upon a promise that they would not take such scholars? Did this argue a conviction in the minds of the Winchester parsons, that Bishop North's was the true religion and that William of Wykham's was the false one? The Church parsons are tolerant enough towards the sects of all descriptions; quite love the Quaker, who rejects baptism and the sacrament; shake hands with the Unitarian, and allow him openly to impugn that which they tell us in the Prayer Book a man cannot be saved if he do not firmly believe in; suffer these, aye, and even Jews, to present to church livings, and refuse that right to Catholics, from whose religion all the church livings came!

Who, then, can doubt of the motive of this implacable hostility, this everlasting watchfulness, this rancorous jealousy that never sleeps? The common enemy being put down by the restoration of Charles, the Church fell upon the Catholics with more fury than ever. This king, who came out of exile to mount the throne in 1660 with still more prodigality than either his father or grandfather, had a great deal more sense than both put together, and in spite of all his well-known profligacy he was, on account of his popular manners, a favourite with his people; but he was strongly suspected to be a Catholic in his heart, and his more honest brother James, his presumptive heir, was an openly declared Catholic. Hence the reign of Charles II. was one continued series of plots, sham or real, and one unbroken scene of acts of injustice, fraud and false swearing. These were plots ascribed to the Catholics, but really plots against them. Even the great fire in London, which took place during this reign, was ascribed to them, and there is the charge to this day going round the base of "the monument," which Pope justly compares to a big, lying bully:-

"Where London's column, pointing to the skies,
Like a tall bully, lifts its head and lies."

The words are these: "This monument is erected in memory of the burning of this Protestant city by the Popish faction, in September. A.D.1666, for the destruction of the Protestant religion and of old English liberty, and for the introduction of Popery and slavery. But the fury of the Papists is not yet satisfied." It is curious enough that this inscription was made by order of Sir Patience Ward, who, as Echard shows, was afterwards convicted of perjury. Burnet (whom we shall find in full tide by-and-by) says that one Hubert, a French Papist, "confessed that he began the fire"; but Higgons (a Protestant, mind) proves that Hubert was a Protestant, and Rapin agrees with Higgons. Nobody knew better than the King the monstrousness of this lie, but Charles II. was a lazy, luxurious debauchee; such men have always been unfeeling and ungrateful, and this king, who had twice owed his life to Catholic priests, and who had in fifty-two instances held his life at the mercy of Catholics (some of them very poor) while he was a wandering fugitive, with immense rewards held out for taking him, and dreadful punishments for concealing him, this profligate king, whose ingratitude to his faithful Irish subjects is without a parallel in the annals of that black sin, had the meanness and injustice to suffer this lying inscription to stand. It was effaced by his brother and successor, but when the Dutchman and the "glorious revolution" came, it was restored; and there it now stands, all the world except the mere mob knowing it to contain a most malignant lie.

By conduct like this, by thus encouraging the fanatical part of his subjects in their wicked designs, Charles II. prepared the way for those events by which his family were excluded from the throne for ever. To set aside his brother, who was an avowed Catholic, was their great object. This was indeed a monstrous attempt; but, legally considered, what was it more than to prefer the illegitimate Elizabeth to the legitimate Mary Stuart? What was it more than to enact that any "natural issue" of the former should be heir to the throne? And how could the Protestant Church complain of it, when its great maker, Cranmer, had done his best to set aside both the daughters of Henry VIII, and to put Lady Jane Grey on the throne? In short, there was no precedent for annulling the rights of inheritance, for setting aside prescription, for disregarding the safety of property and of person, for violating the fundamental laws of the kingdom,

that the records of the "Reformation" did not amply furnish: and this daring attempt to set aside James on account
of his religion might be truly said, as it was said, to be a
Protestant principle; and it was, too, a principle most decidedly acted upon in a few years afterwards.

James II. was sober, frugal in his expenses, economical as
to public matters, sparing of the people's purses, pious and
sincere, but weak and obstinate, and he was a Catholic; and
his piety and sincerity made him not a match for his artful,
numerous, and deeply interested foes. If the existence of a
few missionary priests in the country, though hidden
behind wainscots, had called forth thousands of pursuivants
in order to protect the Protestant Church, if to hear mass in
a private house had been regarded as incompatible with the
safety of that Church, what was to be the fate of that
Church if a Catholic king continued to sit on the throne? It
was easy to see that the ministry, the army, the navy, and all
the offices under the government would soon contain few
besides Catholics, and it was also easy to see that by degrees
Catholics would be in the parsonages and in the episcopal
palaces, especially as the King was as zealous as he was sincere. The "Reformation" had made consciences to be of so
pliant a nature, men had changed under it backward and
forward so many times, that this last (the filling of the
Church with Catholic priests and bishops), would perhaps,
amongst the people in general, and particularly amongst
the higher classes, have produced but little alarm. But not
so with the clergy themselves, who soon saw their danger,
and who, "passive" as they were, lost no time in preparing
to avert it.

James acted, as far as the law would let him, and as far as
prerogative would enable him to go beyond the law, on
principles of general toleration. By this he obtained the
support of the sectaries. But the Church had got the good
things, and it resolved if possible to keep them. Besides this,
though the abbey lands and the rest of the real property of
the Church and the poor had been a long while in the

peaceable possession of the then owners and their predecessors, the time was not so very distant but that able lawyers,
having their opinions backed by a well-organised army,
might still find a flaw in, here and there, a grant of Henry
VIII, Edward VI, and Elizabeth. Be their thoughts what
they might, certain it is that the most zealous and most
conspicuous and most efficient of the leaders of the
"Glorious Revolution," which took place soon afterwards,
and which drove James from the throne, together with his
heirs and his house, were amongst those whose ancestors
had not been out of the way at the time when the sharing
of the abbey lands took place.

With motives so powerful against him, the King ought to
have been uncommonly prudent and wary. He was just the
contrary. He was severe towards all who opposed his views,
however powerful they might be. Some bishops, who presented a very insolent but artful petition to him, he sent to
the Tower, had them prosecuted for a libel, and had the
mortification to see them acquitted. As to the behaviour of
the Catholics, prudence and moderation were not to be
expected from them. Look at the fines, the burning-irons,
the racks, the gibbets, and the ripping-knives of the late
reigns, and say if it were not both natural and just that their
joy and exultation should now be without bounds. These
were, alas! of short duration, for a plan (we must not call it
a plot) having been formed for compelling the King to give
up his tolerating projects, and "to save the kingdom," as it
was called, the planners, without any act of Parliament, and
without consulting the people in any way whatever, invited
William, the Prince of Orange, who was the Stadtholder of
the Dutch, to come over with a Dutch army to assist them
in "settling" the kingdom. All things having been duly prepared, the Dutch guards (who had been suffered to get from
Torbay to London, by perfidy in the English army) having
come to the King's palace and thrust out the English guards,
the King, having seen one "settling" of a sovereign, in the
reign of his father, and apparently having no relish for

another settling of the same sort, fled from his palace and his kingdom and took shelter in France, instead of fleeing to some distant English city and there rallying his people round him, which if he had done, the event would, as the subsequent conduct of the people proved, have been very different from what it was.

Now came, then, the "glorious Revolution," or Reformation the third.

CHAPTER THIRTEEN

The King being gone, the Lord Mayor and Aldermen of London, with a parcel of Common Councilmen, and such lords and members of the late King Charles's Parliaments as chose to join them, went in February, 1688, without any authority from King, Parliament, or people, and forming themselves into "a Convention," at Westminster, gave the crown to William (who was a Dutchman) and his wife (who was a daughter of James, but who had a brother alive), and their posterity for ever; made new oaths of allegiance for the people to take; enabled the new king to imprison at pleasure all whom he might suspect; banished, to ten miles from London, all Papists, or reputed Papists, and disarmed them all over the kingdom; gave the advowsons of Papists to the Universities; granted to their new Majesties excise duties, land-taxes, and poll-taxes, for the "necessary defence of the realm;" declared themselves to be the "two Houses of Parliament as legally as if they had been summoned according to the usual form:" and this they called a "glorious Revolution," as we Protestants call it to this present day. After "Reformation" the second, and upon the restoration of Charles, the palaces and livings, and other indestructible plunder, were restored to those from whom the "thorough godly" had taken it, except however to the Catholic Irish, who had fought for this king's father, who had suffered most cruelly for this king himself, and who were left still to be plundered by the "thorough godly;" which is an instance of ingratitude such as in no other case has been witnessed in the world. However, there were after the restoration men enough to contend that the episcopal palaces and other property, confiscated and granted away by the "thorough godly," ought not to be touched; for that if those grants were resumed why not resume those of Henry VIII? Aye, why not indeed! Here was a question to put to the Church clergy, and to the abbey land-owners! If nine hundred years of quiet possession, and Magna Charta at the back of it, —if it were right to set these at nought for the sake of making only "a godly Reformation," why should not one hundred years of unquiet possession be set at nought for the sake of making "a thorough godly Reformation?" How did the Church clergy answer this question? Why, Dr. Heylyn, who was Rector of Alresford, in Hampshire, and afterwards Dean of Westminster, who was a great enemy of the "thorough godly," though not much less an enemy of the Catholics, meets the question in this way, in the address at the head of his History of Reformation the first, where he says, "that there certainly must needs be a vast disproportion between such contracts as were founded upon acts of Parliament, legally passed by the king's authority, with the consent and approbation of the three estates, and those which have no other ground but the bare votes and orders of both Houses only. By the same logic it might be contended, that the two Houses alone have authority to depose a king."

This church doctor died a little too soon, or he would have seen, not two Houses of Parliament, but a Lord Mayor of London, a parcel of Common Councilmen, and such other persons as chose to join them, actually setting aside one king and putting another upon the throne, and without any authority from King, Parliament, or people; he would have heard this called a "glorious" thing; and if he had lived to our day, he would have seen other equally "glorious" things grow directly out of it; and that not-withstanding Blackstone had told the Americans that a "glorious" revolution was a thing never to be repeated, Doctor Heylyn would have heard them repeating, as applied to George III, almost word for word the charges which the "glorious" people preferred against James II, though they, naughty Yankees, knew perfectly well that, after the "glorious" affair, a King of England (being a Protestant) could "do no wrong!" The doctor's book, written to justify the "Reformation," did, as Pierre Orleans tells us, convert James II. and his first wife to the Catholic religion, but his preface above quoted did not succeed so well with Protestants.

As William and his Dutch army have been called our deliverers, let us see what it really was after all that they delivered the people from; and here, happily, we have the statute-book to refer to, in which there still stands the list of charges drawn up against this Catholic king. However, before we examine these charges, we ought in common justice to notice certain things that James did not do. He did not, as Protestant Edward VI. had done, bring German troops into the country to enforce a change of religion; nor did he, like that young saint, burn his starving subjects with a hot iron on the breast or on the forehead, and make them wear chains as slaves, as a punishment for endeavouring to relieve their hunger by begging. He did not, as Protestant Elizabeth had done, make use of whips, boring irons, racks, gibbets and ripping-knives to convert people to his faith, nor did he impose even any fines for this purpose; but, on the contrary, put, as far as he was able, an end to all persecution on account of religion.

Indictments do not generally come after judgment and execution, but for some cause or other the charges against James were postponed until the next year, when the crown had been actually given to the Dutchman and his wife. No matter; they came out at last, and there they stand, twelve in number, in Act, 2 sess. Wm. and M., chap.2. We will take them one by one, bearing in mind that they contained all that could ever be said against this Popish king.

CHARGE I. "That he assumed and exercised a power of dispensing with and suspending laws and the execution of laws without consent of Parliament." That is to say, he did not enforce those cruel laws against conscientious Catholics which had been enacted in former reigns. But did not Elizabeth and her successor, James I., dispense with or suspend laws when they took a composition from recusants? Again, have we ourselves never seen any suspension of or dispensing with laws without consent of Parliament? Was there, and is there, no dispensing with the law in employing foreign officers in the English army, and in granting pensions from the Crown to foreigners? And was there no suspension of the law when the bank stopped payment in 1797? And did the Parliament give its assent to the causing of that stoppage? And has it ever given its assent to the putting of foreigners in offices of trust, civil or military, or to the granting of pensions from the Crown to foreigners? But did James ever suspend the Habeas Corpus Act? Did his secretaries of state ever imprison whom they pleased, in any gaol or dungeon that they pleased, let the captives out when they pleased? Ah! but what he and his ministers did in this way (if they did anything) was all done "without consent of Parliament;" and who is so destitute of discrimination as not to perceive the astonishing difference between a dungeon with consent of Parliament and a dungeon without consent of Parliament!

CHARGE II. "That he committed and prosecuted divers worthy prelates for humbly petitioning to be excused from concurring to the said assumed powers."

CHARGE III. "That he issued a commission for erecting a court called the Court of Commissioners for Ecclesiastical Causes." Bless us! What! was this worse than "good Queen" Elizabeth's real inquisition under the same name? And, good God! have we no court of this sort now? And did not the revolution Protestants, who drew up the charges against James, leave this law in full force for our benefit?

CHARGE IV. "That he levied money for and to the use of the Crown, by pretence of prerogative, for other time and in other manner than was granted by Parliament." It is not pretended that he levied more money than was granted; but he was not exact as to the time and manner.

CHARGE V. "That he kept a standing army in time of peace without consent of Parliament." Ah! without consent of Parliament, indeed! That was very wicked. There were only seven or eight thousand men, to be sure, and such a thing as a barrack had never been heard of. But without consent of Parliament! Think of the vast difference between the prick of a bayonet coming without consent of a Parliament, and that of one coming with such consent? This King's father had been dethroned and his head had been cut off by an army kept up with consent of Parliament: mind that, however.

CHARGE VI. "That he caused several good subjects, being Protestants, to be disarmed at the same time that Papists were both armed and employed contrary to law."

CHARGE VII. "That he violated the freedom of election of members to serve in Parliament."

CHARGE VIII. "That he promoted prosecutions in the court of King's Bench for matters and things cognizable only in Parliament, and that he did divers other arbitrary and unlawful things." That is to say that he brought before a jury matters which the Parliament wished to keep to itself! Oh, naughty and arbitrary king! to have jury trial for the deeds of Parliament men, instead of letting them try themselves! As to the divers other such arbitrary things, they not being specified we cannot say what they were.

CHARGE IX. "That he caused juries to be composed of partial, corrupt and unqualified persons who were not freeholders." Very bad if true, of which, however, no proof and no instance is attempted to be given. One thing, at any rate; there were no special juries in those days. They, which are "appointed" by the Master of the Crown Office, came after Catholic kings were abolished. But not to mention that Protestant Betsy dispensed with juries altogether when she pleased, and tried and punished even vagabonds and rioters by martial law, do we not now, in our own free and enlightened and liberal Protestant days, see many men transported for seven years without any jury at all? Aye, and that, too, in numerous cases only for being more than fifteen minutes at a time out of their houses (which the law calls their castles) between sunset and sunrise? Ah! but this is with consent of Parliament! Oh! I had forgotten that. That's an answer.

CHARGE X. "That excessive bail hath" (by the judges, of course) "been required of persons committed in criminal cases, to elude the benefit of the laws made for the liberty of the subject."

CHARGE XI. "That excessive fines have been imposed and illegal and cruel punishments inflicted."

CHARGE XII. "That he had made promises and grants of fines before conviction and judgement on the party."

I take these last three charges together. As to fines and bail, look at Protestant Elizabeth's and Protestant James I.'s reign. But coming to our own times, I, for having expressed my indignation at the flogging of English local militia men in the heart of England, under a guard of German troops, was two years imprisoned in a felon's gaol, and at the expiration of the time had to pay a fine of a thousand pounds, and to give bail for seven years, myself in three thousand pounds, with two sureties in two thousand pounds each.

Until, therefore, some zealous admirer of the "glorious revolution" will be pleased to furnish us with something specific as to the bail and fines in James's reign, we ought in prudence to abstain from even any mention of this charge against the unfortunate king, for to talk of them in too censorious a strain may possibly receive a no very charitable interpretation. But there had been illegal and cruel punishments in his reign. What punishments? There had been no people burnt, there had been no racks, as there had been in the reigns of Protestant Elizabeth and James I. Why, Sir

John Cox Hippesley, in a petition to Parliament a year or two ago, asserted that the tread-mill was "cruel and illegal." Yet it stands, and that, too, for very trifling offences. Sir John might be wrong, but this shows that there might also be two opinions about punishments in the time of James, and we have to lament that those who brought in "the deliverer" were so careless as to specify none of those instances which might have enabled us to make as to this matter a comparison between a Catholic king and a Protestant one. But he granted away fines before the conviction of the party. Indeed! What, then, we have in our happy day, under a Protestant king, no fines granted beforehand to informers of any sort? Ah! but this is with consent of Parliament! I had forgotten that again: I am silenced!

These were the offences of King James; these were the grounds, as recorded in the statute-book of the "glorious revolution" made, as the same act expresses, to "deliver this kingdom from Popery and arbitrary power, and to prevent the Protestant religion from being subverted;" and seeing that this was immediately followed by a perpetual exclusion of Catholics, and those who should marry with Catholics, from the throne, it is clear that this was a revolution entirely Protestant, and that it was an event directly proceeding from the "Reformation." But there are still to notice some things which lying history and vulgar prejudice urge against this unfortunate Catholic king, who has been asserted to have been the adviser of his late brother in all those deeds which have been deemed wicked, and especially in the putting of Lord Russell and Algernon Sidney to death for high treason.

Alas! how have we been deluded upon this subject! I used to look upon these as two murdered men. A compulsion to look into realities and to discard romance has taught me the contrary. The Protestants were, in the reign of Charles II, continually hatching Popish plots, and, by contrivances the most diabolical, bringing innocent Catholics to the scaffold and the gibbet; and in the course of these their proceedings they were constantly denying the prerogative of the king to pardon or to mitigate the punishment of their victims. But at last the king got real proof of a Protestant plot! The king was ill, and a conspiracy was formed for setting aside his brother by force of arms if the king should die. The king recovered, but the Protestant plot went on. The scheme was, to rise in arms against the Government, to pay and bring in an army of Protestants from Scotland, and in short, to make now that sort of "Reformation" the third which did not take place till, as we have seen, some years afterwards. In this Protestant plot Russell and Sidney were two great leaders. Russell did not attempt to deny that he had had a part in the conspiracy, his only complaint was that the indictment was not agreeable to law; but he was told, which was true, that it was perfectly agreeable to numerous precedents in cases of trials of Popish plotters! When brought to the place of execution Russell did not deny his guilt, but did not explicitly confess it. That part of his sentence which ordered his bowels to be ripped out while he was yet alive, and his body to be quartered, was, at the intercession of his family, remitted by the king, who, in yielding to their prayer, cuttingly said, "My Lord Russell shall find that I am possessed of that prerogative which, in the case of Lord Strafford, he thought fit to deny me."

As to Sidney, he had been one of the leading men in the "thorough godly" work of the last reign, and had even been one of the Commissioners for trying Charles I. and bringing him to the block, though it is said by his friends he did not actually sit at the trial. At the restoration of Charles II. he had taken refuge abroad. But having confessed the errors of his younger years and promised to be loyal in future, this king, under the guidance of a Popish brother, pardoned him, great as his offences had been. Yet after this he conspired to destroy the government of that king, or, at the very least, to set aside that brother, and this, too, observe, by force of arms, by open rebellion against the king who had pardoned him, and by plunging into all the horrors of another civil war that country which he had before assisted to desolate. If any man ever deserved an ignominious death this Sidney deserved his.

So much for the "good old cause for which Hampden died in the field and Sidney on the scaffold." What credulous creatures we have been, and who more so than myself?

It is said, and I think truly, that Charles II. was at one time in pecuniary treaty with the king of France for the purpose of re-establishing the Catholic Church in England. Well, had not he as much right to do this as Edward VI. had to bring over German troops to root out that ancient Church which had been established for 900 years, and which was guaranteed to the people by Magna Charta? And if doing this by means of French troops were intended by Charles, can that be complained of by those who approve of the bringing in of Dutch troops to "settle" the kingdom?

But now, if James be to be loaded with all those which have been called the bad deeds of his brother's reign, we cannot, with common justice, refuse him the merit of the good deeds of that reign. This reign gave us then, the Act of Habeas Corpus, which Blackstone calls the "second Great Charter of English Liberty." There are many other acts of this reign, tending to secure the liberties and all the rights of the people; but if there had been only this one act, ought not it alone to have satisfied the people that they had nothing to apprehend from a Popishly inclined king on the throne? Here these "Popish tyrants," Charles and James, gave up, at one stroke of the pen, at a single writing of Charles's name, all prerogatives enabling them, as their predecessors had been enabled, to put people into prison and to keep them there in virtue of a mere warrant or order from a minister. And was this a proof of that arbitrary disposition of which we hear them incessantly accused? We are always boasting about this famous Act of Habeas Corpus, but never have we the gratitude to observe that it came from those against whom Russell and Sidney conspired, and the last of whom was finally driven from his palace by the Dutch guards in 1688.

Then again, was this act ever suspended during the reigns of these Popish kings? Never, not even for a single day. But the moment the "glorious revolution" or Reformation the third came, the Dutch "deliverer" was, by the Protestant "Convention," whose grand business it was to get rid of "arbitrary power," — the moment that this "glorious" affair had taken place, that moment was the Dutch "deliverer" authorised to put in prison, and to keep there, any Englishman that he or his ministers might suspect! But why talk of this? We ourselves have seen this "second Great Charter of English liberty" suspended for seven years at a time; and besides this, we have seen the king and his ministers authorised to imprison any one they chose to imprison, in any gaol that they chose, in any dungeon that they chose, to keep the imprisoned person from all communication with friends, wives, husbands, fathers, mothers and children, to prevent them from the use of pen, ink, paper, and books, to deny them the right of being confronted with their accusers, to refuse them a specification of their offence, and the names of their accusers; to put them out of prison (if alive), when they pleased, without any trial; and at last, to hold them to bail for good behaviour, and that too, mind, still without stating to them the names of the witnesses against them, or even the nature of their offence! All this we have seen done in our own dear Protestant times, while our Parliament-house and our pulpits ring with praises of the "glorious revolution" that "delivered us from Popery and slavery."

There was another great thing, too, done in the reigns of these Popish kings, namely; the settling of the Provinces (now States) of America. Virginia had been attempted to be settled under Elizabeth, by that unprincipled minion, Sir Walter Raleigh, who in the next reign lost on the scaffold that life which he ought to have lost thirty years before; but the attempt wholly failed. A little, and very little, was done

in the succeeding reigns. It was not until that of Charles II.
that charters and patents were granted, that property
became real, and that consequent population and prosperity
came. This was a great event, great in itself and greater in
its consequences, some of which consequences we have
already felt, others we are now feeling, but others, and by
far of greater moment, we have yet to feel.

All these fine colonies were made by this Popishly
inclined king and by his really Popish brother. Two of them,
the Carolinas, take their name from the king himself;
another, and now the greatest of all, New York, from the
king's brother, who was duke of the city of that name in old
England. These were the men who planted these the finest
and happiest colonies that the sun ever lighted and warmed.
Then came that "glorious" affair; and it furnished all those
principles by which, at the end of only about seventy years,
this compensation was wrested from us, —and not only this,
but by which was created a power, a great maritime power,
at the very name of which, affect what they may,
Englishmen, once so high and daring, now grow pale.

We shall before the close of the next Chapter, and after
we have taken a view of the torments inflicted on the
Catholics (Irish and English) in the reigns of William,
Anne, and the Georges, trace this "Reformation" the
fourth directly back to "Reformation" the third; and we
shall finally see that this famous and "glorious" affair, all
Protestant as it was, did at last bring, though it crossed the
Atlantic to fetch it, that dawn of liberty which the
Catholics began to behold at the end of a night of cruel
slavery which had lasted for more than two hundred years.
But I must not even here, lest it should not occur to my
mind again, omit to notice, and to request the reader to
notice, that of the above-mentioned colonies the only ones
that wholly abstained from religious persecution, the only
ones that from the first settling proclaimed complete religious liberty, were those granted by patent to the Duke of
York (afterwards the Catholic James II.), to Lord

Baltimore, a Catholic nobleman, and to William Penn, who suffered long imprisonment for his adherence to this Popish king. We shall, by-and-by, find all the colonies cordially united in declaring the character of a Protestant king to be "marked by every act that may define a tyrant;" but this much we know, at any rate, — that the colonies granted to and settled by Catholics, and by Penn, an adherent of James, were the only ones that had from first to last proclaimed and strictly adhered to complete freedom as to matters of religion, and that, too, after the Protestants at home had for more than a hundred years been most cruelly and unremittingly persecuting the Catholics.

CHAPTER FOURTEEN

We have seen that King James and his family were set aside because they were Catholics; and we are to bear that in mind, not forgetting at the same time that Alfred the Great was a Catholic, and that those kings of England who really conquered France and won that title of King of France which George III. gave up, were also Catholics. But we are now particularly to bear in mind that James, an Englishman, was set aside, that William, a Dutchman, was made king in his stead, and that James's heirs were set aside too, because he and they were Catholics. Bearing these things constantly in mind, we shall now see what took place, and how the "Protestant Reformation" worked till it produced the debt, the banks, the stock-jobbers and the American Revolution.

James found faithful adherents in his Irish subjects, who fought and bled in his cause with all that bravery and disregard of life of which so many Irishmen have given proof. But with the aid of Dutch and German armies paid by England the "Deliverer" finally triumphed over James and the Irish, and the whole kingdom submitted to the sway of the former. It is hardly necessary to say that the Catholics were now doomed to suffer punishments heretofore unknown, and that if their faith still existed in the kingdom, it could scarcely be owing to anything short of the immediate superintendence of Providence. The oppressions which they had had to endure under former sovereigns were terrible enough, but now began a series of acts against them such as the world never heard of before. I shall, further on, have to give a sketch at least of these acts, which we shall find going on increasing in number and in severity, and at last presenting a mass of punishment which but to think of makes one's blood run cold, when all of a sudden, in the eighteenth year of George III, came the American Revolution, which grew out of the English Revolution, and (mark the justice of God!) which produced the first relaxation in this most dreadfully penal code.

But how did the American Revolution grow out of the Dutch Deliverer's or "Glorious" Revolution? We shall by-and-by see the American Revolution producing wonderful events, and therefore we must with the greatest possible care trace it to its true source.

King James had, as we have seen, been received in France. Louis XIV. treated him as King of England, Scotland, and Ireland. William hated Louis for this, and England had to pay for that hatred. All those who had assisted in a conspicuous manner to bring in the "Deliverer" were now embarked in the same boat with him. They were compelled to humour and to yield to him. They, historians say, wished to give the crown solely to his wife, because, she being James's daughter, there would have been less of revolution in this than in giving the crown to an utter alien. But he flatly told them that he "would not hold his power by the apron strings," and, the dispute having continued for some time, he cut the matter short with them by declaring that if they did not give him the crown he would go back to Holland and leave them their old sovereign! This was enough; they gave him the crown without more hesitation, and they found that they had got not only a "deliverer" but a master at the same time.

The same reasons that induced a submission to this conduct in the "Deliverer," induced the same parties to go cordially along with him in his war against France. There was James in France; a great part of his people were still for him; if France were at peace with England the communication could not be cut off. Therefore war with France was absolutely necessary to the maintenance of William on the throne; and if he were driven from the throne, what was to become of those who had obtained from him, as the price of their services in bringing him in, immense grants of crown lands and various other enormous emoluments, none of which they could expect to retain for a day if James were restored? Besides this, there was the danger, and very great danger, too, to their own estates and their lives; for though that which they did was and is called a "glorious revolution," it would, if James had been restored, have been called by a very different name; and that name would not have been an empty sound, it would have been applied to very practical purposes, and the chances are that very few of the principal actors would have wholly escaped. And there were, moreover, the possessors of the immense property of the Church founded and endowed by our fathers. The confiscation of this was not yet of so ancient a date as to have been forgotten. Tradition is very long-lived. Many and many then alive knew all the story well. They had heard their grandfathers say that the Catholic Church kept all the poor, that the people were then better off; and they felt, the whole of the people felt, that England had lost by the change. Therefore, in case of the restoration of James, the possessors of Church property, whether they were lay or clerical, might reasonably have their fears.

Thus, all these deeply interested parties, who were also the most powerful parties in the kingdom, were for a war with France, which they rightly regarded as absolutely necessary to the keeping of William on the throne, and to the quiet enjoyment of their great possessions, if not actually to the safety of their lives. This ought therefore to have been called "a war to preserve Church property, crown lands and other great emoluments, to their present possessors." But those who make wars, like those who make confiscations of property belonging to the Church and poor, generally know how to give them a good name, and accordingly this was called and proclaimed as a war "to preserve the Protestant religion, and to keep out Popery and slavery." It was a real "no-popery" war, and though attended with the most dreadful consequences to the nation, it answered all the purposes of its inventors. The history of this war as an affair of fighting is of little consequence to us. It was, indeed, attended in this respect with disgrace enough, but it answered the great object of its inventors. It did not hurt France, it did not get rid of James and his son, but it made the English people identify their old king and his son with the foreign enemies of England! That was what the inventors of the war wanted, and that they completely got. It was in vain that King James protested that he meant no harm to England; it was in vain that he reminded the people that he had been compelled to flee to France; in vain his declarations that the French only wanted to assist in restoring him to his rights. They saw him in France, they saw the French fighting for him and against England, that was quite sufficient. Men do not reason in such a case, and this the inventors of this war knew very well.

But though passion muddles the head, though even honest feeling may silence the reasoning faculties, the purse is seldom to be quieted so easily; and this war, though for "the preservation of the Protestant religion and for keeping out Popery and slavery," soon began to make some most dreadful tugs at this most sensitive part of those accoutrements that almost make part and parcel of the human frame. The expenses of this famous "no-popery" war ... Good God! what has this kingdom not suffered for that horrid and hypocritical cry!... The expenses of this famous "no-popery" war were enormous. The taxes were, of course, in proportion to those expenses, and the people, who already paid more than four times as much as they had paid in the time of James, began not only to murmur but to give no very insignificant signs of sorrow for having been "delivered!" France was powerful, the French king liberal and zealous, and the state of things was ticklish. Force, as far as law and the suspension of law could go, was pretty fairly put in motion; but a scheme was at last hit upon to get the money, and yet not to tug so very hard at that tender part, the purse.

An Act of Parliament was passed in the year 1694, being the 5th year of William and Mary, chapter 20, the title of which act is in the following words, — words that every man should bear in mind, words fatal to the peace and happiness of England, words which were the precursor of a scourge greater than ever before afflicted any part of God's creation: — "An Act for granting to their Majesties several rates and duties upon tonnage of ships and vessels, and upon beer, ale, and other liquors, for securing certain recompenses and advantages in the said Act mentioned, to such persons as shall voluntarily advance the sum of fifteen hundred thousand pounds towards carrying on the war against France." This act lays certain duties, sufficient to pay the interest of this sum of £1,500,000. Then it points out the manner of subscribing, the mode of paying the interest, or annuities, and then it provides that, if so much of the whole sum be subscribed by such a time, the subscribers shall have a charter under the title of "The Governor and Company of the Bank of England"!

Thus arose loans, funds, banks, bankers, bank-notes, and a national debt; things that England had never heard or dreamed of before this war "for preserving the Protestant religion as by law established;" things without which she had had a long and glorious career of many centuries, and had been the greatest and happiest country in the world; things which she never would and never could have heard of, had it not been for what is audaciously called the "Reformation," seeing that to lend money at interest, that is to say, for gain, that is to say to receive money for the use of money, seeing that to do this was contrary and still is contrary to the principles of the Catholic Church, and amongst Christians or professors of Christianity such a thing was never heard of before that which is impudently called "the Reformation." The Rev. Mr. O'Callaghan, in his excellent little work, which I had the honour to republish last winter, and which ought to be read by every man, and especially every young man, in the kingdom, has shown that the ancient philosophers, the Fathers of the Church, and the decisions of Pope and Councils, all agree, all declare that to take money for the use of money is sinful. Indeed, no such thing was ever attempted to be justified until the savage Henry VIII. had cast off the supremacy of the Pope.

This monstrous thing, the usury or funding system, was not only a Protestant invention, not only arose out of the "Reformation," not only was established for the express purpose of carrying on a war for the preservation of this Church of England against the efforts of Popery, but the inventor, Burnet, was the most indefatigable advocate for the "Reformation" that had ever existed.

Burnet, whose first name, as the Scotch call it, was Gilbert, was in the first place a political church parson, next he was a monstrously lying historian, next he was a Scotchman, and lastly he received the thanks of Parliament for his *History of the Reformation*, that is to say, a mass of the most base falsehoods and misrepresentations that ever were put upon paper; so that the instrument was the very fittest that could have been found on earth. This man had, at the accession of James II, gone to Holland, where he became secretary to William (afterwards the "Deliverer"), and where he corresponded with and aided the "Glorious Revolutionizers" in England, and in 1689, the year after the "deliverance," the "Deliverer" made him Bishop of Salisbury as a reward for his "glorious revolution" services.

This was the fittest man in the world to invent that which was destined to be a scourge to England. Though become a bishop he was still a most active politician; who invented, who advised, and who, backed by the "Deliverer," caused to be adopted the schemes of borrowing, of mortgaging the taxes, and of pawning the property and labour of future generations. Pretty "deliverance"! Besides sparing the purses of the people and quieting their discontents on account of taxes, this scheme had a further and still more important object in view, namely, to make all those who had money to lend wish to see the new king and new dynasty and all the grants and emoluments of the "glorious revolution" folks upheld.

The case was this: James II. and his son had been set aside because they were Catholics, a "glorious revolution" had been made, the great makers of it had immense possessions, which had been public or Church possessions. If James were restored all these would be taken from them, together with all the titles of nobility, all the bishoprics, and in short everything granted by the "Deliverer." And as the "Deliverer" was liable to die, it was necessary to these great possessors and "glorious" actors to take care, if possible, that James or his son should not be the successors of the "Deliverer." Acts of Parliament were passed to provide against this danger; but still, experience had shown that acts of Parliament were in some cases of but little avail when the great body of the people, feeling acutely, were opposed to them. Therefore something was wanted to bind great numbers of the people fast to the new dynasty. The cry of "no popery" had some power, but it had not power sufficient to weigh down that which, in later times, Castlereagh had the insolence to call the "ignorant impatience of taxation," and for which impatience the English were in former times always remarkable.

The "Deliverer" and all those who had brought him in, together with all those who had been fattened or elevated by him, were, as I said before, embarked in the same boat: but the great body of the people were not yet thus embarked. But if all, or a great part of those who had money to lend, could by the temptation of great gain be induced to lend their money on interest to the government, if they could be induced to do this, it was easy to see that all this description of persons would then be embarked in the same boat too; and that they who must necessarily be a class having great influence in the community would be amongst the most zealous supporters of the "Deliverer," and the "glorious" aiders, abettors, and makers of the "revolution" which had just taken place.

For these purposes this funding system was invented. It had the two-fold object of raising money to carry on the "no-popery" war and of binding to the "no-popery" government all those persons who wished to lend money at high interest, and these were, as is always the case, the most greedy, most selfish, least public-spirited, and most base and slavish and unjust part of the people. The scheme, which was quite worthy of the mind of the Protestant Bishop Burnet, answered its purposes: it enabled the "Deliverer" to carry on the "no-popery" war, it bound fast to the "Deliverer" and his bringers-in all the base and selfish and greedy and unfeeling part of those who had money. The scheme succeeded in effecting its immediate objects, but, good God! what a scourge did it provide for future generations! What troubles, what shocks, what sufferings it had in store for a people whose rulers, in an evil hour, resorted to such means for the purpose of causing to be trampled under foot those whose only crime was that of adhering to the faith of their fathers!

The sum at first borrowed was a mere trifle. It deceived by its seeming insignificance. But it was very far from being intended to stop with that trifle. The inventors knew well what they were about. Their design was to mortgage, by degrees, the whole of the country, all the lands, all the houses, and all other property, and even all labour, to those who would lend their money to the state. The thing soon began to swell at a great rate, and before the end of the "glorious" no-popery war, the interest alone of the debt, the annual interest, amounted to £1,310,492 a year, which, observe, was a greater sum than the whole of the taxes had yearly amounted to in the reign of the Catholic James II! So that here were taxes laid on for ever, mind that.

However, we must not anticipate. We shall further on see something of the probable ultimate effects of this dreadful scheme. At present we have to see how it, together with the "glorious revolution" out of which it arose, led to and produced the American revolution, or "Reformation" the fourth, by which two things were accomplished; first, the lopping off of a large and valuable part of the dominions of England; secondly, the creating of a new mercantile and naval power, capable of disputing with her that dominion of the sea which has for so many ages been her chief glory, and without possessing which she must become a second-rate power in Europe. These were the things which were accomplished by the American Revolution, and therefore let us now see what it was that produced that revolution, or rather, let us see how it grew directly out of the "glorious revolution" and its "no-popery" wars and debts.

Burnet's contrivance did very well for present use: it made the nation deaf to the voice of all those who foreboded mischief from it, it made all those who were interested in the funds advocates for taxation; the deep scheme set the rich to live upon the poor, and made the former have no feeling for those who bore the burden of the taxes; in short, it divided the nation into two classes, the tax-payers and the tax-eaters, and these latter had the government at their back. The great protection of the people of England always had been, that they could not be taxed without their own consent. This was always in Catholic times the great principle of the English government, and it is expressly and most explicitly asserted in Magna Charta, which was the work of a Catholic archbishop of Canterbury more than of anybody else. But how was it to be expected that this grand principle would be maintained, when a large part of the rich people themselves lived upon taxes; when a man's next-door neighbour received the taxes paid by that man; when, in short, the community was completely divided, one part having a powerful interest in upholding that which was oppressive and ruinous to the other part?

Taxes, of course, went on increasing, and the debt went on in the same way. The Protestant interest demanded more wars, and brought on a couple of civil wars. Taxation marched on with dreadful strides. The people did not like it. At the "glorious revolution" it had been settled and enacted that there should be a new Parliament called every three years at least, and this had been held forth as one of the great gains of the "glorious revolution." Another "great gain" was that no pensioner and no placeman were to sit in the House of Commons. These things were enacted, they were laws of the land, they were held forth to the people as great things gained by "Glorious." This last act was soon repealed, and placemen and pensioners have sat in the House of Commons ever since! But the other act, the act securing the people a fresh choice every three years at least, that was a vital law. That law was in the new state of things, a state of taxes and debts, a state of things which demanded new taxes almost every year; in such a state of things frequent and new Parliaments, new choosings at short intervals, were absolutely necessary to give the people a chance, even so much as a chance of avoiding oppressive taxation, and oppression, indeed, of every sort. It was, in short, the only means of protection that was left to the people.

Yet to uphold the new system it was necessary to demolish even this barrier of liberty and property; and in the year 1715, being the first year of the reign of George I., chap xxxviii., this law, this vital law, this solemn compact between the Protestant dynasty and the people, was repealed and for ever abolished, and the three years were changed for seven, and that too, observe, by the very men whom the people had chosen to sit only for three years! Yes, men chosen by the people to sit for three years enacted that they would sit for seven; that they themselves would sit for seven; and that those who had chosen them, together with their descendants for ever, should have no choice at all unless they voted for men who might at the king's pleasure sit for seven years!

But this Septennial Bill, this measure which is perfectly matchless in its nature, and which has led to such dreadful effects; — this is a thing which we must have in its original black and white, and we must have every word of it too, for here we have a complete "no-popery" law, and of this law we are tasting the effects to the present hour, and we shall taste them for a long while yet to come. The following are the words, all the words, of this memorable Act:-

"Whereas in and by an Act of Parliament made in the sixth year of the reign of their late Majesties King William and Queen Mary (of ever blessed memory) intituled an Act for the frequent meeting and calling of Parliaments: It was among other things enacted that from thenceforth no Parliament whatsoever that should at any time thereafter be called, assembled or held, should have any continuance longer than for three years only at the farthest, to be accounted from the day on which by the writ of summons the said Parliament should be appointed to meet: And whereas it has been found by experience that the said clause hath proved very grievous and burthensome, by occasioning much greater and more continued expenses in order to elections of members to serve in Parliament, and more violent and lasting heats and animosities among the subjects of this realm than were ever known before the said clause was enacted, and the said provision, if it should continue, may probably at this juncture, when a restless and popish faction are designing and endeavouring to renew the rebellion within this kingdom and an invasion from abroad, be destructive to the peace and security of the government." "Be it enacted by the King's most Excellent Majesty, by and with the advice and consent of the Lords Spiritual and Temporal, and Commons, in Parliament assembled, and by the authority of the same, that this present

Parliament, and all Parliaments that shall at any time hereafter be called, assembled or held, shall and may respectively have continuance for seven years and no longer, to be
accounted from the day on which by the writ of summons
this present Parliament hath been or any future Parliament
shall be appointed to meet, unless this present or any such
Parliament hereafter to be summoned, shall be sooner dissolved by his Majesty, his heirs or successors."

So here it is again! The "restless popish faction" was at
work! So that the rights, the most precious rights of the
whole of the people, were to be taken away merely on
account of the designs and wishes of a "popish faction!"
What harm could a mere "faction" do at an election? The
truth is these pretences were false: the people, the great
body of the people, smarting under the lash of enormous
taxation, became disaffected towards the new order of
things; they were strongly disposed to revert to their former
state; it was suspected, and indeed pretty well known, that
they would at the next election have chosen almost everywhere members having the same sentiments, and therefore
it was resolved that they should not have the power of
doing it. However, the deed was done; we have felt the
effects of it from that day to this, and we have now to
remember that even this terrible curtailment of English liberty we owe to the hostility to the religion of our fathers,
that religion during the dominance of which there was
always a new House of Commons every time the
Parliament was assembled; that religion, along with which
were bound up the people's civil and political rights; that
religion, the followers of which, while it was predominant,
never heard of Parliaments for seven years or for three
years, or even for one year, but who, as often as they saw a
Parliament called, saw a Commons' House chosen for that
one session and for no more.

After the passing of the Septennial Act the people
would, of course, lose nearly all the control that they had
ever had with regard to the laying on of taxes and to the

expending of the public money. Accordingly taxes went on increasing prodigiously. The excise system, which had had a little beginning in former Protestant reigns, and the very name of which had never been heard of in Catholic times, now assumed somewhat its present form, and the "castles" of Englishmen became thenceforth things to be visited by excisemen. Things went on in this way until the reign of George III, when, by means of "no-popery" wars and other measures for "preserving the Protestant religion as by law established," the debt from £1,500,000 had swelled up to £146,682,844. The yearly interest of it had swelled up to £4,840,821, which was about four times as much as the whole annual amount of the taxes in the reign of the popish James II! And the whole of the yearly taxes had swelled up to £8,744,682. That is to say, about eight times as much as James had raised yearly on this same "no-popery" people!

In this dilemma, namely, the danger of touching the interest of the debt and the danger of continuing to pay that interest, a new scheme was resorted to, which it was hoped would obviate both these dangers. It was to tax the American colonies, and to throw a part first, and perhaps the whole in the end, of the "no-popery" debt upon their shoulders!

The Septennial gentlemen proceeded at first very slowly in their attempts to shift the pressure of the debt from their own shoulders to that of the Americans. They sent out tea to pay a tax; they imposed a stamp duty on certain things in the colonies; but they had a clever, a sharp-sighted and a most cool and resolute and brave people to deal with. The Americans had seen debts, and funds and taxation, and abject submission creep by slow degrees over the people of England, and they resolved to resist at once the complicated curse. The money-people there were not, like those in England, the owners of stock and funds. They were not, as the money-people of England were, embarked in the same boat with the government; if they had, there would have been more hesitation on the subject of resistance; if they had been entangled in Burnet's artful web, the Americans might at this day have been hardly known in the world, might have been a parcel of bands of poor devils doomed to toil for haughty and insolent masters. Happily for them, the Scotch bishop's deadly trammels had not reached them, and therefore they at once resolved not to submit to the Septennial commands.

It is curious enough that they should, as the "glorious" people had done, call themselves Whigs! But the Septennial people were Whigs too, so that there were now Whigs resisting Whigs. A Whig means, in England, one who approves of the setting of James and his heirs aside. A Whig means, in America, one who approves of the setting of George and his heirs aside. The English Whigs called a convention, so did those of America. The English Whigs published a declaration, containing charges against James; so did those of America against George. The charges against James were twelve in number. This is a favourite number with Whigs, for the American Whigs had twelve charges against George. We have seen what Protestants accused a Popish king of, and it is but fair for us to see what Protestants, and Catholics too, accused a Protestant king of. Blackstone, in justifying the "glorious" affair, took good care to say that the like was never to take place again, and the Septennial gentlemen declared, and I think enacted, that the king in future (being, of course, a Protestant) could do no wrong. Now the Americans seemed to think it hard that they should thus be positively forbidden to do what was so "glorious" in Englishmen. Blackstone had told them that to justify another revolution all the same circumstances must exist; not a part of them, but the whole of them. The king must not only endeavour to subvert the laws, he must not only commit acts of tyranny, but he must be a Catholic, and must have a design to overthrow the Protestant religion, and he must, into the bargain, have abdicated his authority by going out of the kingdom. So that, according to this lawyer, there never could by any possibility be a "glorious" revolution again, seeing that two essential circumstances must in any future case be wanting, as no Catholic was ever to be king again, and as no king was ever to do wrong any more.

But, alas! these American Whigs did not listen to Blackstone, though he had talked so piously about the "dark ages of monkish ignorance and superstition." They thought, nay they said, that a Protestant king might do wrong and had done wrong. They thought, or at least they said, that a king might abdicate his authority, not only without going out of the country, but also without ever having been in it! In short, they drew up, à la "glorious," charges against their Protestant king, his late Majesty; and as the charges against James II. are found in an Act of Parliament, so the charges against George III. are found in an Act of Congress, passed on the memorable 4th of July, 1776. These charges were as follows:-

"The history of the present King of Great Britain is a history of repeated injuries and usurpations, all having in direct object the establishment of an absolute tyranny over these States. To prove this, let facts be submitted to a candid world.

"I. He has refused to pass laws for the accommodation of large districts of people, unless those people would relinquish the right of representation in the legislature — a right inestimable to them, and formidable to tyrants only.

"II. He has called the legislative bodies at places unusual, uncomfortable, and distant from the repository of their public records, for the sole purpose of fatiguing them into compliance with his measures.

"III. He has dissolved representative houses repeatedly, for opposing with firmness his invasions on the rights of the people.

"IV. He has obstructed the administration of justice, by refusing his assent to laws for establishing judiciary powers.

"V. He has made judges dependent on his will alone for the tenure of their offices and the amount and payment of their salaries.

"VI. He has created a multitude of new offices, and sent hither swarms of officers to harass our people and eat their substance.

"VII. He has kept among us, in times of peace, standing armies without the consent of our legislatures.

"VIII. He has affected to render the military independent of, and superior to, civil power.

"IX. He has combined with others to subject us to a jurisdiction foreign to our constitution and un-acknowledged by our laws; giving his assent to their acts of pretended legislation.

"X. He has imposed taxes on us without our consent.

"XI. He has deprived us in many cases of the benefits of trial by jury.

"XII. He has abdicated government here, by declaring us out of his protection and waging war against us. In every stage of these oppressions we have petitioned for redress in the most humble terms: our repeated petitions have been answered by repeated injury. A prince whose character is thus marked by every act which defines a tyrant is unfit to be the ruler of a free people."

Now, justice to the memory of the late king demands that we expressly assert that here are some most monstrous exaggerations, and especially at the close; but does not that same justice demand of us, then, to be cautious how we give full credit to the charges made against James II? However, the question with us at the present moment is, not whether the grounds of one of these revolutions were better than those of the other, but whether the last revolution grew directly out of the former; and of the affirmative of this question no man who has read this chapter can, I think, entertain a doubt.

CHAPTER FIFTEEN

We have now traced the "Reformation," in its deeds, down from the beginning, in the reign of Henry VIII, to the American Revolution; and all that remains is to follow it along through the French Revolution and unto the present day.

The American Revolution, which, as we have seen, grew directly out of those measures which had been adopted in England to crush the Catholics and to extinguish their religion for ever, did, at its very outset, produce good to those same Catholics by inducing the English government to soften, for the sake of its own safety, that penal code by which they had so long been scourged.

We have seen how cruelly the Catholics were treated under Queen Elizabeth and James I. We have seen that Charles I, for whom they afterwards fought against Cromwell, treated them as cruelly as the two former. We have seen Charles II. most unmercifully abandon them to the persecutions of the Church by law established; and during this reign we have seen that the Protestants had the baseness, and the king the meanness, to suffer the lying inscription to be put on the Monument on Fish Street Hill, in the City of London, though Lord Clarendon (whose name the Law-Church holds in so much honour), in that work which the University of Oxford publishes at the "Clarendon Press," expressly says that a committee of the House of Commons, "who were very diligent and solicitous to make the discovery, never were able to find any probable evidence that there was any other cause of that woeful fire than the displeasure of Almighty God." What infamy then to charge the Catholics with it; what an infamy to put the lying inscription on the pillar; what an act of justice in James II. to efface it; what a shame to William to suffer it to be restored; and what is it to us, then, who now suffer it to remain without petioning its erasure!

But it was after James II. was set aside that the penal code grew really horrible. And here it is of the greatest consequence to the cause of truth that we trace this code to its real authors, namely, the clergy of the Established Church. This is evident enough throughout the whole of this Church's history; but until the reign of James II. the sovereign was of the Church religion, so that the persecutions appeared to come from him or her. But now, when the king was for softening the penal code, when the king was for toleration, now the world saw who were the real persecutors; and this is a matter to be fully explained and understood before we come to a more minute account of the code and to the causes which finally led to its, in great part, abolition.

James II. wished to put an end to the penal code, he wished for general toleration; he issued a proclamation suspending all penal laws relating to religion, and granting a general liberty of conscience to all his subjects. This was his offence. For this he and his family were set aside for ever! No man can deny this. The clergy of the Church set themselves against him. Six of the bishops presented to him an insolent petition against the exercise of this his prerogative, enjoyed and exercised by all his predecessors. They led the way in that opposition which produced the "glorious revolution," and they were the most active and most bitter of all the foes of that unfortunate king, whose only real offence was his wishing to give liberty of conscience to all his subjects, and by showing respect to whose mortal remains (displaced by the French Revolutionists) our present king has done himself very great honour.

Now we are going to see a sketch of this terrible code. It must be a mere sketch. It went on increasing in bulk and in cruelty from the coronation of Elizabeth till nearly twenty years after that of George III. It consisted, at last, of more than a hundred acts of Parliament. The code differed, in some respects, in its application with regard to England and Ireland respectively.

In England this code (1) stripped the peers of their

hereditary right to sit in Parliament; (2) it stripped gentle-men of their right to be chosen members of the Commons' House; (3) it took from all the right to vote at elections, and though Magna Charta says that no man shall be taxed without his own consent, it double-taxed every man who refused to abjure his religion and thus become an apostate; (4) it shut them out from all offices of power and trust, even the most insignificant; (5) it took from them the right of presenting to livings in the Church, though that right was given to Quakers and to Jews; (6) it fined them at the rate of £20 a month for keeping away from that Church to go to which they deemed apostacy; (7) it disabled them from keeping arms in their houses for their defence, from main-taining suits at law, from being guardians or executors, from practising in law or physic, from travelling five miles from their houses, and all these under heavy penalties in case of disobedience; (8) if a married woman kept away from church, she forfeited two-thirds of her dower, she could not be executrix to her husband, and might, during her hus-band's lifetime, be imprisoned, unless ransomed by him at £10 a month; (9) it enabled any four justices of the peace, in case a man had been convicted of not going to church, to call him before them, to compel him to abjure his religion, or, if he refused, to sentence him to banishment for life (without judge or jury), and if he returned he was to suffer death; (10) it enabled any two justices of the peace to call before them, without any information, any man that they chose above sixteen years of age, and if such man refused to abjure the Catholic religion and continued in his refusal for six months, he was rendered incapable of possessing land, and any land the possession of which might belong to him came into possession of the next Protestant heir, who was not obliged to account for any profits; (11) it made such man incapable of purchasing lands, and all contracts made by him or for him were null and void; (12) it imposed a fine of £10 a month for employing a Catholic schoolmaster in a private family, and £2 a day on the schoolmaster so employed; (13) it imposed £100 fine for sending a child to a Catholic foreign school, and the child so sent was disabled from ever inheriting, purchasing, or enjoying lands or profits, goods, debts, legacies, or sums of money; (14) it punished the saying of mass by a fine of £120, and the hearing of mass by a fine of £60; (15) any Catholic priest who returned from beyond the seas and who did not abjure his religon in three days afterwards, and also any person who returned to the Catholic faith, or procured another to return to it, this merciless, this sanguinary code punished with hanging, ripping out of bowels, and quartering.

In Ireland the code was still more ferocious, more hideously bloody, for in the first place all the cruelties of the English code had, as the work of a few hours, a few strokes of the pen, in one single act been inflicted on unhappy Ireland; and then, in addition, the Irish code contained, amongst many other violations of all the laws of justice and humanity, the following twenty most savage punishments:- (1) A Catholic schoolmaster, private or public, or even usher to a Protestant, was punished with imprisonment, banishment, and finally as a felon. (2) The Catholic clergy were not allowed to be in the country without being registered and kept as a sort of prisoners at large, and rewards were given (out of the revenue raised in part on the Catholics) for discovering them, £50 for an archbishop or bishop, £20 for a priest, and £10 for a schoolmaster or usher. (3) Any two justices of the peace might call before them any Catholic, order him to declare on oath where and when he heard mass, who were present, and the name and residence of any priest or schoolmaster that he might know of; and if he refused to obey this inhuman inquisition, they had power to condemn him (without judge or jury) to a year's imprisonment in a felon's gaol or to pay £20. (4) No Catholic could purchase any manors, nor even hold under a lease for more than thirty-one years. (5) Any Protestant, if he suspected any one of holding property in trust for a Catholic, or of being concerned in any sale, lease, mort-

gage, or other contract for a Catholic, any Protestant thus
suspecting might file a bill against the suspected trustee and
take the estate or property from him. (6) Any Protestant
seeing a Catholic tenant of a farm, the produce of which
farm exceeded the amount of the rent by more than one-
third, might dispossess the Catholic and enter on the lease
in his stead. (7) Any Protestant seeing a Catholic with a
horse worth more than five pounds might take the horse
away from him upon tendering him five pounds. (8) In
order to prevent the smallest chance of justice in these and
similar cases, none but known Protestants were to be jury-
men in the trial of any such cases. (9) Horses of Catholics
might be seized for the use of the militia, and besides this
Catholics were compelled to pay double towards the militia. (10) Merchants whose ships and goods might be taken
by privateers during a war with a Catholic prince were to be
compensated for their losses by a levy on the goods and
lands of the Catholics only, though, mind, Catholics were
at the same time impressed and compelled to shed their
blood in the war against that same Catholic prince. (11)
Property of a Protestant whose heirs at law were Catholics
was to go to the nearest Protestant relation, just the same as
if the Catholic heirs had been dead, though the property
might be entailed on them. (12) If there were no Protestant
heir, then, in order to break up all Catholic families, the
entail and all heirship were set aside, and the property was
divided, share and share alike, amongst all the Catholic
heirs. (13) If a Protestant had an estate in Ireland he was
forbidden to marry a Catholic in or out of Ireland. (14) All
marriages between Protestants and Catholics were
annulled, though many children might have proceeded
from them. (15) Every priest who celebrated a marriage
between a Catholic and a Protestant, or between two
Protestants, was condemned to be hanged. (16) A Catholic
father could not be guardian to, or have the custody of, his
own child, if the child, however young, pretended to be a
Protestant; but the child was taken from its own father and

put into the custody of a Protestant relation. (17) If any child of a Catholic became a Protestant, the parent was to be instantly summoned and to be made to declare upon oath the full value of his or her property of all sorts, and then the Chancery was to make such distribution of the property as it thought fit. (18) "Wives, be obedient unto your own husbands," says the great Apostle. "Wives, be disobedient to them," said this horrid code; for if the wife of a Catholic chose to turn Protestant it set aside the will of the husband and made her a participator in all his possessions in spite of him, however immoral, however bad a wife or bad a mother she might have been. (19) "Honour thy father and thy mother, that thy days may be long in the land which the Lord thy God giveth thee." "Dishonour them," said this savage code; for if any one of the sons of a Catholic father became a Protestant, this son was to possess all the father had, and the father could not sell, could not mortgage, could not leave legacies or portions out of his estate by whatever title he might hold it, even though it might have been the fruit of his own toil. (20) Lastly "the Church, as by law established" was, in her great indulgence, pleased not only to open her doors, but to award (out of the taxes) thirty pounds a year for life to any Catholic priest who would abjure his religion and declare his belief in hers!

Englishmen! is there a man, a single man, bearing that name, whose blood will not chill at this recital, who, when he reflects that these barbarities were inflicted on men because and only because they adhered with fidelity to the faith of their and our fathers, to the faith of Alfred, the founder of our nation, to the faith of the authors of Magna Charta and of all those venerable institutions of which we so justly boast, who, when he thus reflects, and when he, being as I am, a Protestant of the Church of England, further reflects that all these cruelties were inflicted for the avowed purpose of giving and preserving predominance to that Church, will not with me not only feel deep sorrow and shame for the past, but heartily join me in best endeavours to cause justice to be done to the sufferers for the time to come?

And is this the "tolerant, the mild, the meek Church as by law established"? Have we here the proofs of Protestant faith and good works? Was it thus that St. Austin and St. Patrick introduced, and that St. Swithun, and Alfred, and William of Wykham inculcated the religion of Christ? Was it out of works like these that the cathedrals, and the palaces, and the universities, and the laws, and the courts of justice arose?

But now, all of a sudden, in 1778, the face of things began to change; the Church as by law established was all at once thought capable of existing in safety with a great relaxation of the penal code! And without even asking it, the Catholics found the code suddenly softened by divers Acts of Parliament in both countries, and especially in Ireland! This humanity and generosity will surprise us; we shall wonder whence it came; we shall be ready to believe the souls of the parties to have been softened by a sort of miracle, until we look back to the last few paragraphs of Chapter 14. There we see the real cause of this surprising humanity and generosity; there we see the Americans unfurling the standard of independence, and having been backed by France, pushing on towards success, and thereby setting an example to every oppressed people in every part of the world, unhappy, trodden-down Ireland not excepted. Thus was fear gratified in a moment, at the very first demand, with a surrender of that which had for ages been refused to the incessant pleadings of justice and humanity.

This great event was soon followed by another still greater, namely, the French Revolution, or "Reformation" the fifth. Humiliation greater than the English government had to endure in the above event it is difficult to conceive; but the French Revolution taught the world what "Reformations" can do when pushed to their full and natural extent. In England the "Reformation" contented itself with plundering the convents and the poor of their all, and the secular clergy in part. But in France they took the whole, though we ought to mark well this difference, that in France they applied this whole to the use of the public; a bad use, perhaps, but to public use they applied the whole of the plunder, while in England the plunder was scrambled for and remained divided amongst individuals!

Well, but here was a great triumph for the clergy of the "Church as by law established"! They, above all men, must have hailed with delight the deeds of the French "Reformation"! No: but on the contrary were amongst the foremost in calling for war to put down that "Reformation"! What? Not like this "Reformation"? Why, here were convents broken up and monks and nuns dispersed; here were abbey lands confiscated; here was the Catholic religion abolished; here were Catholic priests hunted about and put to death in almost as savage a manner as those of England had been; here were laws, seemingly translated from our own code, against saying or hearing mass, and against priests returning into the kingdom; here was a complete annihilation (as far as legislative provisions could go) of that which our Church clergy called "idolatrous and damnable"; here was a new religion "established by law"; and, that no feature might be defective in the likeness, here was a royal family set aside by law for ever by what they called a "glorious revolution"; and there would have been an abdicating king, but he was by mere accident stopped in his flight, brought back and put to death, not, however, without an example to plead in the deeds of the English double-distilled Protestant "Reformation" people.

The French Revolution, though it caused numerous horrid deeds to be committed, produced, in its progress and in its end, a great triumph for the Catholics. It put the fidelity of the Catholic priests and the Protestant pastors to the test; and while not one of the former was ever seen to save his life by giving up his faith, all the latter did it without hesitation. It showed, at last, the people of a great kingdom returning to the Catholic worship by choice, when they might have been, and may now be, Protestants without the loss of any one right, immunity, or advantage, civil or military. But the greatest good that it produced fell to the lot of ill-treated Ireland. The Revolutionists were powerful, they were daring; they, in 1793, cast their eyes on Ireland; and now, for the second time, a softening of the penal code took place, making a change which no man living ever expected to see! Those who had been considered as almost beneath dogs, were now made capable of being magistrates; and now, amongst many other acts of generosity we saw established at the public expense a college for the education of Catholics exclusively, thus doing by law that which the law-givers had before made high treason! Ah! But there were the French with an army of four hundred thousand men, and there were the Irish people, who must have been something more or less than men if their breasts did not boil with resentment. Alas! that it should be said of England that the Irish have never appealed with success but to her fears!

And shall this always be said? Shall it ever be said again? Shall we not now, by sweeping away for ever every vestige of this once horrible and still oppressive code, reconcile ourselves to our long ill-treated brethren and to our own consciences? The code is still a penal code; it is still a just ground of complaint; it has still disqualifications that are greatly injurious, and distinctions that are odious and insulting. (1) It still shuts Catholic peers out of those seats in the House of Lords which are their hereditary right, and Catholic gentlemen out of the House of Commons. (2) Then, as if caprice were resolved not to be behindhand with injustice, this code, which allows Catholic freeholders in Ireland to vote at elections for members of Parliament of the now "United Kingdom," refuses that right to all Catholics in England! (3) It excludes Catholics from all corporations. (4) It excludes them from all offices under the government of England, but admits them to inferior offices in Ireland. (5) It takes from them the right of presenting to any ecclesiastical benefice, though Quakers and Jews are allowed to enjoy that right. (6) It prevents them from endowing any school or college for educating children in the Catholic religion; and this, too, while there is now, by law established, a college for this very purpose supported out of the taxes! Here is consistency, and here is, above all things, sincerity! What! maintain out of the taxes a college to teach exclusively that religion which you call "idolatrous and damnable"? (7) This code still forbids Catholic priests to appear in their canonical habiliments, except in their chapels or in private houses; and it forbids the Catholic rites to be performed in any building which has a steeple or bells! What! forbid the use of steeples and bells to that religion which created all the steeples and all the bells; that built and endowed all the churches, all the magnificent cathedrals, and both the Universities! And why this insulting, this galling, prohibition? Why are you, who are the most gentle, amiable, and beautiful Church that law ever created —why, I say, are you so anxious to keep your rival out of sight? Nay, and out of hearing, too!

Well, then, is this code, is any fragment of it, longer to continue? Is it to continue now, when all idea of conversion to Protestantism is avowedly abandoned, and when it is notorious that the Catholic faith has, in spite of ages of persecution, done more than maintain its ground?

Here, then, we are, at the end of three hundred years from the day when Henry VIII. began the work of "Reformation"; here we are, after passing through scenes of plunder and of blood such as the world never beheld before; here we are with these awful questions still before us; and here we are, too, with forty sorts of Protestant religion, instead of the one fold in which our forefathers lived for nine hundred years; here we are, divided and split up into sects, each condemning all the rest to eternal flames; here we are, a motley herd of Church people, Methodists, Calvinists, Quakers, and Jews, chopping and changing with every wind; while the faith of Saint Austin and Saint

Patrick still remains what it was when it inspired the heart and sanctified the throne of Alfred.

Such, as far as religion is concerned, have been the effects of what is called the "Reformation": what its effects have been in other respects, how it has enfeebled and impoverished the nation, how it has corrupted and debased the people, and how it has brought barracks, taxing-houses, poor-houses, mad-houses and gaols, to supply the place of convents, hospitals, guilds, and alms-houses, we shall see in the next chapter.

CHAPTER SIXTEEN

This chapter is to conclude my task, which task was to make good this assertion, — that the event called the "Reformation" had impoverished and degraded the main body of the people of England and Ireland; and that as to its more remote consequences, they are, some of them, now before us in that misery, that beggary, that nakedness, that hunger, that everlasting wrangling and spite, which now stare us in the face and stun our ears at every turn, and which the "Reformation" has given us in exchange for the ease and happiness and harmony and Christian charity enjoyed so abundantly, and for so many ages, by our Catholic forefathers.

But I choose to be better rather than worse than my word: I did not pledge myself to prove anything as to the population, wealth, power, and freedom of the nation; but I will now show not only that the people were better off, better fed and clad, before the "Reformation" than they ever have been since, but that the nation was more populous, wealthy, powerful and free before than it ever has been since that event. But writers have, for ages, been so dependent on the government and the aristocracy, and the people have read and believed so much of what they have said, and especially in praise of the "Reformation" and its effects, that is is no wonder that they should think that in Catholic times England was a poor, beggarly spot, having a very few people on it, and that the "Reformation" and the house of Brunswick and the Whigs have given us all we possess of wealth, of power, of freedom, and have almost created us, or at least, if not actually begotten us, caused nine-tenths of us to be born. These are all monstrous lies, but they have succeeded for ages. Few men dared to attempt to refute them, and if anyone made the attempt he obtained few hearers, and ruin, in some shape or other, was pretty sure to be the reward of his virtuous efforts.

Populousness is a thing not to be proved by positive facts, because there are no records of the numbers of the people in former times, and because those which we have in our own day are notoriously false. That England was more populous in Catholic times than it is now we must believe, when we know that in the three first Protestant reigns thousands of parish churches were pulled down, that parishes were united in more than two thousand instances, and when we know from the returns now before Parliament, that out of 11,761 parishes in England and Wales, there are upwards of a thousand which do not contain a hundred persons each, men, women and children. Then, again, the size of the churches. They were manifestly built, in general, to hold three, four, five or ten times the number of their present parishioners, including all the sectarians. What should men have built such large churches for? We are told of their "piety and zeal;" yes, but there must have been men to raise the buildings. The Lord might favour the work, but there must have been hands as well as prayers. And what motive could there have been for putting together such large quantities of stone and mortar, and to make walls four feet thick, and towers and steeples, if there had not been people to fill the buildings? And how could the labour have been performed? There must have been men to perform the labour; and can anyone believe that this labour would have been performed if there had not been a necessity for it? Appendix 7: Population of England and Ireland examines the issues.

The wealth of the country is a question easily decided. In the reign of Henry VIII, just before the "Reformation," the whole of the lands in England and Wales had, according to Hume, been rated, and the annual rental was found to be three millions; and, as to this, Hume quotes undoubted authorities. Appendix 8 sets out what I calculate the purchasing power of money and the value of rents to be as compared with the present day.

As to the power of the country compared with what it is now, what do we want more than the fact that for many centuries before the "Reformation" England held possession of a considerable part of France; that the "Reformation" took, as we have seen, the two towns of Boulogne and Calais from her, leaving her nothing but those little specks in the sea, Jersey and Guernsey? What do we want more than this? France was never a country that had any pretensions to cope with England until the "Reformation" began. Since the "Reformation" she has not only had such pretensions, but she has shown to all the world that the pretensions are well founded. She even at this moment holds Spain in despite of us, while in its course the "Reformation" has wrested from us a large portion of our dominions, and has erected them into a state more formidable than any we have ever before beheld. We have, indeed, great standing armies, arsenals, and barracks, of which our Catholic forefathers had none; but they were always ready for war nevertheless. They had the resources in the hour of necessity. They had arms and men; and those men knew what they were to fight for before they took up arms. It is impossible to look back, to see the respect in which England was held for so many, many ages, to see the deference with which she was treated by all nations, without blushing at the thought of our present state. None but the greatest potentates presumed to think of marriage alliances with England. Her kings and queens had kings and princes in their train. Nothing petty ever thought of approaching her. She was held in such high honour, her power was so universally acknowledged, that she had seldom occasion to assert it by war. And what has she been for the last hundred and fifty years? Above half the time at war; and with a debt never to be paid, the cost of that war, she now rests her hopes of safety solely on her capacity of persuading her well-known foes that it is not their interest to assail her. Her warlike exertions have been the effect, not of her resources, but of an anticipation of those resources. She has mortgaged, she has spent beforehand, the resources necessary for future defence. And there she now is, inviting insult and injury by her well-known weakness, and, in case of attack, her choice lies between foreign victory over her or internal convulsion. Power is relative. You may have more strength than you had, but if your neighbours have gained strength in a greater degree, you are, in effect, weaker than you were. And can we look at France and America, and can we contemplate the inevitable consequences of war, without feeling that we are fast becoming, and indeed that we are already become a low and little nation? Can we look back to the days of our Catholic ancestors, can we think of their lofty tone and of the submission instantly produced by their threats, without sighing, "Alas! those days are never to return"?

And as to the freedom of the nation, where is the man who can tell me of any one single advantage that the

"Reformation" has brought, except it be freedom to have forty religious creeds instead of one? Freedom is not an empty sound; it is not an abstract idea; it is not a thing that nobody can feel. It means, — and it means nothing else, — the full and quiet enjoyment of your own property. If you have not this, if this be not well secured to you, you may call yourself what you will, but you are a slave. Now, our Catholic forefathers took special care upon this cardinal point. They suffered neither kings nor parliaments to touch their property without cause clearly shown. They did not read newspapers, they did not talk about debates, they had no taste for "mental enjoyment;" but they thought hunger and thirst great evils, amd they never suffered anybody to put them to board on cold potatoes and water. They looked upon bare bones and rags as indubitable marks of slavery, and they never failed to resist any attempt to affix these marks upon them. You may twist the word freedom as long as you please, but at last it comes to quiet enjoyment of your own property, or it comes to nothing. Why do men want any of those things that are called political rights and privileges? Why do they, for instance, want to vote at elections for members of parliament? Oh! because they shall then have an influence over the conduct of those members. And of what use is that? Oh! then they will prevent the members from doing wrong. What wrong? Why, imposing taxes that ought not to be paid. That is all; that is the use, and the only use, of any right or privilege that men in general can have. Now how stand we in this respect compared with our Catholic ancestors? They did not perhaps all vote at elections. But do we? Do a fiftieth part of us? And have the main body of us any, even the smallest, influence in the making of laws and in the imposing of taxes? But the main body of the people had the Church to protect them in Catholic times. The Church had great power, and it was naturally the guardian of the common people; neither kings nor parliaments could set its power at defiance: the whole of our history shows that the Church was invariably on the side of the people, and that in all the much and justly boasted triumphs which our forefathers obtained over their kings and nobles the Church took the lead. It did this because it was dependent upon neither kings nor nobles; because, and only because, it acknowledged another head; but we have lost the protection of the Church, and have got nothing to supply its place; or rather, whatever there is of its power left has joined, or rather been engrossed by, the other branches of the state, leaving the main body of the people to the mercy of those other branches. "The liberties of England" is a phrase in every mouth, but what are those liberties? The laws which regulate the descent and possession of property; the safety from arrest, unless by due and settled process; the absence of all punishment without trial before duly authorised and well-known judges and magistrates; the trial by jury; the precautions taken by the divers writs and summonses; the open trial; the impartiality in the proceedings. These are the "liberties of England." And had our Catholic forefathers less of these than we have? Do we not owe them all to them? Have we one single law that gives security to property or to life which we do not inherit from them? The treadmill, the law to shut men up in their houses from sunset to sunrise, the law to banish us for life if we utter anything having a tendency to bring our "representatives" into contempt; these indeed we do not inherit, but may boast of them, and of many others of much about the same character, as being unquestionably of pure Protestant origin.

Poverty, however, is after all the great badge, the never-failing badge of slavery. Bare bones and rags are the true marks of the real slave. What is the object of government? To cause men to live happily. They cannot be happy without a sufficiency of food and of raiment. Good government means a state of things in which the main body are well fed and well clothed. It is the chief business of a government to take care that one part of the people do not cause the other part to live miserable lives. There can be no morality, no virtue, no sincerity, no honesty, amongst a people continually suffering from want; and it is cruel in the last degree to punish such people for almost any sort of crime, which is in fact, not crime of the heart, not crime of the perpetrator, but crime of his all-controlling necessities.

To what degree the main body of the people in England are now poor and miserable, how deplorably wretched they now are, this we know but too well; and now we will see what was their state before this vaunted "Reformation." I shall be very particular to cite my authorities here. I will infer nothing; I will give no "estimate," but refer to authorities such as no man can call in question, such as no man can deny to be proofs more complete than if founded on oaths of credible witnesses, taken before a judge and jury. I shall begin with the account which Fortescue gives of the state and manner of living of the English in the reign of Henry VI., that is, in the fifteenth century, when the Catholic Church was in the height of its glory. Fortescue was Lord Chief Justice of England for nearly twenty years; he was appointed Lord High Chancellor by Henry VI. Being in exile in France, in consequence of the wars between the Houses of York and Lancaster, and the King's son, Prince Edward, being also in exile with him, the Chancellor wrote a series of letters addressed to the prince, to explain to him the nature and effect of the laws of England, and to induce him to study them and uphold them. This work, which was written in Latin, is called *De Laudibus Legum Angliae* or *Praise the Laws of England*. This book was many years ago translated into English, and it is a book of law authority quoted frequently in our courts at this day. No man can doubt the truth of facts relating to such a work. It is a work written by a famous lawyer for a prince, it was intended to be read by other contemporary lawyers, and by all lawyers in future. The passage that I am about to quote, relating to the state of the English, was purely incidental; it was not intended to answer any temporary purpose. It must have been a true account.

The Chancellor, after speaking generally of the nature of the laws of England, and of the difference between them and the laws of France, proceeds to show the difference in their effects by a description of the state of the French people, and then by a description of the state of the English. His words, — words that, as I transcribe them, make my cheeks burn with shame ,— are as follows: "Besides all this, the inhabitants of France give every year to their king the fourth part of all their wines, the growth of that year; every vintner gives the fourth penny of what he makes of his wine by sale. And all the towns and boroughs pay to the king yearly great sums of money, which are assessed upon them for the expenses of his men-at-arms. So that the king's troops, which are always considerable, are subsisted and paid yearly by those common people who live in the villages, boroughs, and cities. Another grievance is, every village constantly finds and maintains two cross-bow-men at the least,— some find more, —well arrayed in all their accoutrements, to serve the king in his wars as often as he pleaseth to call them out, which is frequently done. Without any consideration had of these things, other very heavy taxes are assessed yearly upon every village within the kingdom for the king's service; neither is there ever any intermission or abatement of taxes. Exposed to these and other calamities, the peasants live in great hardship and misery. Their constant drink is water, neither do they taste throughout the year any other liquor, unless upon some extraordinary times or festival days. Their clothing consists of frocks or little jerkins made of canvas, no better than common sackcloth; they do not wear any woollens except of the coarsest sort, and that only in the garments under their frocks; nor do they wear any trowse but from the knees upwards, their legs being exposed and naked. The women go barefoot except on holidays. They do not eat flesh, except it be the fat of bacon, and that in very small quantities, with which they make a soup. Of other sorts, either boiled or roasted, they do not so much as taste, unless it be of the inwards and offals of sheep and bullocks, and the like, which are killed for the use of the better sort of people and the merchants, for whom also quails, partridges, hares, and the like, are reserved upon pain of the galleys: as for their poultry, the soldiers consume them, so that scarce the eggs, slight as they are, are indulged them by way of a dainty. And if it happen that a man is observed to thrive in the world and become rich, he is presently assessed to the king's tax, proportionably more than his poorer neighbours, whereby he is soon reduced to a level with the rest." Then comes his description of the English at the same time; those "priest-ridden" English whom Chalmers and Hume, and the rest of that tribe would fain have us believe were a mere band of wretched beggars. "The king of England cannot alter the laws or make new ones without the express consent of the whole people in parliament assembled. Every inhabitant is at his liberty fully to use and enjoy whatever his farm produceth, the fruits of the earth, the increase of his flock, and the like; all the improvements he makes, whether by his own proper industry or of those he retains in his service, are his own to use and to enjoy without the let, interruption, or denial of any. If he be in anywise injured or oppressed, he shall have his amends and satisfactions against the party offending. Hence it is that the inhabitants are rich in gold, silver, and in all the necessaries and conveniences of life. They drink no water, unless at certain times upon a religious score, and by way of doing penance. They are fed in great abundance with all sorts of flesh and fish, of which they have plenty everywhere; they are clothed throughout in good woollens; their bedding and other furniture in their houses are of wool, and that in great store. They are also well provided with all other sorts of household goods and necessary implements for husbandry. Every one according to his rank hath all things which conduce to make life easy and happy."

Go and read this to the poor souls who are now eating sea-weed in Ireland, who are detected in robbing the pig-troughs in Yorkshire, who are eating horse flesh and grains (draff) in Lancashire and Cheshire, who are harnessed like horses and drawing gravel in Hampshire and Sussex, who have 2d. a day allowed them by the magistrates in Norfolk, who are all over England worse fed than the felons in gaols. Go and tell them, when they raise their hands from the pig-trough or from the grains-tub and with their dirty tongues cry "No Popery," go, read to the degraded and deluded wretches this account of the state of their Catholic forefathers, who lived under what is impudently called "Popish superstition and tyranny," and in those times which we have the audacity to call "the dark ages."

Look at the then picture of the French; and, Protestant Englishmen, if you have the capacity of blushing left, blush at the thought of how precisely that picture fits the English now! Look at all the parts of the picture, the food, the raiment, the game. Good God! If anyone had told the old Chancellor that the day would come when this picture, and even a picture more degrading to human nature, would fit his own boasted country, what would he have said? What would he have said if he had been told that the time was to come when the soldier in England would have more than twice, nay, more than thrice the sum allowed to the day-labouring man; when potatoes would be carried to the field as the only food of the ploughman; when soup-shops would be opened to feed the English; and when the judges, sitting on that very bench on which he himself had sat for twenty years, would (as in the case last year of the complaint against the magistrates at Northallerton), declare that bread and water were the general food of working-people in England? What would he have said? Why, if he had been told that there was to be a "Reformation," accompanied by a total devastation of Church and Poor property, upheld by wars, creating an enormous debt and enormous taxes, and requiring a constantly standing army, — if he had been told this he would have foreseen our present state and would have wept for his country; but if he had, in addition, been told that even in the midst of all this suffering we should still have the ingratitude and the baseness to cry "No Popery," and the injustice and the cruelty to persecute those Englishmen and Irishmen who adhered to the faith of their pious, moral, brave, free and happy fathers, he would have said, "God's will be done: let them suffer."

But it may be said that it was not, then, the Catholic Church but the laws that made the English so happy, for the French had that Church as well as the English. Aye! But in England the Church was the very basis of the laws. The very first clause of Magna Charta provided for the stability of its property and rights. A provision for the indigent, an effectual provision, was made by the laws that related to the Church and its property; and this was not the case in France, and never was the case in any country but this; so that the English people lost more by a "Reformation" than any other people could have lost.

Fortescue's authority would of itself be enough, but I am not to stop with it. White, the late rector of Selbourne, in Hampshire, gives, in his history of that once famous village, an extract from a record, stating that for disorderly conduct men were punished by being "compelled to fast a fortnight on bread and beer!" This was about the year 1380 in the reign of Richard II. Oh! miserable "dark ages"! This fact must be true. White had no purpose to answer. His mention of the fact, or rather his transcript from the record, is purely incidental; and trifling as the fact is, it is conclusive as to the general mode of living in those happy days. Go, tell the harnessed gravel-drawers in Hampshire to cry "No Popery," for that if the Pope be not put down he may in time compel them to fast on bread and beer, instead of suffering them to continue to regale themselves on nice potatoes and pure water.

But let us come to Acts of Parliament, and first to the Act of the 24th year of Henry VIII, chapter 3. That Act fixes the price of meat. After naming the four sorts of meat, beef, pork, mutton and veal, the preamble has these words: "These being the food of the poorer sort." This is conclusive. It is an incidental mention of a fact. It is an Act of Parliament. It must have been true; and it is a fact that we know well, that even the judges have declared from the bench, that bread alone is now the food of the poorer sort. What do we want more than this to convince us that the main body of the people have been impoverished by the "Reformation?"

But I will prove by other Acts of Parliament this Act of Parliament to have spoken truth. These Acts declare what the wages of workmen shall be. There are several such Acts, but one or two may suffice. The Act of 23rd of Edward III. fixes the wages, without food, as follows. There are many other things mentioned, but the following will be enough for our purpose:-

	s.	d.
A woman hay-making or weeding corn for the day	0	1
A man filling dung-cart	0	3
A reaper	0	4
Mowing an acre of grass	0	6
Threshing a quarter of wheat	0	4

The price of shoes, cloth, and of provisions, throughout the time that this law continued in force was as follows:

	£	s.	d.
A pair of shoes	0	0	4
Russet broad-cloth the yard	0	1	1
A stall-fed ox	1	4	0
A grass-fed ox	0	16	0
A fat sheep unshorn	0	1	8
A fat sheep shorn	0	1	2
A fat hog two years old	0	3	4
A fat goose	0	0	2½
Ale, the gallon, by proclamation	0	0	1
Wheat the quarter	0	3	4
White wine the gallon	0	0	6
Red wine the gallon	0	0	4

These prices are taken from the *Preciosum* of Bishop Fleetwood, who took them from the accounts kept by the bursars of convents. All the world knows that Fleetwood's book is of undoubted authority.

We may, then, easily believe that "beef, pork, mutton and veal were the food of the poorer sort," when a dung-cart filler had more than the price of a fat goose and a-half for a day's work, and when a woman was allowed for a day's weeding the price of a quart of red wine! Two yards of the cloth made a coat for the shepherd, and as it cost 2s. 2d., the reaper would earn it in six and a half days; and the dung-cart man would earn very nearly a pair of shoes every day! The dung-cart filler would earn a fat shorn sheep in four days; he would earn a fat hog two years old in 12 days; he would earn a grass-fed ox in twenty days; so that we may easily believe that 'beef, pork, veal and mutton" were "the food of the poorer sort." And, mind, this was "a priest-ridden people," a people "buried in Popish superstition!" In our days of "Protestant light" and of "mental enjoyment" the "poorer sort" are allowed by the magistrates of Norfolk threepence a day for a single man able to work. That is to say, a halfpenny less than the Catholic dung-cart man had; and that threepence will get the "no popery" gentleman about six ounces of old ewe mutton, while the Popish dung-cart man got for his day rather more than the quarter of a fat sheep.

There! That settles the matter; and if the Bible Society and the "Education" and the "Christian knowledge" gentry would, as they might, cause this little book to be put into the hands of all their millions of pupils, it would, as far as relates to this kingdom, settle the question of religion for ever and ever. I have now proved that Fortescue's description of the happy life of our Catholic ancestors was correct. There wanted no proof, but I have given it. I could refer to divers other Acts of Parliament, passed during several centuries, all confirming the truth of Fortescue's account. And there are in Bishop Fleetwood's book many things that prove that the labouring people were most kindly treated by their superiors, and particularly by the clergy; for instance, he has an item in the expenditure of a convent, "30 pair of autumnal gloves for the servants." This was sad "superstition." In our "enlightened" and Bible-reading age, who thinks of gloves for ploughmen? We have priests as well as the "dark ages" people had; ours ride as well as theirs, but, theirs fed at the same time; both mount, but theirs seem to have used the rein more and the spur less. It is curious to observe that the pay of persons in high situations was, as compared with that of the present day, very low when compared with the pay of the working classes. If you calculate the year's pay of the dung-cart man, you will find it, if multiplied by 20 (which brings it to our money) to amount to £91 a year, while the average pay of the judges did not exceed £60 a year of the then money, and, of course, did not exceed £1,200 a year of our money. So that a judge had not so much pay as fourteen dung-cart fillers. To be sure, judges had in those "dark ages," when Littleton and Fortescue lived and wrote, pretty easy lives; for Fortescue says that they led lives of great "leisure and contemplation," and that they never sat in court but three hours in a day, from 8 to 11. Alas! if they had lived in this "enlightened age" they would have found little time for their "contemplation"! They would have found plenty of work, they would have found that theirs was no sinecure, at any rate, and that ten times their pay was not adequate to their enormous labour. Here is another indubitable proof of the great and general happiness and harmony and honesty and innocence that reigned in the country. The judges had lives of leisure! In that one fact, incidentally stated by a man who had been twenty years Chief Justice of the Queen's Bench, we have the true character of the so long calumniated religion of our fathers.

The Act, 27 Henry VIII, chap. 25, began the poor laws. The monasteries were not actually seized on till the next year; but the fabric of the Catholic Church was, in fact, tumbling down, and instantly the country swarmed with necessitous people, and open begging, which the government of England had always held in great horror, began to disgrace this so lately happy land. To put a stop to this the above Act authorised sheriffs, magistrates, and churchwardens to cause voluntary alms to be collected; and at the same time it punished the persevering beggar by slicing off part of his ears, and, for a second offence, put him to death as a felon! This was the dawn of that "Reformation" which we are still called upon to admire and to praise!

"The pious young Saint Edward," as Fox the Martyr-man most impiously calls him, began his Protestant reign, 1st year Edward VI, chap. 3, by an Act, punishing beggars by burning them with a red-hot iron and by making them slaves for two years, with power in their masters to make them wear an iron collar, and to feed them upon bread and water and refuse meat! For even in this case still there was meat for those who had to labour: the days of cold potatoes and of bread and water alone were yet to come; they were reserved for our "enlightened" and Bible-reading days, our days of "mental enjoyment." And as to horse flesh and draff (grains), they appear never to have been even thought of. If the slave ran away, or were disobedient, he was by this Protestant Act to be a slave for life. This Act came forth as a sort of precursor of the Acts to establish the Church of England. Horrid tyranny! The people had been plundered of the resource which Magna Charta, which justice, which reason, which the law of nature gave them. No other resource had been provided, and they were made actual slaves, branded and chained because they sought by their prayers to allay the cravings of hunger!

Next came "good Queen Bess," who, after trying her hand eight times without success to cause the poor to be relieved by alms, passed that compulsory Act which is in force to the present day. All manner of shifts had been resorted to in order to avoid this provision for the poor. During this and the two former reigns licences to beg had been granted. But at last the compulsory assessment came, that true mark, that indelible mark of the Protestant Church as by law established. This assessment was put off to the last possible moment, and it was never relished by those who had got the spoils of the Church and poor. But it was a measure of absolute necessity. All the racks, all the law-martial of this cruel reign could not have kept down the people without this Act, the authors of which seem to have been ashamed to state the grounds of it, for it has no preamble whatever. The people so happy in former times, the people described by Fortescue, were now become a nation of ragged wretches. Defoe, in one of his tracts, says that Elizabeth in her progress through the kingdom, upon seeing the miserable looks of the crowds that came to see her, frequently exclaimed, "pauper ubique jacet," that is, the poor cover the land. And this was that same country in which Fortescue left a race of people, "having all things which conduce to make life easy and happy"!

Things did not mend much during the reigns of the Stuarts, except in as far as the poor-law had effect. This rendered unnecessary the barbarities that had been exercised before the passing of it; and as long as taxation was light the paupers were comparatively little numerous. But when the taxes began to grow heavy, the projectors were soon at work to find out the means of putting down pauperism. Amongst these was one Child, a merchant and banker, whose name was Josiah, and who had been made a knight or baronet, for he is called Sir Josiah. His project, which was quite worthy of his calling, contained a provision, in his proposed Act, to appoint men to be called "Fathers of the poor;" and one of the provisions relating to these "Fathers" was to be, "that they may have power to send such poor as they may think fit into any of his Majesty's plantations!" That is to say, to transport and make slaves of them! And, gracious God! this was in Fortescue's country! This was in the country of Magna Charta! And this monster dared to publish this project! And we cannot learn that any man had the soul to reprobate the conduct of so hard-hearted a wretch.

When the "Deliverer" had come, when a "glorious revolution" had taken place, when a war had been carried on and a debt and a bank created, and all for the purpose of putting down Popery for ever, the poor began to increase at such a frightful rate that the Parliament referred the subject to the Board of Trade, to inquire and to report a remedy. Locke was one of the commissioners, and a passage in the Report of the Board is truly curious. "The multiplicity of the poor, and the increase of the tax for their maintenance, is so general an observation and complaint that it cannot be doubted of; nor has it been only since the last war that this evil has come upon us; it has been a growing burden on the kingdom this many years, and the last two reigns felt the increase of it as well as the present. If the cause of this evil be looked into, we humbly conceive it will be found to have proceeded, not from the scarcity of provisions, nor want of employment for the poor; since the goodness of God has blessed these times with plenty no less than the former; and a long peace during three reigns gave us as plentiful a trade as ever. The growth of the poor must therefore have some other cause, and it can be nothing else but the relaxation of discipline and corruption; virtue and industry being as constant companions on the one side, as vice and idleness are on the other."

So the fault was in the poor themselves! It does not seem to have occurred to Mr. Locke that there must have been a cause for this cause. He knew very well that there was a time when there were no paupers at all in England; but being a fat placeman under the "Deliverer," he could hardly think of alluding to that interesting fact, "relaxation of discipline"! What discipline? What did he mean by discipline? the taking away of the Church and the poor's property, the imposing of heavy taxes, the giving of low wages compared with the price of food and raiment, the drawing away of the earnings of the poor, to be given to paper-harpies and other tax-eaters, these were the causes of the hideous and disgraceful evil; this he knew very well, and therefore it is no wonder that his report contained no remedy.

After Locke came, in the reign of Queen Anne, Defoe, who seems to have been the father of the present race of projectors, Malthus and Lawyer Scarlett being merely his humble followers. He was for giving no more relief to the poor; he imputed their poverty to their crimes, and not their crimes to their poverty; and their crimes he imputed to "their luxury, pride and sloth." He said the English labouring people ate and drank three times as much as foreigners! How different were the notions of this insolent French Protestant from those of the Chancellor Fortescue, who looked upon the good living of the people as the best possible proof of good laws, and seems to have delighted in relating that the English were "fed in great abundance with all sorts of flesh and fish"!

If Defoe had lived to our "enlightened age" he would, at any rate, have seen no "luxury" amongst the poor, unless he would have grudged them horse-flesh, draff (grains), seaweed, or the contents of the pig-trough. From his day to the present there have been a hundred projects and more than fifty laws to regulate the affairs of the poor. But still the pauperism remains for the Catholic Church to hold up in the face of the Church of England. "Here," the former may say to the latter, "here, look at this; here is the result of your efforts to extinguish me; here, in this one evil, in this never ceasing, this degrading curse, I am more than avenged, if vengeance I were allowed to enjoy; urge on the deluded potato-crammed creatures to cry, 'No Popery' still; and when they retire to their straw, take care not to remind them of the cause of their poverty and degradation."

Hume, in speaking of the sufferings of the people in the first Protestant reign, says, that at last those sufferings "produced good," for that they "led to our present situation." What, then; he deemed our present situation a better one than that of the days of Fortescue! To be sure Hume wrote fifty years ago, but he wrote long after Child, Locke, and Defoe. Surely enough the "Reformation" has led to "our then present, and our now present situation." It has "at last" produced the bitter fruit of which we are now tasting. Evidence given, by a clergy-man too, and published by the House of Commons in 1824, states the labouring people of Suffolk to be a nest of robbers, too deeply corrupted ever to be reclaimed; evidence of a Sheriff of Wiltshire (in 1821) states the common food of the labourers in the field to be cold potatoes; a scale, published by the magistrates of Norfolk, in 1825, allows threepence a day to a single labouring man; the judges of the Court of King's Bench (1825) have declared the general food of the labouring people to be bread and water; intelligence from the northern counties (1826), published upon the spot, informs us that great numbers of people are nearly starving, and that some are eating horse-flesh and grains, while it is well known that the country abounds in food; and while the clergy have recently put up from the pulpit the rubrical thanksgiving for times of plenty, a law recently passed, making it felony to take an apple from a tree, tells the world that our characters and lives are thought nothing worth, or that this nation, once the greatest and most moral in the world, is now a nation of incorrigible thieves, and, in either case, the most impoverished, the most fallen, the most degraded that ever saw the light of the sun.

I have now performed my task. I have made good the positions with which I began. Born and bred a Protestant of the Church of England, having a wife and numerous family professing the same faith, having the remains of most dearly beloved parents lying in a Protestant churchyard, and trusting to conjugal or filial piety to place mine by their side, I have in this undertaking had no motive, I can have had no motive, but a sincere and disinterested love of truth and justice. It is not for the rich and the powerful of my countrymen that I have spoken; but for the poor, the persecuted, the proscribed. I have not been unmindful of the unpopularity and the prejudice that would attend the enterprise; but when I considered the long, long triumph of calumny over the religion of those to whom we owe all that we possess that is great and renowned; when I was convinced that I could do much towards the counteracting of that calumny; when duty so sacred bade me speak, it would have been baseness to hold my tongue, and baseness superlative would it have been, if, having the will as well as the power, I had been restrained by fear of the shafts of falsehood and of folly. To be clear of self-reproach is amongst the greatest of human consolations; and now, amidst all the dreadful perils which the event that I have treated of has at last surrounded my country, I can, while I pray God to save her from still further devastation and misery, safely say that neither expressly nor tacitly am I guilty of any part of the cause of her ruin.

APPENDICES

APPENDIX 1

PAYMENTS TO THE POPE

The money of England went to the Pope. Popes cannot live, and keep courts and ambassadors, and maintain great state, without money, any more than other people. A part of the money of England went to the Pope; but a part also of that of every other Christian nation took the same direction. This money was not, however, thrown away. It was so much given for the preservation of unity of faith, peace, good will, and charity and morality. We shall, in the broils that ensued, and in the consequent subsidies and bribes to foreigners, soon see that the money which went to the Pope was extremely well laid out. But how we Protestants strain at a gnat, while we swallow camels by whole caravans! We have since given more to foreigners in one single year than the Popes ever received from our ancestors in four centuries. We have bowed, for years, to a Dutchman, who was no heir to the crown any more than one of our workhouse paupers, and who had not one drop of English blood in his veins; and we have sent annually to Hanoverians and other foreigners, under the name of half-pay, more money than was ever sent to the Pope in twenty years. From the time of the "Glorious Revolution" we have been paying two thousand pounds a year to the heirs of "Marshal Schomberg," who came over to help the Dutchman, and this is, mind, to be paid as long as there are such heirs of Marshal Schomberg, which, to use the elegant, and logical, and philosophical phrase of our great "Reformation" poet, will, I dare say, be "for ever and a day." And have we forgotten the Bentincks, and all the rest of the Dutch tribe. who had estates of the crown heaped upon them? and do we talk, then, of the degradation and the loss of money occasioned by the supremacy of the Pope?

If, however, we still insist that the Pope's supremacy and its accompanying circumstances produced ignorance, super-stition and slavery, let us act the part of sincere, consistent and honest men. Let us knock down, or blow up, the cathe-drals and colleges and old churches: let us sweep away the three courts, the twelve judges, the circuits and the jury boxes; let us demolish all that we inherit from those whose religion we denounce, and whose memory we affect so heartily to despise; let us demolish all this, and we shall have left — all our own — the capacious jails and peniten-tiaries, the stock-exchange, the hot, ankle and knee-swelling and lung-destroying cotton-factories; the whiskered standing army and its splendid barracks; the par-son-captains, parson-lieutenants, parson-ensigns and par-son-justices, the poor-rates and the pauper-houses; and, by no means forgetting that blessing which is peculiarly and doubly and "gloriously" Protestant, — the National Debt. Ah! people of England, how have you been deceived!

APPENDIX 2

OTHER AUTHORS' VIEWS
OF THE BENEFITS OF MONASTICISM

In Chapters 4 and 5 I appeared to content myself with the authority of the Protestant Bishop Tanner, as a defender of monastic institutions against the attacks of Hume; I had in reserve other authorities in abundance, some of which I should then have cited. Bishop Tanner goes, indeed, quite home to every point; but the matter is of such great impor-tance, when we are about to view the destruction of these institutions, that out of fifty authorities that I might refer to I will select four. I will take one foreign and two English; and, observe, they are all Protestant authorities.

Mallet, History of the Swiss, vol. i, p.105: "The monks

softened by their instructions the ferocious manners of the people, and opposed their credit to the tyranny of the nobility, who knew no other occupation than war and grievously oppressed their neighbours. On this account the government of monks was preferred to theirs. The people sought them for judges. It was an usual saying, that it was better to be governed by the bishop's crozier than the monarch's sceptre."

Drake, Literary Hours, vol.ii, p.435: " The monks of Cassins," observes Wharton, " were distinguished not only for their knowledge of sciences, but for their attention to polite learning and an acquaintance with the classics. Their learned abbot Desiderius collected the best Greek and Roman authors. The fraternity not only composed learned treatises on music, logic, astronomy, and the Vitruvian architecture, but likewise employed a portion of their time in transcribing Tacitus, etc.. This laudable example was followed with great spirit and emulation by many English monasteries."

Bates, Rural Philosophy, p. 322: "It is to be lamented that while the Papists are industrially planting nunneries and other religious societies in this kingdom, some good Protestants are not so far excited to imitate their example as to form establishments for the education and protection of young women of serious disposition, or who are otherwise unprovided, where they might enjoy at least a temporary refuge, be instructed in the principles of religion, and in all such useful and domestic arts as might qualify them who were inclined to return into the world for a pious and laudable discharge of the duties of the common life. Thus might the comfort and welfare of many individuals be promoted for the great benefit of society at large; and the interests of Popery, by improving on its own principles, be considerably counteracted."

APPENDIX 3

MONASTIC AND
CONTEMPORARY HOSPITALITY

If I look at the county of Surrey, in which I myself was born, and behold the devastation of that county, I am filled with indignation against the ruffian devastators. Surrey has very little of natural wealth in it. A very considerable part of it is mere heath-land. Yet this county was, from one end if it to the other, ornamented and benefited by the establishments which grew out of the Catholic Church. At Bermondsey there was an abbey; at St. Mary Overy there was a priory, and this convent founded that very St. Thomas' Hospital which now exists in Southwark. This hospital also was seized by the ruffians, but the building was afterwards given to the City of London. At Newington there was a hospital, and after its revenues were seized the master obtained a licence to beg! At Merton, there was a priory, then, going across to the Sussex side, there was another priory at Reigate. Coming again near the Thames, and more to the west, there was a priory at Shene. Still more to the west there was an abbey at Chertsey. At Tandridge there was a priory. Near Guildford, at Sende, there was a priory; and at the lower end of the county, at Waverley, in the parish of Farnham, was an abbey. To these belonged cells and chapels at a distance from the convents themselves; so that it would have been a work of some difficulty for a man so to place himself, even in this poor heathy county, at six mile distance from a place where the door of hospitality was always open to the poor, to the aged, the orphan, the widow, the stranger. Can any man now place himself, in that whole county, within any number of miles of any such door? No, nor in any other county. All this is wholly changed, and all is changed for the worse.

There is now no hospitality in England. Words have changed their meaning. We now give entertainment to those who entertain us in return. We entertain people because we like them personally, and very seldom because they stand in need of entertainment. A hospital, in those days, meant a place of free entertainment, and not a place merely for the lame, the sick, and the blind; and the very sound of the words "Old English Hospitality" ought to raise a blush on every Protestant cheek. But besides this hospitality exercised invariably in the monasteries, the weight of their example was great with all the opulent classes of the community, and thus to be generous and kind was the character of the nation at large; a niggardly, a base, a money-loving disposition could not be in fashion, when those institutions to which all men looked with reverence set an example which condemned such a disposition.

APPENDIX 4

VERACITY OF FOX'S BOOK OF MARTYRS

From the 277 Protestant martyrs stated on the authority of Fox there must be taken such as were still alive when he first published his book, and who expressly begged to decline the honour of being enrolled amongst its "Martyrs." As a proof of Fox's total disregard of truth, there was in the next reign a Protestant parson, as Anthony Wood (a Protestant) tells us, who in a sermon related, on authority of Fox, that a Catholic of the name of Grimwood had been, as Fox said, a great enemy of the Gospellers, had been "punished by a judgment of God," and that "his bowels fell out of his body". Grimwood was not only alive at the time when the sermon was preached, but happened to be present in the church to hear it, and he brought an action of defamation against the preacher! Another instance of Fox's falseness related to the death of Bishop Gardiner. Fox and Burnet, and other vile calumniators of the acts and actors in Queen Mary's reign, say that Gardiner, on the day of the execution of Latimer and Ridley, kept dinner waiting till

the news of their suffering should arrive, and that the Duke
of Norfolk, who was to dine with him, expressed great cha-
grin at the delay; that when the news came, "transported
with joy" they sat down to table, where Gardiner was suddenly seized with the disury, and died in horrible torment in
a fortnight afterwards. Now Latimer and Ridley were put to
death on the 16th of October, and Collier, in his
Ecclesiastical History, p.386, states that Gardiner opened
Parliament on the 21st of October, that he attended in
Parliament twice afterwards, that he died on the 12th of
November of the gout, and not of disury, and that as to the
Duke of Norfolk, he had been dead a year when that event
took place. What a hypocrite, then, must be the man be
who pretends to believe in this Fox! Yet this infamous book
has, by the arts of the plunderers and their descendants,
been circulated to a boundless extent amongst the people of
England, who have been taught to look upon all the
thieves, felons and traitors whom Fox calls "Martyrs," as
sufferers resembling St. Stephen, St. Peter and St. Paul!

APPENDIX 5

THE POOR UNDER ELIZABETH

The Catholic Church rendered all municipal laws about
the poor unnecessary; but when that Church had been
plundered and destroyed, when the greedy leading
"Reformers" had sacked the convents and the churches,
when those great estates which of right belonged to the
poorer classes had been taken from them, when the parsonages had been first well pillaged and the remnant of their
revenues given to married men, then the poor (for poor
there will and must be in every community) were left destitute of the means of existence other than the fruits of begging, theft and robbery. Accordingly, when Elizabeth had
put the finishing hand to the plundering of the Church and

poor, once happy and free and hospitable England became a den of famishing robbers and slaves. Strype, a Protestant, and an authority to whom Hume appeals and refers many hundreds of times, tells us of a letter from a Justice of the Peace in Somersetshire to the Lord Chief Justice, saying, "I may justly say that the able men that are abroad seeking the spoil and confusion of the land, are able, if they were reduced to good subjection, to give the greatest enemy her Majesty hath a strong battle, and as they are now are so much strength to the enemy. Besides, the generation that daily springeth from them is likely to be most wicked: these spare neither rich nor poor, but, whether it be great gain or small, all is fish that cometh to net with them; and yet I say both they and the rest are trussed up apace." The same Justice says: "In default of justice many wicked thieves escape; for most commonly the most simple countrymen and women, looking no farther than to the loss of their own goods, are of the opinion that they would not procure any man's death for all the goods in the world." And while Elizabeth complained bitterly of the non-execution of her laws, the same Protestant historian tells us that "she executed more than five hundred criminals in a year,and was so little satisfied with that number that she threatened to send private persons to see her penal laws executed for 'profit and gain's sake.' " It appears that she did not threaten in vain, for soon after this complaint was made in Parliament that the stipendiary magistrate of that day was " a kind of living creature, who for half a dozen of chickens would dispense with a dozen penal statutes." She did not , however, stop with this "liberal" use of the gallows. Such was the degree of beggary, of vagabondage, and of thievishness and robbery, that she resorted, particularly in London and its neighbourhood, to martial law. This fact is so complete a proof of the horrible effects of the "Reformation" upon the moral state of the people, and it is so fully characteristic of the government which the people of England had, in consequence of that Reformation, become so debased as to submit to, that I must take the statement as it stands in Hume, who gives the very words of "good and glorious Bess's" commission to her head murderer upon this occasion. "The streets of London were very much infested with idle vagabonds and riotous persons; the Lord Mayor had endeavoured to repress this disorder, the Star-chamber had exerted it authority and inflicted punishment on these rioters; but the Queen, finding these remedies ineffectual, revived (What does he mean "revived"?) "martial law, and gave Sir Thomas Wilford a commission as provost-martial, 'granting him authority and commanding him, upon signification given by the justices of the peace in London or the neighbouring counties of such offenders worthy to be speedily executed by martial law, to take them, and according to the justice of martial law to execute them upon the gallows or gibbet.'" And yet this is she whom we have been taught to call "good Queen Bess;" this is she of the "glories" of whose reign there are men of learning base enough to talk even to this day.

APPENDIX 6

ALGERNON SIDNEY AND TREASON

Sidney did not deny, he could not deny, that the conspiracy had existed, and that he was one of its chiefs. He had no complaint but one, and that related to the evidence against him. There was only one parole witness to his acts, and in cases of high treason, the law of England required two. And here it was that a blush might (if it were possible) have been raised upon the cheeks of these revilers of Popery; for this very law which has saved the lives of so many innocent persons, this law which ought to engrave gratitude to its author on the heart of every Englishman, this law came from that very Popish Queen Mary, whom artful knaves have taught generations of thoughtless people to call "bloody," while, too, she was the wife of, and had for coadjutor, that Philip II., whom to hold up as a sanguinary Popish tyrant has been a great object with all our base deluders.

Seeing, however, that Sidney had such a strong attachment to this Popish law, and that there really was but one witness against him, the crown lawyers (all Protestants, mind, who had abjured the "damnable errors of Popery") contrived to accommodate him with a couple by searching his drawers and making up a second witness out of his own papers. It was in vain that he rested upon this flaw in the proceedings; all men knew that hundreds of Catholics had suffered death upon evidence slight indeed compared with that against him; men were not to be amused with this miserable special plea, and all men of sense and justice concurred in the opinion that he received substantial justice and no more.

APPENDIX 7

POPULATION OF ENGLAND AND IRELAND

The modern writings on the subject of ancient population are mere romances, or they have been put forth with a view of paying court to the government of the day. George Chalmers, a placeman, a pensioner, and a Scotchman, has been one of the most conspicuous in this species of deception. He, in what he calls an "Estimate," states the population of England and Wales in 1377 at 2,092,978. The half of these were, of course, females. The males then were 1,046,486. The children, the aged, the infirm, the sick, made a half of these; so that there were 523,243 left of able-bodied men in this whole kingdom! Now the churches and the religious houses amounted at that time to upwards of 16,000 in number. There was one priest to every church, and these priests, together with the monks and friars, must have amounted to about 40,000 able men, leaving 483,243 able men. So that, as there were more than 14,000 parish churches, there were not quite twelve able-bodied men to each! Do we want, can we want, anything more than this in answer, in refutation of these writers on the ancient population of the country? The same may be said with regard to Ireland, where there were, according to Archdall, 742 religious houses in the reign of Henry VIII., and, of course, one of these to every piece of land six miles each way; and where there was a parish church to every piece of land a little more than two miles and a half each way. Why these churches? What were they built for? By whom were they built? And how were all these religious houses maintained? Alas! Ireland was in those days a fine, a populous, and a rich country. Her people were not then half-naked and half-starved. There were then no projects for relieving the Irish by sending them out of their native land!

APPENDIX 8

PURCHASING POWER AND RENTS

The wealth of the country is a question easily decided. In the reign of Henry VIII., just before the "Reformation," the whole of the lands in England and Wales had, according to Hume, been rated, and the annual rental was found to be three millions; and, as to this, Hume quotes undoubted authorities. Now, in order to know what these three millions were worth in our money we must look at the Act of Parliament, 24th year of Henry VIII., chapter 3, which says, that "no person shall take for beef or pork above a halfpenny, and for mutton or veal above three-farthings a pound, avoirdupois weight, and less in those places where they be now sold for less." This is by retail, mind. It is sale in the butchers' shops. So that, in order to compare the then with the present amount of the rental of the country, we must first see what the annual rental of England and Wales now is, and then we must see what the price of meat now is. I wish to speak here of nothing that I have not unquestionable authority for, and I have no such authority with regard to the amount of the rental as it is just at this moment; but I have that authority for what the rental was in the year 1804. A return, printed by order of the House of Commons, and dated 10th July, 1804, states, that "the returns to the Tax-office (property tax) prove the rack-rental of England and Wales to be thirty-eight millions a year." Here, then, we have the rental to a certainty; for what was there that could escape the all-searching, taxing eye of Pitt and his understrappers? King Henry's inexperience must have made him a poor hand, compared with Pitt, at finding out what people got for their land. Pitt's return included the rent of mines, canals, and of every species of real property; and the rental, the rack-rental, of the whole amounted to thirty-eight millions. This, observe, was in time of bank restriction, in time of high prices, in time of monstrously high rents, in time of high price of meat: that very year I gave eighteen shillings a score for fat hogs, taking head, feet, and all together; and for many years before and after, and including 1804, beef, pork, mutton and veal were, taken on the average, more than tenpence a pound by retail. Now, as Henry's Act orders the meat to be sold, in some places, for less than the half-penny and the three-farthings, we may, I think, fairly presume that the general price was a half-penny. So that a half-penny of Henry's money was equal in value to tenpence of Pitt's money; and, therefore, the three millions of rental in the time of Henry ought to have become sixty millions in 1804; and it was, as we have seen, only thirty-eight millions. In 1822, Mr. Curwin said, the rental had fallen to twenty millions. But, then, meat had also fallen in price. It is safer to take 1804, where we have undoubted authority to go on. This proof is of a nature to bid defiance to cavil. No man can dispute any of the facts, and they are conclusive as to the point that the nation was more wealthy before the "Reformation" than it is now. When Cardinal Pole landed at Dover, in the reign of Queen Mary, he was met and escorted on his way by two thousand gentlemen of the country on horseback. What! 2,000 country gentlemen in so beggarly a country as Chalmers describes it! Aye, and they must have been found in Kent and Surrey too. Can we find such a troop of country gentlemen there now? In short, everything shows that England was then a country abounding in men of real wealth, and that it so abounded precisely because the king's revenue was small.

LITTLETON, THOMAS (1422-81), celebrated judge and writer on legal matters; his short book, *Tenures*, originally written in French for his son, Richard, was the principle work on the law of real property in England of its day.

LOCKE, JOHN (1632-1704), philosopher and writer on political economy. He was a Commissioner of Trade and Plantations under William and Mary. His *Report of the Board of Trade respecting relief and employment of the poor* was published in 1697.

MALTHUS, THOMAS ROBERT (1766-1834), curate of Albury in Surrey; his *An Essay on the Principle of Population*, first published in 1793, and heavily revised in a second edition of 1803, argued for the need to control population growth, with regulation of sexual activity as a means of keeping it in check.

MILNER, JOHN (1753-1826), Catholic prelate who wrote on ecclesiastical antiquities and theology; Vicar-Apostolic of the Midlands from 1803. His *Letters to a Prebendary* was an acute and learned defence of Catholic doctrine in response to John Sturges' *Reflections on Popery*.

NORTH, ROGER (1653-1734), author of *Examen*, published posthumously in 1740, which was designed to vindicate the honour of Charles II against the attacks of White Kennett in his *Complete History of England*.

O'CALLAGHAN, REV J , author of *Usury or Lending at Interest*, published in England by Cobbett in 1825; Cobbett saw the introduction of usury as a key aspect of the Reformation.

RYMER, THOMAS (16?-1713), critic, poet and antiquary; his collection of treaties and diplomatic documents, *Fœdera, conventiones, cujuscumque Generis Acta publica inter Reges Angliæ, et alios Principes*, was published from 1704 onwards.

SPELMAN, SIR HENRY (1561-1641), Protestant historian and author of *History of Sacrilege*.

STOWE, JOHN (1525-1605), chronicler and antiquary; charged with popish writings in 1569-70, but avoided punishment; his works include *The Chronicles of England* (1580) and *A Survey of London* (1598 and 1603).

STRYPE, JOHN (1643-1717), ecclesiastical historian; he wrote *Annales of the Reformation*, and lives of Cranmer, Parker and Whitgift.

STURGES, JOHN (?-1807) theological writer, and prebendary of Winchester; his *Reflections on Popery* was a response to a work of Dr. Milner on the history of Winchester; Dr Milner responded with *Letters to a Prebendary*.

TANNER, THOMAS (1674-1735), Bishop of St Asaph and author of *Notitia Monastica*, or an account of all the monastic houses in England and Wales; though a Protestant, Tanner gave full credit to the value of monasteries in their contribution to the preservation of culture and the support of the poor and elderly.

TILLOTSON, JOHN (1630-94), latitudinarian prelate, who preached strongly against freedom of conscience for Roman Catholics; he was appointed Archbishop of Canterbury by William III.

TURNER, SHARON (1768-1847) lawyer and historian; author of a *History of England*; he was admired for his use of primary sources; legal adviser to the *Quarterly Review*.

WHITE, GILBERT (1720-93) vicar of Selbourne in Hampshire and author of the *Natural History of Selbourne* (1788).

WHITAKER, JOHN (1735-1808), rector of Ruhan-Lanyhorne in Cornwall; his *Vindication of Mary Queen of Scots* (3 Vols, 1787) attacked the lack of humanity of Queen Elizabeth.

WOOD, à, ANTHONY (1632-95), historian and antiquary, who wrote *Athenæ Oxonienses* (1691-2), a biographical dictionary of Oxford writers and bishops.

ALSO FROM FISHER PRESS
G K CHESTERTON
A SHORT HISTORY OF ENGLAND
Illustrated by Mary Tyler

Chesterton's classic *A Short History of England* was written during the
Great War. While his brother and their young friends were in the
trenches of France, he felt a need to define how the country for which
they were fighting came about. Chesterton proudly claims that he is writing as an ordinary member of the public for others like himself. It is not a
history for the specialist, but a consideration of the past so as to better
understand the present. His starting point is his reflection on the English
landscape and buildings. and his insight into how these physical features
came to be what they are. The neglected side of English history, he
argues in the introductory chapter, does not consist of the little things
which the learned obscurely conceal, but rather of the large things, such
as common lands and the ruins of the monasteries, which the learned
frequently ignore. Though an "amateur" history his short work is shaped
with consummate skill; it is continuously entertaining, full of Chesterton
wit and paradox, and often prophetic. *The Observer* has said of him that
"he is at once the most concise and fullest historian."

Chesterton shows in detail how the rights of ordinary people were
gradually taken from them by the destruction of the guilds of craftsmen,
the enclosure movement, and the rise of trading monopolies. The dissolution of the monasteries is seen in large part as a means whereby a small
elite enriched itself. Chesterton had himself written a book on William
Cobbett, who had come to the same conclusion. To Chesterton, the
19th century reforms widening the franchise were primarily a means
whereby the continuing elite staved off revolution. They were far from a
genuine attempt to restore to the English people their traditional free-
doms: those of association, ownership of land, and of the equipment
needed to earn their livelihood. This new edition of Chesterton's *History*
is timely now that the ordinary individual's freedom is in danger of being
further eroded as more and more decisions on how he lives his life are
taken by powerful forces residing elsewhere.

Fisher Press
£6.99   ISBN 1 874037 09 4

If you have difficulty in obtaining Fisher Press books from your local
bookshop you can order them direct from Post Office Box 41, Sevenoaks,
Kent TN15 6YN. England. Telephone/Fax 01732-761830

ALSO FROM FISHER PRESS
HUGH DORMER D.S.O.
WAR DIARY

With a facsimile of a leaf from his secret diary, maps, military sketch plan, and a drawing by John Dormer, the artist brother of the author.

Nothing in World War II fiction captures the excitement and terror of SOE's clandestine operations so well as Hugh Dormer's authentic *Diary* of 15 months in 1943-44. Although many other young Englishmen sacrificed their lives for the people of France, few had the talent to describe the daring events both accurately for intelligence purposes, and in a way which is of lasting literary value.The commemoration of the end of the War would be incomplete without a new edition of this classic account.

Several years of training with the Irish Guards Armoured Division for the long-awaited D Day landing made Hugh Dormer restless for action. In October 1942 he volunteered for subversion work in German-occupied France, despite his strong English accent when speaking French. He was twice parachuted into France in 1943, leading small bands of men to dynamite key components of industrial plants being operated for the German military machine. The diary record of these attacks, much of it written in secret at the time, and of his escapes through occupied France and over the Pyrenees at night is totally absorbing.

Yet it is the clarity of his understanding of the war as nothing less than the defence of Christian civilization, for which the martyrs in earlier times had also died, which gives the *War Diary* its greatness. For while on the run in France he observes at close hand what can happen when men and nations begin to lose the moral and spiritual values which they had acquired over so many centuries. The results were horrific: men betraying their neighbours, rejecting their children, sending their compatriots to death camps; indiscriminate bloody reprisals; the forced labour of the young; above all the paralysis of knowing what should be done, but failing to act out of cold fear. It was to help the French believe once more that it was possible to be free of tyranny and again act rightly and honourably that motivated Hugh Dormer. Readers will be fully engaged in his internal struggle when he decides that, despite his D.SO. and the offer of a leading role with SOE in Western France, his final contribution to French liberation should be, not as a modern-day Scarlet Pimpernel, but as a soldier with his beloved Irish guardsmen. The diary ends with his account of the D day landings, and the armoured push into Normandy in which he was killed.

Fisher Press
£7.99   ISBN 1 874037 11 6

If you have difficulty in obtaining Fisher Press books from your local bookshop you can order them direct from Post Office Box 41, Sevenoaks, Kent TN15 6YN. England. Telephone/Fax 01732-761830

BIBLIOGRAPHY

BOOKS AND AUTHORS
MENTIONED BY COBBETT

ARCHDALE, MERVYN (1723-91), Protestant clergyman and antiquary, and author of *Monasticon Hibernicum, an History of the Abbies, Priories and other Religious Houses in Ireland*, published in 1786.

BLACKSTONE, SIR WILLIAM (1723-80), first Vinerian Professor of English Law at Oxford and Solicitor-General. His *Commentaries on the Laws of England* (4 vols, 1765-9) was criticised by Cobbett for defending a legal system which deprived Catholics of their civil rights.

BURNET, GILBERT (1645-1715), adviser to William of Orange; he was appointed Bishop of Salisbury on William's accession to the English Throne. His *History of the Reformation in England* in 3 vols (1679, 1681, and 1715) was a key work in establishing the Whig view of Tudor and Stuart history, which Cobbett opposed.

CRANMER, THOMAS (1489-1556), Archbishop of Canterbury; favoured Henry VIII's divorce of Queen Catherine, supported the King's claim to be Head of the Church, and supervised the writing of the first prayer book in English after the breach with the Pope. *His Book of Homilies* was published in 1547, and his *Catechism*, based on the Lutheran *Nuremburg Catechism*, in 1548.

DEFOE, DANIEL (1660-1731), novelist and satirist; Cobbett attacked his *Family Instructor* (1715) in which he opposed relief for the poor. An enlarged edition in 1727 denounced popery.

D'ORLEANS, PIERRE (1644-98), French historian and a Jesuit; his *History of the Revolution in England under the Stuarts* appeared in English in 1722.

FORTESCUE, SIR JOHN (?1394-?1476), Chief Justice of England under Henry VI and the earliest constitutional lawyer; he wrote in both Latin and English.

FLEETWOOD, WILLIAM (1656-1723), Bishop of Ely, antiquarian and student of economic history; author of *Chronicon Preciosum or an Account of the English Money , the Price of Corn etc.*

FOX[E], JOHN (1517-87), promoter of the protestant cause and author of *Acts and Monuments*, known as *Fox[e]'s Book of Martyrs*, which describes the punishment of Protestants and those opposed to Catholic teaching under Mary I.

GOLDSMITH, OLIVER (1730-74), poet, critic and playwright. His *A History of England* in a series of letters from a nobleman to his son (1764) is criticised by Cobbett as providing young people with little more than a romance.

HERBERT, EDWARD, LORD (1582-1648), public servant and philosopher; with Thomas Master he wrote a detailed official history of Henry VIII's reign, from which Cobbett takes his account of the execution of the Countess of Salisbury.

HEYLY[I])N, PETER (1602-62), Dean of Westminster and author of *Ecclesia Restaurata or History of the Reformation* (1661). Although written to defend the Protestant Reformation, Pierre d'Orleans, the French historian, said it contributed to the conversion to Catholicism of the future James II and his wife.

HUME, DAVID (1711-76), philosopher,economist and historian. His *History of Great Britain* (1754-62) was immensely popular; in it he showed himself particularly hostile to the monastic ideal.

LINGARD, JOHN (1771-1851), major historian and Catholic priest; his *History of England*, published in 13 vols between 1819 and 1830, is renowned for its careful research; Cobbett used the work as a major source for his History of the Protestant Reformation; Lingard's work confirmed Cobbett's own perception that the Reformation had had disastrous consequences for the ordinary people of England and Ireland.